Practical Cryptography in Python

Learning Correct Cryptography by Example

Seth James Nielson
Christopher K. Monson

Apress®

Practical Cryptography in Python: Learning Correct Cryptography by Example

Seth James Nielson
Austin, TX, USA

Christopher K. Monson
Hampstead, MD, USA

ISBN-13 (pbk): 978-1-4842-4899-7
https://doi.org/10.1007/978-1-4842-4900-0

ISBN-13 (electronic): 978-1-4842-4900-0

Managing Director, Apress Media LLC: Welmoed Spahr
Acquisitions Editor: Susan McDermott
Development Editor: Laura Berendson
Coordinating Editor: Rita Fernando

Cover designed by eStudioCalamar

Distributed to the book trade worldwide by Springer Science+Business Media New York, 233 Spring Street, 6th Floor, New York, NY 10013. Phone 1-800-SPRINGER, fax (201) 348-4505, e-mail orders-ny@springer-sbm.com, or visit www.springeronline.com. Apress Media, LLC is a California LLC and the sole member (owner) is Springer Science + Business Media Finance Inc (SSBM Finance Inc). SSBM Finance Inc is a **Delaware** corporation.

For information on translations, please e-mail rights@apress.com, or visit http://www.apress.com/rights-permissions.

Apress titles may be purchased in bulk for academic, corporate, or promotional use. eBook versions and licenses are also available for most titles. For more information, reference our Print and eBook Bulk Sales web page at http://www.apress.com/bulk-sales.

Any source code or other supplementary material referenced by the author in this book is available to readers on GitHub via the book's product page, located at www.apress.com/9781484248997. For more detailed information, please visit http://www.apress.com/source-code.

Printed on acid-free paper

For Saige, who hopes to be a Computer Scientist like Daddy.
—Seth

To Mom and Dad, who valued good writing
and never settled for less than my best.
—Chris

Table of Contents

About the Authors

Seth James Nielson is the Founder and Chief Scientist of Crimson Vista, Inc., a boutique computer security research and consulting company. He is also an adjunct professor at Johns Hopkins University where he teaches network security and has also served as the Director of Advanced Research Projects in the Information Security Institute. As part of his Hopkins work, he co-founded the https://cryptodoneright. org knowledge base, through a generous grant from Cisco.

Christopher K. Monson has a PhD in machine learning and has spent over a decade at Google in various engineering, machine learning, and leadership roles. He has broad experience writing and teaching programming courses in multiple languages and has worked in document password recovery, malware detection, and large-scale secure computing. He is serving as the Chief Technology Officer at Data Machines Corp. and teaches Cloud Computing Security at the Johns Hopkins University Information Security Institute.

About the Technical Reviewer

 **Mike Ounsworth** is a Software Security Architect at Entrust Datacard. He holds an undergraduate degree in computer science with concentrations in mathematics and physics and an MSc in computer science in robotics and artificial intelligence. Professionally, his day job is mainly application security architecture and penetration testing, with some research side projects in cryptography and post-quantum cryptography. Outside of work, he mentors teams competing in the high-school-age FIRST Robotics Competition.

Introduction

The interconnected world of the current era has drastically changed everything, including banking, entertainment, and even statecraft. Despite differences in users, purposes, and security profiles, these digital applications have at least one thing in common: they all require properly applied cryptography to work correctly.

Informally, cryptography is the mathematics of secrets. We need secret codes to make messages unreadable to unauthorized eyes, to make messages unchangeable, and to know who sent the message. Practical cryptography is the design and use of these codes in real systems.

This book is primarily for computer programmers with little or no previous background with cryptography. Although mathematics makes brief appearances in the book, the overall approach is to teach introductory cryptography concepts by example.

Our journey begins with some introductory components, including hashing algorithms, symmetric encryption, and asymmetric encryption. Next, we go beyond encryption and into the realm of digital certificates, signatures, and message authentication codes. The final chapters show how these various elements come together in interesting and useful combinations, such as Kerberos and TLS.

Another important part of cryptography by example is cryptography by bad example! In this book we will break things on purpose to help the reader appreciate what motivates accepted best practices. Exercises and examples include walk-throughs of real vulnerabilities that have afflicted the Internet. The bad examples will help the reader gain a greater intuition of what goes wrong in cryptography and why.

CHAPTER 1

Cryptography: More Than Secrecy

Welcome to the world of practical cryptography! The intent of this book is to teach you enough about cryptography that you can reason about what it does, when certain types can be effectively applied, and how to choose good strategies and algorithms. There are examples and exercises throughout each chapter, usually with a follow-along exercise right at the beginning to help you get your bearings. These examples are often accompanied by some fictitious stage setting to add some context. After you've had some exposure and experience, the technical terms that follow those examples should make more sense and be more memorable. We hope you like it.

Setting Up Your Python Environment

In order to dive in, we'll need a place to swim, and that's a Python 3 environment. If you are already a Python 3 pro and have no trouble installing modules that you discover you need, skip this section and do some actual diving. Otherwise, read on, and we'll get through the setup steps quickly.

All of the examples in this book are written using Python 3 and the third-party "cryptography" module.

If you do not want to mess around with your system Python environment, we suggest creating a Python virtual environment using the venv module. This will configure a selected directory with a Python interpreter and associated modules. Using an "activate" script, the shell is directed to use this custom environment for Python rather than the system-wide installation. Any modules you install are only locally installed.

© Seth James Nielson, Christopher K. Monson 2019
S. J. Nielson and C. K. Monson, *Practical Cryptography in Python*,
https://doi.org/10.1007/978-1-4842-4900-0_1

We will walk through installing the system in Ubuntu Linux in this section. Installation will be slightly different for other versions of Linux or Unix and may be considerably different for Windows.

First, we need to install Python 3, Pip, and the venv module:

```
apt install python3 python3-venv python3-pip
```

Next, we use venv to set up the environment in an env directory:

```
python3 -m venv env
```

This will set up the interpreter and modules within the path. Once the installation is complete, the environment can be used at any time by the following command:

```
source env/bin/activate
```

You should now see a prefix to your shell prompt with the name of your environment. Once your environment is activated, install the cryptography module. Remember to activate your Python virtual environment first if you don't want cryptography installed system-wide.

```
pip install cryptography
```

We will be using the cryptography module throughout the book. Many times we will refer directly to the module's documentation that can be found online at https://cryptography.io/en/latest/.

For some practices, we will also need the gmpy2 module. This *does* require a few system-wide packages.

```
apt install libmpfr-dev libmpc-dev libgmp-dev python3-gmpy2
```

Once you have these packages installed, you can install the Python gmpy2 module within your virtual environment

```
pip install gmpy2
```

Note that within the virtual environment, you can use "python" instead of "python3" and "pip" instead of "pip3." This is because when you created the environment with venv, you did so using Python3. Within the virtual environment, Python3 is the only interpreter and there is no need to differentiate between version 2 and version 3. If you install any of these packages system-wide, you may need to use pip3 instead of just pip. Otherwise, the packages might be installed for Python 2.

If you have trouble with gmpy2 or do not wish to install all the system-wide packages, you can skip this step. There are only a few exercises you will not be able to complete.

Now let's get diving!

Caesar's Shifty Cipher

The two (made-up) countries of East Antarctica (EA) and West Antarctica (WA) don't like each other very much and are spying on each other incessantly. In this scenario, two spies from EA, with code names "Alice" and "Bob," have infiltrated their western neighbors and are sending messages back and forth through covert channels.

They don't like it when their adversaries in West Antarctica read their messages, so they communicate using a secret code.

Unfortunately, East Antarctica is not particularly advanced in the realm of cryptography. For a code, the East Antarctica Truth-Spying Agency (EATSA) creates a simple substitution by replacing each letter with another letter later in the alphabet. Both countries use the standard ASCII alphabet with the letters "A" through "Z."

Suppose for a moment that they choose to code their messages using this substitution technique with the *shift distance* set to 1. In that case, the letter "A" would be replaced with "B," the letter "B" would be replaced with "C," and so on. The last letter of the alphabet, "Z," would wrap around to the beginning and be replaced with "A." This table shows the whole (uppercase) mapping of **plaintext** (original, untouched) letters to **ciphertext** (coded) letters. Non-letters like spaces and punctuation are left intact.

A	B	C	D	E	F	G	H	I	J	K	L	M
B	C	D	E	F	G	H	I	J	K	L	M	N
N	O	P	Q	R	S	T	U	V	W	X	Y	Z
O	P	Q	R	S	T	U	V	W	X	Y	Z	A

Using this table, HELLO WORLD encodes to IFMMP XPSME.

Now try it with distance 2, where "A" goes to "C," "B" goes to "D," and so on until "Y," which maps to "A," and "Z," which maps to "B."

A	B	C	D	E	F	G	H	I	J	K	L	M
C	D	E	F	G	H	I	J	K	L	M	N	O
N	O	P	Q	R	S	T	U	V	W	X	Y	Z
P	Q	R	S	T	U	V	W	X	Y	Z	A	B

Now, the message HELLO WORLD is encoded as JGNNQ YQTNF.

Happy with their simple *shift cipher*, the East Antarctica Truth-Spying Agency (EATSA) decides to create a Python program to handle encoding and decoding messages.

Tip: Write Code

This book walks through a lot of sample Python programs. At the beginning of each one, we will list the requirements and perhaps a hint or an overview of a cryptographic API. You should go ahead and try to write the program yourself first. It's fine if you get stuck or make mistakes. Even if you can't figure everything out on your own, your experience with trying to write the program will help you understand the provided samples much better.

EXERCISE 1.1. SHIFT CIPHER ENCODER

Create a Python program that encodes and decodes messages using the shift cipher described in this section. The amount of shift must be configurable.

Let's walk through this exercise together. We use Python 3 for all exercises.

First, let's create a simple function for creating our substitution tables. For simplicity, we will create two Python dictionaries: one containing the encoding table and one creating the decoding table. We will also only encode and decode uppercase ASCII letters, as shown in Listing 1-1.

Listing 1-1. Creating Substitution Tables

```
1    # Partial Listing: Some Assembly Required
2
3    import string
4
5    def create_shift_substitutions(n):
6        encoding = {}
7        decoding = {}
8        alphabet_size = len(string.ascii_uppercase)
9        for i in range(alphabet_size):
10           letter      = string.ascii_uppercase[i]
11           subst_letter = string.ascii_uppercase[(i+n)%alphabet_size]
12
13           encoding[letter]        = subst_letter
14           decoding[subst_letter] = letter
15       return encoding, decoding
```

Observe that this function is parameterized on n, the shift parameter. We don't have any error checking in this function; we will check parameters elsewhere. Note, though, that any integer value of n is valid because Python handles negative modulus in a reasonable way. Even the value 0 is okay: it just produces a mapping from each character to itself! Values larger than 26 also work fine because we apply a final modulus of alphabet_size before indexing into the alphabet.

Now, for encoding and decoding, we simply substitute each letter in a message for one in the corresponding dictionary, shown in Listing 1-2.

Listing 1-2. Shift Encoder

```
1    # Partial Listing: Some Assembly Required
2
3    def encode(message, subst):
4        cipher = ""
5        for letter in message:
6            if letter in subst:
7                cipher += subst[letter]
8            else:
```

```
 9                    cipher += letter
10          return cipher
11
12    def decode(message, subst):
13          return encode(message, subst)
```

Note: Compactness vs. Clarity

We tend to favor universal clarity over compactness when there is a conflict between them. We will even write things in ways that might not be widely considered idiomatic if it helps to illustrate what is happening.

The code in Listing 1-2 has a nice example of favoring clarity over common idioms. An idiomatic function body would probably be a one-liner:

```
def encode(message, subst):
    return "".join(subst.get(x, x) for x in message)
```

That's a lovely bit of Python if you're used to it, but we're trying not to make too many assumptions here.

In our implementation, the encode function takes an incoming message and a substitution dictionary. For each letter in the message, we replace it if a substitution is available. Otherwise, we just include the character itself with no transformation (preserving spaces and punctuation).

Obviously, the decode operation in this listing is completely unnecessary, but we have included it to emphasize that encoding and decoding in a substitution cipher work exactly the same. Only the dictionary needs to change.

These functions are sufficient to build an application, but for fun we will add in another function in Listing 1-3 to take a substitution dictionary and create a string that shows the mapping. This will allow us to print out our different tables created from different shift values.

Listing 1-3. Printable Substitutions

```
1   # Partial Listing: Some Assembly Required
2
3   def printable_substitution(subst):
4       # Sort by source character so things are alphabetized.
5       mapping = sorted(subst.items())
6
7       # Then create two lines: source above, target beneath.
8       alphabet_line = " ".join(letter for letter, _ in mapping)
9       cipher_line = " ".join(subst_letter for _, subst_letter in mapping)
10      return "{}\n{}".format(alphabet_line, cipher_line)
```

Using these functions, we can build a simple application for encoding and decoding messages, shown in Listing 1-4.

Listing 1-4. Shift Cipher Application

```
1   # Partial Listing: Some Assembly Required
2
3   if __name__ == "__main__":
4       n = 1
5       encoding, decoding = create_shift_substitutions(n)
6       while True:
7           print("\nShift Encoder Decoder")
8           print("--------------------")
9           print("\tCurrent Shift: {}\n".format(n))
10          print("\t1. Print Encoding/Decoding Tables.")
11          print("\t2. Encode Message.")
12          print("\t3. Decode Message.")
13          print("\t4. Change Shift")
14          print("\t5. Quit.\n")
15          choice = input(">> ")
16          print()
17
18          if choice == '1':
19              print("Encoding Table:")
```

```
20              print(printable_substitution(encoding))
21              print("Decoding Table:")
22              print(printable_substitution(decoding))
23
24          elif choice == '2':
25              message = input("\nMessage to encode: ")
26              print("Encoded Message: {}".format(
27                  encode(message.upper(), encoding)))
28
29          elif choice == '3':
30              message = input("\nMessage to decode: ")
31              print("Decoded Message: {}".format(
32                  decode(message.upper(), decoding)))
33
34          elif choice == '4':
35              new_shift = input("\nNew shift (currently {}): ".format(n))
36              try:
37                  new_shift = int(new_shift)
38                  if new_shift < 1:
39                      raise Exception("Shift must be greater than 0")
40              except ValueError:
41                  print("Shift {} is not a valid number.".format(new_
                     shift))
42              else:
43                  n = new_shift
44                  encoding, decoding = create_shift_substitutions(n)
45
46          elif choice == '5':
47              print("Terminating. This program will self destruct in 5
                 seconds .\n")
48              break
49
50          else:
51              print("Unknown option {}.".format(choice))
```

The encoding and decoding program completed, the East Antarctica Truth-Spying Agency (EATSA) sends Alice and Bob off to their covert destinations hopeful that their communications, if intercepted, will not be readable by the West Antarctica Central Knights Office (WACKO).

The problem is this code is quite easy to break. Can you see why? There are all kinds of ways to figure it out by clever guessing. For example, try to break this:

```
FA NQ AD ZAF FA NQ FTMF UE FTQ CGQEFUAZ
```

Using a couple of simple two-letter words such as "if," "or," "in," "to," and so forth, it quickly becomes obvious that this phrase is

```
TO BE OR NOT TO BE THAT IS THE QUESTION
```

The preserved spaces make it easy to figure out. For this reason, real spies before modern cryptography would typically remove all of the spaces in their messages, like this:

```
FANQADZAFFANQFTMFUEFTQCGQEFUAZ
```

With this change, at least it isn't obvious where to try easy word substitutions. But even if Alice and Bob remove all spaces and punctuation, it is still trivial to break their codes. Although this code is so trivial it can be broken with pen and paper, we are going to write a Python program to crack it. Do you already see how? If so, go ahead and do it yourself. If not, keep reading!

The problem with the substitution cipher used by EATSA is that there are only 25 unique and effective shifts. You can easily construct a Python program to try all possible 25 combinations.

How do we know when we are using the same shift as Alice and Bob? We'll know it when we see it because it will be readable.

Let's switch sides in this Antarctic cold war and work for the West Antarctica Central Knights Office (WACKO). They know that spies have infiltrated their country, and they are monitoring for communications between those spies and EATSA. One of their counter-intelligence agents, code named "Eve," has just come across the following message:

```
FANQADZAFFANQFTMFUEFTQCGQEFUAZ
```

With this message, Eve *also* has intel that EA agents are using substitution ciphers. She decides to construct a program for encoding and decoding such messages. In an amazing coincidence, she constructs a Python program just like EATSA!

Running the program, she tries decoding the message with a shift of 1, producing this:

```
EZMPZCYZEEZMPESLETDESPBFPDETZY
```

That doesn't look right. So Eve tries again with shifts 2, 3, and so forth.

```
 1:   EZMPZCYZEEZMPESLETDESPBFPDETZY
 2:   DYLOYBXYDDYLODRKDSCDROAEOCDSYX
 3:   CXKNXAWXCCXKNCQJCRBCQNZDNBCRXW
 4:   BWJMWZVWBBWJMBPIBQABPMYCMABQWV
 5:   AVILVYUVAAVILAOHAPZAOLXBLZAPVU
 6:   ZUHKUXTUZZUHKZNGZOYZNKWAKYZOUT
 7:   YTGJTWSTYYTGJYMFYNXYMJVZJXYNTS
 8:   XSFISVRSXXSFIXLEXMWXLIUYIWXMSR
 9:   WREHRUQRWWREHWKDWLVWKHTXHVWLRQ
10:   VQDGQTPQVVQDGVJCVKUVJGSWGUVKQP
11:   UPCFPSOPUUPCFUIBUJTUIFRVFTUJPO
12:   TOBEORNOTTOBETHATISTHEQUESTION
```

Using a shift of 12, Eve sees a string of obviously English text. This is clearly the message.

This type of substitution cipher is often called a Caesar cipher because Julius Caesar used it for his secret messages [3]. This cipher is more than 2000 years old. Obviously, we've come a long way since then. This technology is quite obsolete.

Even so, there are a lot of principles of modern cryptography that can be discussed using the Caesar cipher, including

1. Key size

2. Block size

3. Preserved structure (structure that survives encoding)

4. Brute-force attacks

We will be learning about all of these concepts in this book in the context of modern cryptography. Mathematical advances have enabled new ciphers that are almost impossible to break *if used correctly*. Before we go on, though, here are a few additional exercises for the intellectually curious.

EXERCISE 1.2. AUTOMATED DECODING

In our example, Eve tried decoding various messages until she saw something that looked like English. Try automating this.

- Get a data structure containing a few thousand English words.[1]

- Create a program that takes in an encoded string, then try decoding it with all 25 shift values.

- Use the dictionary to try to automatically determine which shift is most likely.

Because you have to deal with messages with no spaces, you can simply keep a count of how many dictionary words show up in the decoded output. Occasionally, one or two words might appear by accident, but the correct decoding should have significantly more hits.

EXERCISE 1.3. A STRONG SUBSTITUTION CIPHER

What if instead of shifting the alphabet, you randomly jumbled the letters? Create a program that encodes and decodes messages using this kind of substitution.

Some newspapers publish puzzles like this called *cryptograms*.

EXERCISE 1.4. COUNT THE DICTIONARIES

How many substitution dictionaries are possible for the cryptogram-style substitution in the previous exercise?

---

[1]You can find lists of such words online, and your program can automatically populate your data structure with them.

EXERCISE 1.5. IDENTIFYING THE DICTIONARY

Modify your cryptogram program so that you can identify and pick the jumbled character substitution map with a number. That is, each mapping has a unique number that identifies it: picking substitution *n* should create the same substitution mapping every time. This exercise is a little tougher than the others. Do your best!

EXERCISE 1.6. BRUTE FORCE

Try having your cryptogram-decoding program brute force a message. How long would it take to test every possible mapping? Can you write a program that can speed this up with any kind of "smart guess"?

A Gentle Introduction to Cryptography

With the example out of the way, we are ready to get into some real cryptography. Welcome! Hopefully you had fun with the substitution cipher. As mentioned earlier, this particular form of encryption is called a "Caesar cipher" because it was used by Julius Caesar for protecting important documents.

Like Caesar, most of us have information that we would like to keep secret. In cryptography terms, we would like to keep it *confidential*. Encryption is a cornerstone of data confidentiality.

What do you think of Caesar's cipher? Even without a computer, how long do you think it would take you to break something like that? Perhaps in Caesar's time it was reasonably effective if Caesar's enemies were not well educated. This is an important lesson in cryptography and computer security. The effectiveness of cryptography is typically *dependent on context*. Good cryptography is effective no matter how well educated your adversaries are, how many computers they have, whether they know the algorithms you use, or how motivated they are.

In short, you're better off when you aren't too dependent on context, at least context that is out of your control.

Good security will *always* depend on *your choices*, however. The goal of this book is to help cryptographic beginners understand a little bit about how certain cryptographic algorithms work and a little bit about the contexts they are designed for. This book is directed at programmers and thus uses a lot of source code to teach and illustrate concepts. As we use the Python programming language, Python programmers will especially enjoy these exercises. However, the concepts are not language-dependent.

Thus, we assume some familiarity with programming. Python is easy enough to learn to read that it should be easy for anyone to at least follow the examples, and we try to stay away from very special Python idioms to facilitate that.

We do *not*, however, assume that the reader has any prior familiarity with cryptography. If you know cryptography a little, please be patient with some of the explanations in the book that may be directed to the absolute beginner. If you are a beginner, this book is for you. We hope that you enjoy getting your feet wet.

Uses of Cryptography

You are probably aware that cryptography is everywhere in today's modern interconnected world. The world's people are exchanging information in mind-boggling quantities and at mind-boggling speeds. A 2018 Forbes article reported the following statistics [10]:

1. 2.5 *quintillion* bytes of data are created each day, and that number is accelerating.

2. Google processes 3.5 billion searches each day.

3. Snapchat users share 500,000 photos *per second*.

4. More than 16 million text messages are sent every second.

5. More than 150 million email messages are sent every second.

What's amazing from an information security perspective is that the vast majority of these transmissions are meant to be protected in some way. There are nearly 4 billion users of the Internet at the time of this writing, but almost all of the data transmitted is meant for a vanishingly small percentage of them. Even when someone posts to social media publicly for the world to see, they are posting *to a specific platform*. The communication is meant for Facebook, or Twitter, or Snapchat, or Instagram *first*, and the platform then makes it available publicly.

Cryptography is the primary tool for protecting information. Cryptography can be used to help provide the following protections:

Confidentiality: Only authorized parties can *read* the protected information. This is probably the first thing that you think of when you think about encryption or secret codes.

Authentication: You know that you are talking to the *right entity/person* and that they have *not delegated their identity* (they're "present"). Many people know that the little lock icon in their browser means that their data is encrypted, but fewer know that it also means the service's *identity* (e.g., your bank) has been verified by a trusted authority. That is pretty important, after all: encrypting data to the wrong party doesn't really help.

Integrity: A message hasn't been *changed* between the sender and receiver. This applies equally to plaintext and to encrypted messages. It may seem unintuitive in some cases, but it is possible to change an encrypted message without being able to read it, even in ways that "make sense" to the receiver.

While there are a lot of books on cryptography, not many of them are focused on programming as the primary method of teaching the algorithms and associated principles. Our goal is to walk you, the computer programmer, through hands-on exercises that will help make these concepts understandable and useful.

What Could Go Wrong?

Unfortunately, there are a lot of ways to use cryptography incorrectly. In fact, there are a lot more ways to use it incorrectly than correctly. There are many reasons for this, but two that we will focus on here.

First, cryptography is based on a lot of pretty esoteric mathematics that most programmers and IT professionals have little experience with. You don't have to know the mathematics to use the cryptography, but sometimes not knowing the math behind it makes it difficult to have correct intuition about what will work and what will not.

Second, and perhaps the biggest problem, is that correct usage is also dependent on context. It is rare to find a universal "this is how you should always do it under all circumstances" algorithm. A big part of learning cryptography is learning how various *parameter settings* impact the operation.

We will talk about this a lot in the book. In fact, many of your exercises will be to *break* cryptography that has been set up incorrectly. Looking at something break is a great way to understand how it works. It is also a lot of fun.

YANAC: You Are Not A Cryptographer

Warning   This Section Is Critical. Please Read It Carefully

To repeat, there are more ways to mess up cryptography than you can possibly imagine. The pages of cryptography history are filled with stories of very smart people that unintentionally created vulnerable algorithms and systems. Many times, non-experts learned just enough to be dangerous and threw together a cryptography-based module that provided little more than a false sense of security. Even some of the very best cryptographic minds have had to correct their protocols after finding out they overlooked a subtle edge case.

If this book is your first exposure to cryptography, you will still not be an expert by the time you finish. This book will not prepare you to create algorithms and protocols that provide industrial strength protections. Please, *please*, do not finish reading this book and then think that you are ready to slap together your own custom cryptography for a real application.

Even for experts, the current best thinking in the cryptography community is to *not* create new or custom mechanisms. This is typically stated as, "Don't roll your own crypto." Instead, find and use existing libraries, protocols, and algorithms that have been heavily tested and are both well documented and consistently maintained. When new algorithms are truly needed, these are typically created and tested to within an inch of their lives by committees of experts, then presented for peer review and public comment before ever being trusted to protect sensitive data.

So why read this book at all? If only the experts should develop cryptography, why should non-experts learn this stuff?

First and foremost, cryptography is fun! Regardless of how ready you are to secure data communications between an app you write and a back-end server, learning cryptography is interesting, enjoyable, and worthwhile. Moreover, maybe after you get a taste for it you will want to do the hard work required to *become* an expert yourself! Perhaps this book will be the first step in your journey to becoming a cryptography wiz!

Second, we live in an imperfect world. You may be working on a project where former contributors (unfortunately) did roll their own cryptography. If you are in that situation, you need to encourage your organization to replace it as quickly as possible. Such situations are like a land mine just waiting to go off and may require a significant financial investment to fix. Your organization may need to hire a cryptography consultant to investigate and assess the risks. Without giving advance notice to the bad guys, you may need to send mandatory security patches to all of your customers. As bad as this situation is, it is still better to discover it yourself than to wait for the bad guys to find it for you. Reading this book can help you to recognize these issues and make a preliminary assessment of what you are dealing with.

Third, even when you are using a reputable algorithm (or better yet, third-party library), it is helpful to understand the underlying cryptography principles at least a little bit. It is handy to know how to use cryptography and particularly how to set parameters of various cryptographic methods. There is a big push from some in the cryptography community to create libraries with APIs that require minimal configuration and are nearly impossible to use incorrectly (we will talk about an example of this later in the book). Even for these, however, if a weakness is found *inside* these black boxes, an informed user can better understand how that weakness affects the security of the system and thus better select mitigation strategies.

Finally, an informed user is better able to recognize good advice and trustworthy experts. Let's discuss this point a little more in the next couple of sections.

"Jump Off This Cliff"—The Internet

Most of us that write code depend heavily on the Internet. It is common to search for API documentation, example code, and even best practices. But please be cautious when searching the Web for recommendations about cryptography. Many answers are good, but many more are terrible. If you're not an expert, it can be hard to recognize the difference.

For example, some researchers published a research paper in 2017 entitled "Stack Overflow Considered Harmful? The Impact of Copy&Paste on Android Application Security" [5]. They detailed over 4000 posts on the Stack Overflow web site that included security-related code snippets. After forensically examining 1.3 million Android applications, they found that a full 15% included code copied from these posts, most of which were insecure to some degree or another.

One of the first things you can do is educate yourself about cryptography in practice, and this is one of our goals in writing this book. You do not have to be an expert to be well-informed. Most of you reading this book know enough about computer hardware to not get taken advantage of by a pushy salesman even though you aren't personally designing circuit boards. Similarly, knowing just a little more about cryptography fundamentals can help you recognize good advice from bad. And it can help you know when you can figure it out yourself and when you should get expert help.

The cryptodoneright.org Project

One of the authors is a founding member of the Crypto Done Right project. The goal of this project is to bring together in one place the very best in practical cryptographic guidance. At the cryptodoneright.org web site, we are creating and maintaining a collection of cryptography recommendations designed for software developers, IT professionals, and managers. The goal is to bridge the gap between the crypto experts that know all the crazy math and the users of cryptography that just need an application to communicate securely with a cloud-based server.

Anyone can submit or suggest an entry to Crypto Done Right, but an editorial board of the very best experts ensure correct content. At the time of this writing, editorial control is still located with the Johns Hopkins University, but moving this into an independent, community-driven organization is on the road map.

We encourage you to use this web site as an authoritative source on cryptographic best practices, and we endorse the content. As a general knowledge base, it will never have everything that everyone needs or answer every question about every application. But it is a good start to understand how cryptographic algorithms work, which parameters matter, and what common problems to avoid. If you are trying to figure out what to do with cryptography in your development project, start there and then branch out to other sources for more detailed recommendations applicable to your situation. Crypto Done Right can sensitize you to the relevant issues so that you can recognize which sources are trustworthy.

Enough Talk, Let's Sum Up

This book is a Python programming book. We will write a lot of very fun, very interesting code to learn about cryptography. To keep things interesting, we are going to rely on Alice, Bob, and Eve throughout the book. Computer security people actually talk about scenarios this way where "Alice" represents "Party A," Bob represents "Party B," and Eve represents the "Eavesdropper." There are sometimes other common names, but these will be our three most common actors.

We will motivate a lot of our examples using a hypothetical cold war between East and West Antarctica, which are *totally fictitious*. Please do not read anything political into any of this. We use Antarctica because it was the least political place we could think of. If we have inadvertently offended you, we apologize in advance.

Although the sample code is written to be entertaining, it is also written to be relevant and illuminating. Take time to play around with the examples. Try out your own experiments. Learn from positive and negative examples.

Please be very careful not to ever use sample "bad" code in your projects. Even the "good" code should not just be copied and pasted into applications without carefully deciding that it is appropriate.

The rest of the book is organized as follows:

In Chapter 2, we will get started with *hashing*. You are probably familiar with hashes to some degree or another already, but we will do some interesting experiments in brute-force attacks against a hash algorithm and even talk a little about Proof of Work like what is used in Bitcoin. From a security perspective, hashes are extremely important for password protection. They are also useful for file integrity and will make a reappearance in later chapters when we talk about message integrity and digital signatures.

In Chapter 3, we really get into encryption with a discussion of *symmetric encryption*. If you have heard of AES, that is an example of a symmetric encryption scheme. It's called "symmetric" because the same key that encrypts the data is used to decrypt the data. These algorithms are fast and used almost exclusively for encrypting most data whether in transit or on disk.

In contrast to symmetric algorithms, Chapter 4 dives into *asymmetric encryption*. This kind of cryptography involves two keys that work together. What one encrypts, the other decrypts. These types of algorithms are used in certificates and digital signatures, although in that chapter we will focus on the algorithms themselves.

Although most people think of encryption when they hear of cryptography, it has other uses. Chapter 5 focuses on integrity and authentication. Integrity is making sure that messages don't change between the sender and the receiver. You might be surprised to learn that even if you cannot read a message, you might still be able to change it in useful and meaningful ways. We will explore some neat examples of this when we get to that chapter. Also, we will look at digital signatures and certificates, bringing together our asymmetric tools from Chapter 4 and our hashing tools from Chapter 2.

Chapter 6 introduces how to use asymmetric and symmetric encryption together and why you want to, and Chapter 7 explores additional modern algorithms for symmetric encryption.

In Chapter 8, we will look very specifically at the TLS protocol used, among other things, for securing HTTPS traffic. This chapter will bring together almost everything we have looked at in the entire book because TLS is a complicated protocol that builds on all of these tools. Don't worry about the complicated stuff though; you will find that it's a great review of the book and a helpful way to see everything come together.

Onward

We have now had a quick introduction to the basics of cryptography, including simple ciphers and the fact that it isn't all about secrecy: there are other important factors as well. Ideally, you now have a good Python environment set up, have tried some code on your own, and are ready to learn more.

Let's get going!

CHAPTER 2

Hashing

Hashing is a cornerstone of cryptographic security. It involves the concept of a *one-way function* or *fingerprint*. Hash functions only work well when a couple of things are true about them:

- They produce *repeatable, unique values* for every input.
- The output value *provides no clues* about the input that produced it.

Some hashing functions are better at satisfying these requirements than others, and we'll talk about some good ones (SHA-256) and some not-so-good ones (MD5, SHA-1) to demonstrate both how they work and why choosing a good one is so terribly important.

Hash Liberally with `hashlib`

WARNING: MD5 Is No Good

We are going to use an algorithm called MD5 for about the first half of the chapter. MD5 is deprecated and **should not be used for any security-sensitive operations**, or really any operations at all, except when you have to interact with legacy systems.

This discussion is for introducing the concept of hashing and for providing historical context. MD5 is nice for that because it produces short hashes, has a rich history, and *gives us something to break*.

When we last left our two favorite spies from East Antarctica, Alice and Bob were working out some codes using simple substitution ciphers. Even though the cipher was very weak, it provided a rudimentary form of message *confidentiality*.

© Seth James Nielson, Christopher K. Monson 2019
S. J. Nielson and C. K. Monson, *Practical Cryptography in Python*,
https://doi.org/10.1007/978-1-4842-4900-0_2

It did nothing, however, for message *integrity*. If you haven't already guessed, message **confidentiality** means that nobody but the authorized parties can *read* the message. Message **integrity** means that no unauthorized parties can *change* the message without the change being noticed.

It is important to understand the distinction. Even with modern ciphers, just because a message can't be read doesn't mean it can't be altered, even in ways that make sense after decryption.

Also, when Alice and Bob go through customs at the WA border, sometimes their laptops are inspected. It would be nice to know that none of the files have been tampered with during that process.

Fortunately for Alice and Bob, their new technology officer introduces them to something called a "message digest" to "fingerprint" their files and message transmissions. He explains that they can combine their messages' *contents* with message *digests*, then using the two together, they can tell whether part of any message was altered. That sounds like just the thing!

Since they don't know anything about digests, it's time for some training. Let's follow along with their instructor in our own Python interpreter, starting with Listing 2-1.

Listing 2-1. Intro to hashlib

```
>>> import hashlib
>>> md5hasher = hashlib.md5()
>>> md5hasher.hexdigest()
'd41d8cd98f00b204e9800998ecf8427e'
```

Importing a library called `hashlib` seems straightforward enough, but what is `md5`?

The instructor explains that the "MD" in MD5 stands for "message digest." We'll get into some interesting details in just a moment, but for now, a digest like MD5 converts a document of any length (even an empty document) into a large number that takes up a fixed amount of space. It should have at least these features:

- The same document always produces the same digest.

- The digest "feels" random: if you have a digest, it gives you no clues about the document.

In this way, a digest is like a fingerprint and is sometimes called one: it is a small amount of data that stands in for the document's *identity*; every document we might ever care about should have a completely unique digest.

Human fingerprints are similar in other ways. If you have a person at hand, it's easy to produce a (relatively) consistent and unique fingerprint; but if the only thing you have is a fingerprint, it's not so easy to find out whose it is. Digests work the same way: given a document, it's easy to calculate its digest; but given only a digest, it's very hard to find out what document produced it. *Very* hard. The harder, the better, in fact.

The MD5 digest creates a number that always occupies 16 bytes of memory. In our example interpreter session, we asked it to produce a digest for the *empty document*, which is why we didn't add any data to the md5hasher before asking it to produce a digest for us. The use of hexdigest is shown to demonstrate a more human-readable format for the number, where each of the 16 bytes in the digest is shown as a two-character hexadecimal value.

The instructor, anxious to move on, asks Alice and Bob to hash each of their names (expressed as bytes). To the interpreter, and Listing 2-2!

Listing 2-2. Hash Names

```
>>> md5hasher = hashlib.md5(b'alice')
>>> md5hasher.hexdigest()
'6384e2b2184bcbf58eccf10ca7a6563c'
>>> md5hasher = hashlib.md5(b'bob')
>>> md5hasher.hexdigest()
'9f9d51bc70ef21ca5c14f307980a29d8'
```

For short strings like these, it's not uncommon to combine operations, like Listing 2-3.

Listing 2-3. Combine Operations

```
>>> hashlib.md5(b'alice').hexdigest()
'6384e2b2184bcbf58eccf10ca7a6563c'
>>> hashlib.md5(b'bob').hexdigest()
'9f9d51bc70ef21ca5c14f307980a29d8'
```

"So, Alice, Bob, what did you learn from this?" the instructor asks. When neither one answers, she suggests that they experiment some more. Let's follow along.

Python differentiates between Unicode strings and raw byte strings. A full explanation of the differences is beyond the scope of this book, but for almost all cryptographic purposes, you *must* use bytes. Otherwise you can end up with some very nasty surprises when the interpreter attempts (or refuses) to convert Unicode strings into bytes for you. We forced our string literals to be bytes using the b'' string syntax. In other examples where user input requires us to start with Unicode strings, we will encode those to bytes ensuring that it is safe to do so.

EXERCISE 2.1. WELCOME TO MD5

Compute more digests. Try computing the MD5 sum of the following inputs:

- `b'alice'` (again)
- `b'bob'` (again)
- `b'balice'`
- `b'cob'`
- `b'a'`
- `b'aa'`
- `b'aaaaaaaaaa'` (ten copies of the letter "a")
- `b'a'*100000` (100,000 copies of the letter "a")

What did you learn about MD5 sums from Exercise 2.1? We will talk about these further in the chapter, but let's jump back to our intrepid Antarcticans.

"Okay, Alice and Bob," the instructor says. "A couple of things. These digest objects don't require the entire input all at once. It can be inserted a chunk at a time using the update method," as shown in Listing 2-4.

Listing 2-4. Hash Update

```
>>> md5hasher = hashlib.md5()
>>> md5hasher.update(b'a')
>>> md5hasher.update(b'l')
>>> md5hasher.update(b'i')
>>> md5hasher.update(b'c')
>>> md5hasher.update(b'e')
```

The instructor asks Alice and Bob, "What do you think the output of the `md5hasher.hexdigest()` instruction will be?" Try it out and see if you got it right!

"Great," the instructor says when they've finished. "Your introductory training is almost over. Just one more exercise!"

EXERCISE 2.2. GOOGLE KNOWS!

Do a quick Google search using the following hashes (enter the hashes literally into the Google search bar):

1.   5f4dcc3b5aa765d61d8327deb882cf99

2.   d41d8cd98f00b204e9800998ecf8427e

3.   6384e2b2184bcbf58eccf10ca7a6563c

Making a Hash of Education

Within the realm of computer security, the terms "hashing" or "hash function" always refer to *cryptographic* hash functions, unless otherwise stated. There are some very useful non-cryptographic hash functions as well. In fact, you were taught a very simple one in grade school: computing whether a number is even or odd. Let's see how this simple, familiar function illustrates principles that apply to all hash functions.

Hash functions are fundamentally trying to map an enormous (even infinite) number of things onto a (relatively) small set of things. When using MD5, for example, no matter how big our document is, we end up with a 16-byte number. In discrete algebra terms, this means that the *domain* of a hash function is much larger than its *range*. Given a very, very large number of documents, chances are that many of them will produce the same hash.

Hash functions are therefore *lossy*. We lose information going from our source document to a digest or **hash**. This is actually critical to their function, because without a loss of information, there would be a way to go backward from the hash to the document. We really don't want that, and we'll see why soon.

Thus, computing whether a number is even or odd fits this description quite well. No matter how large or interesting the (integer) number, we can squash it down into a single bit of space: 1 for odd, 0 for even. That's a hash! Given any number of any size, we can efficiently produce its "oddness" value, but given its oddness, we would be hard-pressed to figure out which number produced it. We can create a very, very large number of *possible* inputs, but we can't know *which one specifically* was used to make that answer.

An "even or odd" bit is sometimes called a "parity" bit and has often been used as a rudimentary error detection code.

The even/odd hash example illustrates this principle of "squashing" an input down to a fixed size value. This value is *consistent*, meaning you won't get a different value out if you put the same number into it twice. It *compresses* large inputs into a fixed-size space (just one bit!), and it is *lossy*: you can't tell me which number was used as input by examining only the output.

All hash functions, including non-cryptographic hash functions, have the fundamental qualities of **consistency**, **compression**, and **lossiness** and have all kinds of important applications in computer science. These qualities alone, however, are not enough for a hash function to be *cryptographic* or *secure*: for those, a hash function needs a few more properties [11, Chap. 9]:

- Preimage resistance

- Second-preimage resistance

- Collision resistance

We'll talk about each of these important qualities in turn.

Preimage Resistance

Informally, a **preimage** is the set of inputs for a hash function *that produce a specific output*. If we were to apply that to our parity example from earlier, the preimage for an odd parity bit is the (infinite!) set of all odd integers. Similarly, the preimage for an even parity bit is the set of all even integers.

What does this mean for a cryptographic hash? Earlier, we computed that the MD5 hash value 6384e2b2184bcbf58eccf10ca7a6563c could be generated by the input b'alice'. Thus, the preimage of

$$MD5(x) = 6384e2b2184bcbf58eccf10ca7a6563c$$

contains the element x == b'alice'.

This is important, so let's state it in more precise terms (using integers in our domain and range—remember, a document is ordered bits and is therefore just a big integer):

Preimage: A *preimage* for a hash function *H* and a hash value *k* is the *set of values* of *x* for which *H(x) = k*.

For cryptographic hash functions, this concept of the preimage is important. If I give you a digest value, there might (should) be infinitely many input numbers that could be used to produce it. Those numbers are the preimage for that digest. Remember, every document is just a large integer number from the computer's point of view. It's all just bytes, and we're just performing a mathematical operation on them. The preimage is therefore just an infinite set of integer numbers.[1]

The idea of **preimage resistance** is basically this: if you hand me a digest and I don't already know how you got it, *I can't even find one element in the preimage for it* without doing a ridiculous amount of work. Ideally I would have to do an *impossible* amount of work.

It's already hard to (in general) find *the entire* preimage; it's way too big. What we're really interested in is making it tough to find *any element* in the preimage unless you already happen to know one. That's where lossiness comes in: the digest should give us *no information whatsoever* about the document that produced it. Without any

---

[1]If thinking about the domain helps, a good quality for every preimage of a hash function would be that all of its elements are very spread out with unpredictable spacing. That way you are very unlikely to accidentally choose one by guessing (they're really spread out), and given a hit, you're just as unlikely to find any others (unpredictable spacing). That last part is something we'll dive into in just a moment.

information to guide us, the best we can do is random guessing or trying everything until we accidentally land on one that produces the right digest. *That* is preimage resistance.

The process of attempting to find an element in the preimage for a given output is called **inverting** the hash: trying to run it backward to get an input for a given output. Preimage resistance means that finding any inverse is hard.

This is why the even/odd function is a potentially *useful* hash function, but not a *secure* hash function. If I give you an even/odd value, you can readily come up with *something* that matches. I say "even," you say "2," for example. That's not very preimage-resistant, because you just told me an input that produces the given output, and you didn't have to think very hard to do it. In fact, you can describe the entire preimage without much trouble: "all even integers." For cryptographic hash functions, if I tell you MD5(x) = `ca8a0fb205782051bd49f02eae17c9ee`, you (ideally) can't tell me what x is unless you can find someone who already knows and is willing to tell you. MD5 is hard to invert.

Now, you could just try random (or ordered) documents to see if any of them produce `ca8a0fb205782051bd49f02eae17c9ee`, and you might get (very!) lucky. That approach is one kind of a **brute-force attack** because you just have to pick your way through every single straw in the haystack to find the needle you are looking for. All you can do is commit to looking at an awful lot of straw, relying on raw stamina to carry you through.

Because consistency is a property of hashes, if you already happen to have an input that maps to a given output, or you can find it by searching Google, for example, then that particular output is trivially inverted. The ASCII text "alice" always maps to "6384e2b2184bcbf58eccf10ca7a6563c" when run through MD5, no matter what, so if you happen to know that those two things go together, you can easily find "alice" from the digest. For that particular output, MD5 is trivially inverted. That doesn't mean MD5 is not preimage-resistant, though: to break that you would need to find an easy way to *always* find an input given an output *without knowing one beforehand*.

That leaves us with brute force again. How long would it take you to "guess" an element of the preimage for an MD5 hash using a brute-force technique (either random guessing or sequential searching)? To answer this, we first need to look at how many possible hash values there are. We know that MD5 always produces a 16-byte digest, and we can use that to figure out how hard it should ideally be to invert MD5. To do so, we'll need some understanding of binary (base-2), decimal (base-10), and hexadecimal (base-16) positive integers (plus 0, but we usually just say "non-negative").

If you already understand those pretty well, feel free to skip to the next section.

Byte into Some Non-negative Integers

Most computers use binary to represent everything. The binary number system is represented in base 2. One nice way to be introduced to it is through counting. Here we have the familiar base-10 (decimal) number on the left and the corresponding binary number on the right:

```
0    0
1    1
2    10
3    11
4    100
5    101
6    110
7    111
8    1000
9    1001
```

How does counting work in this system? We start with 0, which is nice and familiar. Adding 1 gives us 1, which is expected. So far, so good. But then, since we're in base 2, we run out of digits when we try to do it again! Just like there is no single digit representing the number "10" in our decimal system, there is no single digit representing "2" in binary!

What do we do when we run out of digits in base 10? We use place values. The very number "10" shows this: there is "1 ten" and "0 ones" in that number. It's the number that comes after "9."

Binary is similar. When we move up one number from "1," we run out of digits, so we put a "1" in the "twos column" and start over at "0" in the "ones column."

What might seem remarkable is the fact that you can represent every non-negative integer this way, just like you can with decimal. The base value ("base-2," "base-10," "base-16," etc.) tells you how many digits you have to work with and therefore what the place values mean. Here are a few place values in different number systems. Note that people get a little bit careless with these things, using decimal to *talk about them*, but really the number system is arbitrary. When it comes to that, there are ten kinds of people in the world: those who understand binary and those who don't.[2]

---

[2]An old joke. You're welcome. And we're sorry.

That's a big problem when teaching number systems: what does "10" mean without knowing what base we're operating in? The default is to assume it means "ten" unless the base is explicitly stated, or is *really obvious*, like with hexadecimal, where we see "a"–"f" along with the more common decimal digits. We'll do that here too: if you don't see a base or you can't easily tell what it is, you are looking at decimal.

	Place 3	Place 2	Place 1	Place 0
Binary	8	4	2	1
Decimal	1000	100	10	1
Hexadecimal	4096	256	16	1

Or, put another way:

	Place 3	Place 2	Place 1	Place 0
Binary	2^3	2^2	2^1	2^0
Decimal	10^3	10^2	10^1	10^0
Hexadecimal	16^3	16^2	16^1	16^0

All of these number systems work in the same way: place value is determined by adding one to an exponent on the base.

In decimal, therefore, the number 237 really means $2 \cdot 10^2 + 3 \cdot 10^1 + 7 \cdot 10^0 = 200 + 30 + 7$.

The same number in hex (we'll use x_h to mean "x in hexadecimal") is ed_h, which means $e_h \cdot 10_h^1 + d_h \cdot 10_h^0$. But what does *that* mean? Well, $e_h = 14_d$ in decimal, and $d_h = 13_d$. Since 10_h has a 1 in the sixteens column, we get (in decimal) $14 \cdot 16 + 13 = 237$.

Why do we care about hexadecimal in the first place, other than its relative compactness? Hexadecimal (or "hex") is useful because its place values are multiples of 2 (they're multiples of 2^4, to be exact), so it lines up nicely with binary. Consider the following table with hex on the left and binary on the right:

0	0
1	1
2	10
3	11
4	100
5	101
6	110
7	111
8	1000
9	1001
A	1010
B	1011
C	1100
D	1101
E	1110
F	1111

We ran out of digits in hex at exactly the same time that we needed to go from four columns to five in binary! That's really helpful, because it means we can trivially convert back and forth between a computer's native and sprawling binary numbers to the much more human-friendly and compact hex numbers. People even get good enough at this that they can just translate them on sight. Here's an example with binary on top and hex underneath:

```
101 1100 1010 0011 0111
5    c    a    3    7
```

No matter how big a binary number gets, you can take every four bits and write them as a single hexadecimal digit.

The point of walking through this review of binary is to emphasize once again that *every* sequence of bits in a computer is a *number*. What if those bits are a document? That's a number. What about if they represent an image? That's just a big number.

The "meaning" of those bits is not in the computer, it's *in our minds*.

We may display the bits a certain way, but *we humans* choose to do that based on what we think they mean. The computer has *no idea* what they really mean. They're just numbers. Can we store the *meaning itself* somehow? Well, sure, but that would force us to encode the meaning *as a number*, because numbers are all that computers understand. Even their instructions are just numbers.

Philosophize much, do we? It's actually a pretty important thing to understand if you really want to know how computers work, and we definitely need people in the world who do. Data and code are just big numbers, and computers basically just fetch, store, and do arithmetic on them.

How Hard a Hash!

With that little side trip, we can now answer what we wanted to answer in the first place: how hard would it be, in general, to invert MD5 using brute force? We can take a stab at this by looking at the size of its output. MD5 outputs a value in 16 bytes, which is $16 \cdot 8 = 128$ bits. With n bits we can express 2^n individual values, so MD5 can output a lot of different digests. This many, in fact (in decimal):[3]

340,282,366,920,938,463,463,374,607,431,768,211,456.

Even if you checked 1 million values *per second* (and were guaranteed that nothing you checked produced an output you had seen before), it would still take you about 10^{26} years (100 million billion billion!) to find a suitable input by brute force. By comparison, our sun is only expected to continue sustaining earth life for at most another 5 billion years; your computer would need to keep running for many, many times that long.

If you have a cryptographic algorithm whose only means of being broken is brute force, you have a good algorithm. The trouble is, you don't necessarily *know that it's good*. But this gives us an upper bound on how long it would take to find an input that produces a particular hash in MD5. At least it won't take longer!

---

[3]In hex, this number is much more tightly related to binary and looks a little more sensible: 10000 00000000000000000000000000000.

Second-Preimage and Collision Resistance

Once preimage resistance is understood, the other two properties are relatively easy to grasp. We wandered a bit into brute force and binary near the end of that last section, so let's quickly review:

> **Preimage resistance** means it is really hard to find a document that produces a particular digest, unless you already know one.

Second-Preimage Resistance

Second-preimage resistance means that if you already have *one* document that produces a particular digest, it's still really hard to find a *different* document that produces that same digest.

In other words, just because you know that

$$MD5(alice) = 384e2b2184bcbf58eccf10ca7a6563c,$$

it doesn't mean you can find another value to put into **MD5**($\cdot$) that will give you the same value. You would have to resort to brute force again.

To tie it back to its name, if you have one member of the preimage already, it is not any easier to find a second member of the preimage; there is no exploitable pattern in the preimage.

Collision Resistance

Collision resistance is a bit more subtle than either of the preimage characteristics we just mentioned. Collision resistance means that it's hard to find *any two inputs that produce the same output*: not a *specific* output, just *the same* output.

A classic way of describing this is by using birthdays.[4] Suppose you are in a room full of people and you want to find two of them whose birthday is February 3. How likely is that? Not necessarily very likely, if you really picked it at random.

But now let's say you want to do something else. You want to know whether any two people have *the same birthday*. You don't care what day of the year it falls on, you just want to know whether anyone's birthday overlaps with anyone else's. How likely is

---

[4]The "birthday problem" is a classic problem in probability theory, of uncertain origin.

that? It turns out that, in general, it is far, *far* more likely. After all, we just removed the constraint of a particular day, and now all we want is a collision on *any day*.

That's the basic idea behind collision resistance. When a hash algorithm is resistant to collision, it is resistant to being able to purposefully create or pick any two inputs that produce the same digest, without deciding what that digest should be beforehand.

MD5 appears to be fairly collision-resistant. One property that helps with this is the fact that small changes in input can produce very large changes in output. Consider Exercise 2.1, where you produced hashes for very similar values like "a" and "aa," or "bob" and "cob." The digests resulting from performing MD5 on these values were not just different, they were *wildly* different:

bob: 9f9d51bc70ef21ca5c14f307980a29d8
cob: 386685f06beecb9f35db2e22da429ec9

There is no discernible pattern that would tie one to the other. This is due to a property shared by many hashes and cryptographic ciphers called the **avalanche property**: a change to the input, no matter how small, creates a large and unpredictable change in the output. Ideally, 50% of the output bits should be altered for small input changes [11, Chap. 7]. Did we achieve that with "bob" and "cob"? Let's take a look at the digests in binary using some Python to aid our exploration (note that our bit string is quite long, so it is broken over two lines in Listing 2-5).

Listing 2-5. Avalanche

```
>>> hexstring = hashlib.md5(b'bob').hexdigest()
>>> hexstring
'9f9d51bc70ef21ca5c14f307980a29d8'
>>> binstring = bin(int(hexstring, 16))
>>> print("{}\n{}".format(binstring[2:66], binstring[66:]))
1001111110011101010100011011110001110000111011110010000111001010
0101110000010100111001100000111100110000000101000101001110011000
```

The following illustration visualizes the changes in bits when given inputs b'bob' and b'cob',

MD5(bob):

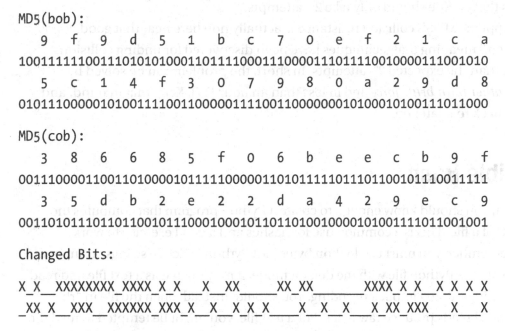

```
  9    f    9    d    5    1    b    c    7    0    e    f    2    1    c    a
10011111100111010101000110111100011100001101111001000011001010
  5    c    1    4    f    3    0    7    9    8    0    a    2    9    d    8
01011100000101001110011000001111001100000010100010100111011000
```

MD5(cob):

```
  3    8    6    6    8    5    f    0    6    b    e    e    c    b    9    f
00111000011001101000010111110000011010111101110110010111001111
  3    5    d    b    2    e    2    2    d    a    4    2    9    e    c    9
00110101110110110010111000100010110110100100001010011111011001001
```

Changed Bits:

```
X_X__XXXXXXX_XXXX_X_X__X__XX_____XX_XX_____XXXX_X_X__X_X_X_X
_XX_X__XXX__XXXXXX_XXX_X__X__X_X_X_____X__X__X__X_XX_XXX___X___X
```

In this example, the difference between the hash of "bob" and "cob" impacted 64 bits out of 128. Not bad! Avalanche is an important property, and we will see it again with ciphers in Chapter 3.

EXERCISE 2.3. OBSERVING AVALANCHE

Compare the bit changes between a wide range of input values.

Avalanche helps collision resistance, because it is hard to produce a document, then come up with predictable changes that will still cause it to produce the same digest. If a small change in a document produces an unpredictable and large change in the digest, then creating collisions on purpose is likely to be a difficult problem, pushing us toward brute force again to solve it.

Remember the birthday analogy from earlier? Finding collisions is not as hard as finding a value in the preimage. Preimage resistance for an n-bit digest means an attacker would expect to compromise your hash after trying 2^n, where it would only take $2^{(n/2)}$ attempts to find a collision. That's not half as many tries, that's a number of tries with half as many *zeros* in it. The difference is astounding. Concretely for MD5, finding a document for a given digest should take about 2^{128} attempts, where finding two documents that collide should only take 2^{64} attempts.

As it happens, MD5's collision resistance is actually nowhere near that good. It has been "broken," meaning that techniques have been discovered for finding collisions in far fewer than the expected 2^{64} attempts. In short, the problem can be solved by something *other than brute force* and in less than an hour [17]. Keep that in mind, and we'll come back to it later on.

Digestible Hash

By this point, you should know enough to create a Python program that computes the MD5 digest[5] of a file. This is a common use for hashes and a good exercise to work through. Remember, you must use Python bytes, not Python Unicode strings, as inputs. If you try to open a Python file with the default mode, it may open it as a text file and read the data as strings, doing implicit decoding. You should, instead, open the file in "rb" mode so that all reads produce raw bytes. For a text file, you might be tempted to read the data as a string and then use the string's encode method to convert to bytes, but *depending on configuration, this encoding may not be what you expect and lead to nasty surprises.*

EXERCISE 2.4. MD5 OF A FILE

Write a python program that computes the MD5 sum of the data in a file. You don't need to worry about any of the file's metadata, such as last modified time or even the file's name, only its contents.

You should check your work for Exercise 2.4. If you're using an Ubuntu Linux system, the md5sum utility is already installed. Run this utility from the command line with a file as input and see if it produces the same hex digest as your utility.

Speaking of Ubuntu, this is a perfect example of using hashes for file integrity. Visit the web site for Ubuntu releases. At the time of this writing, the web site is https://releases.ubuntu.com. If you take a look at the "Bionic Beaver" distribution, for example,

---

[5]Sometimes called the "MD5 sum," where "sum" is short for "checksum," a name with some interesting (and long) history of its own, from error detection in digital transmissions.

you will find that there are number of files available for download. In particular, there are two ISOs, but they are available directly or through other downloading technologies such as BitTorrent.

There's also a file called MD5SUMS. Take a look. For this distribution, the contents of this file should be as follows:

```
f430da8fa59d2f5f4262518e3c177246 *ubuntu-18.04.1-desktop-amd64.iso
9b15b331455c0f7cb5dac53bbe050f61 *ubuntu-18.04.1-live-server-amd64.iso
```

Once downloaded, you can verify that the data is uncorrupted by running an MD5 sum on the ISO.

How is the MD5 hash value helpful? It will not protect you from somebody that has compromised the Ubuntu web site. If they upload a fake Ubuntu to the web server, they can upload a fake MD5 sum as well.

The MD5 sum *does*, however, make it easier for you to obtain the Ubuntu ISO from other sources and know that it's authentic. For example, suppose that you were about to download the ISO file directly from the Ubuntu web site when a coworker stops by and says that you can use the already-downloaded one they have on a USB drive. You can download the (relatively small) file of MD5 sums from Ubuntu's official site and check them against the (much larger) files on the drive before trusting them.

Looking in the Ubuntu directory, you will also see a file called SHA1SUMS and SHA256SUMS. What are these?

So far, we've only talked about MD5 as a way of teaching some of the principles of hashing. MD5 was a standard approach to cryptographic hashing for a long time too, but it has been broken: people have discovered methods much faster than brute force for inducing collisions, so it is being phased out in favor of other hash functions.

Interestingly enough, being "broken" often means "someone can solve a problem in an order of magnitude less time than brute force." For example, that might mean that preimage values can be found in 2^{127} tries on average instead of 2^{128}. That's still hard, just not as hard as it should be. When looking at articles indicating that something has been broken, it's important to find out *exactly what that means*. Does it mean one of the fundamental properties no longer holds? Does it mean it holds, but isn't as hard to get around? What if it's more than one property? These things matter.

With MD5, researchers have found a way to "break" preimage resistance [12]. They showed that they could find a preimage for an MD5 hash faster than 2^{128} tries. How much faster? Well, their algorithm takes slightly longer than 2^{123} tries or, in decimal, 10,633,

823,966,279,326,983,230,456,482,242,756,608 tries. This attack is considered theoretical because it is still not useful in practice: 2^{123} is still *huge*.

On the other hand, MD5 has been shown to be very, very broken where *collision resistance* is concerned. It is reasonably easy to create two inputs that produce the same MD5 output. This has been shown to enable a practical attack for getting a false certificate for use in TLS, which is used for all kinds of secure Internet communication. We won't get into the details here, because we haven't talked about certificates yet, but we'll revisit this when we get to TLS at the end of the book.

On the other hand, collision resistance is not the same as second-preimage resistance. Remember that second-preimage resistance prevents you for finding a second member of the preimage for an output when you already have the first. Even though MD5's collision resistance is broken, its preimage resistance is not. Returning to our Ubuntu distribution example, if you're getting your distribution from an intermediary, they are not able to create an alternate distribution with the same MD5 digest.

The Ubuntu organization, however, could exploit the MD5 collision resistance weakness to create two separate distributions that have the same MD5 sum. Perhaps, in conjunction with a government, they could sell one distribution with all kinds of tracking software to another government hostile to the first. The MD5 sum could not be used to ensure that the same ISO was being distributed to all parties.

Also, once a cryptographic algorithm is broken in one way, there is increased suspicion that it is broken in other ways as well. So even though nobody has demonstrated a practical attack on MD5's preimage or second-preimage resistance, many cryptographers worry that such vulnerabilities exist.

To reiterate the warning at the beginning of the chapter, **DO NOT USE MD5**. It has been deprecated for over 10 years (decimal), and some of its security flaws have been known for two decades.

The SHA-1 hash is another algorithm that was widely viewed as the replacement for MD5. SHA-1's collision resistance has *also* recently been broken, however, as researchers have shown that it is relatively easy to create two inputs that hash to the same output [13]. So, as with MD5, **DO NOT USE SHA-1**, either.

At the time of this writing, best practice is to use SHA-256. Fortunately, this means very little to you if you are using `hashlib`: just change the hasher, as shown in Listing 2-6.

Listing 2-6. Change to SHA-256

```
>>> import hashlib
>>> hashlib.md5(b'alice').hexdigest()
'6384e2b2184bcbf58eccf10ca7a6563c'
>>> hashlib.sha1(b'alice').hexdigest()
'522b276a356bdf39013dfabea2cd43e141ecc9e8'
>>> hashlib.sha256(b'alice').hexdigest()
'2bd806c97f0e00af1a1fc3328fa763a9269723c8db8fac4f93af71db186d6e90'
```

You should notice that these different hash algorithms have different lengths. MD5, of course, outputs 16 bytes (128 bits). If it isn't obvious, SHA-1's output is 20 bytes (160 bits). And, more simply, SHA-256's output is 32 bytes (256 bits).

If you thought it would take a long time to invert MD5 (find a preimage for a given output), take a look at SHA-1. Because the output is 160 bits, it will take 2^{160} tries, or

1,461,501,637,330,902,918,203,684,832,716,283,019,655,932,542,976

tries to find a preimage. And SHA-256 requires 2^{256} tries, or

115,792,089,237,316,195,423,570,985,008,687,907,853,269,984,665,640,564,039,457,
584,007,913,129,639,936.

Good luck with that!

Pass Hashwords...Er...Hash Passwords

Another common use for hash functions is password storage. When you create an account on a web site, for example, they almost never store your password. Typically, they store a *hash* of the password. That way, if the web site is ever compromised and the password file is stolen, the attacker cannot recover anyone's password.

What does this mean? When you send your password (over a secure channel, via HTTPS), the server doesn't need to store it to check it. When you registered, your password was hashed, and the hash was stored. We'll call that H(password). When you go to log in later, you send a password that we'll call the "proposal": you're proposing that this is your true password, and the server needs to verify that.

So, you attempt to log in by sending your proposed password over a secure connection, and the server now has two things for you: it can look up H(password) from your username, and it has the proposal that you just submitted. All it has to do is check that H(proposal) = H(password) and let you through if they are the same.

What if you don't trust the service to not actually store your password? That can be a valid worry, particularly since we've seen so many sites with stolen passwords in recent years. Why not use the power of JavaScript to hash your password in the browser, then send *that* to the server? Then the server never even sees your password in memory, let alone in its database!

There are a few big problems with this:

- The code that hashes the password in your browser *came from that server in the first place*, so you still have to trust the service.

- If you don't have a secure channel for your password, then someone can read it in transit. If you do have a secure channel, then you might as well just send the password. You have to trust the service already.

- If you send a hash successfully, that just became your password. Yes, you can generate it from some other easy-to-remember thing, but now you have to protect that hash value as well. The server has to hash your hash anyway, so that an attacker that makes off with the database can't just log in using what's stored there.

In short, if you were to use a hash as your password, the right way is to generate that hash from your password and the site name of interest *using a tool separate from your browser*, and then use the result as your password. This is essentially the same thing as just creating a brand new password and remembering it in a secure place, like a password manager.

Just do that instead. Then the server will never see a password that you use somewhere else, because you created a brand new random one for it.

Far better than trying to solve security with a hash is to use multiple forms of authentication that are proven to make it harder to steal your identity online, typically involving a hardware token attached to your computer.

Most common forms of two-factor authentication don't help and actually make things worse. Secret questions are one of those. It's usually easy to get answers to them, and if it isn't, they're just one more hard thing to remember, unless written down. Plus, now you have *several* things that can be used as a password for the site, which means attackers have more opportunities to get in by guesswork. SMS has been shown to be critically weak and easy to hijack as well, so having a code sent via SMS to your phone is no good.

Properly deployed challenge-response hardware tokens don't have any of these problems. They are something you possess instead of just another thing you know, and they can't be guessed or spoofed by people listening in on the connection or pretending to be some other site's login form. They can't be given over the phone accidentally, and they can't be forged.

Ultimately you need two or more factors for authentication *anyway* for true security. "Fixing passwords" is the wrong place to look for a complete solution.

If server-side hashing is correctly used and if an attacker steals the password file, they will see something like this. From looking at it, can you tell smithj's password?

```
...
smithj,5f4dcc3b5aa765d61d8327deb882cf99
...
```

Look closely. Have you seen that hash value before?

The eagle-eyed reader will remember that hash value from the beginning of the chapter exercises. You were asked to look for that value online. What did you find?

That hash value is the MD5 hash of "password," and yes, that password is still used far too often. But the deeper problem here is that hash values are deterministic: the same input always hashes to the same output. If an attacker has seen the MD5 sum of "password" once, he will be able to look for that same digest in every password file stolen. How can we fix this?

First, let's not assume that we can make people stop using dumb passwords.

Let's assume that they're going to and we need to fix it anyway. We'll start with the digest itself.

Recall that MD5 is *not* broken (in practice) with respect to preimage resistance or second-preimage resistance. So there is no practical attack, at present, for inverting this hash value to the password. Nevertheless, **MD5 is broken and should not be used!** So let's take a look at a new password file.

```
...
smithj,5baa61e4c9b93f3f0682250b6cf8331b7ee68fd8
...
```

Any idea what smithj's password is now? Yes, it is still "password" but now it's hashed under SHA-1. That's better, right? Oh yeah, **SHA-1 is broken and should not be used!** Let's try one more time!

```
...
smithj,5e884898da28047151d0e56f8dc6292773603d0d6aabbdd62a11ef721d1542d8
...
```

There! Finally! We're using a hash algorithm without known vulnerabilities. That's better, but the problem with deterministic hashing is still a problem. If the attacker knows that this hash maps to the SHA-256 of "password," smithj is still compromised.

This is where the idea of a "salt" comes into play. A salt is a publicly known value that is mixed in with the user's password before hashing. By mixing in a salt value, the user's password will not be immediately discernible as it is now.

This salt has to be chosen correctly. It needs to be unique, and it needs to be sufficiently long. One way of doing this is to use `os.urandom` and `base64.b64encode` to generate a strong, random[6] salt:

```
>>> import hashlib
>>> hashlib.md5(b'alice').hexdigest()
'6384e2b2184bcbf58eccf10ca7a6563c'
>>> hashlib.sha1(b'alice').hexdigest()
'522b276a356bdf39013dfabea2cd43e141ecc9e8'
>>> hashlib.sha256(b'alice').hexdigest()
'2bd806c97f0e00af1a1fc3328fa763a9269723c8db8fac4f93af71db186d6e90'
```

---

[6]The requirement is *uniqueness*, not *randomness*, but randomness provides us with a simple approach that works well for our examples.

Obviously, your salt output will be different from that shown in the code listing and will be different every time you call it.

Once you have the salt, you store it, then mix the password and the salt with concatenation. For example, prepend the password with the salt before hashing. Now, if the attacker gets your password file, it will be impossible to "recognize" the password from any kind of pre-computed table.

They can still try hashing the salt plus "password" to see if anything matches, though. Guesswork is always a strategy, and it's a particularly good one for most people's password choices.

It should be easy to see that the same salt has to be used every time for checking a user's password. But should the same salt be used for multiple users? Could you generate the salt once for an entire web site and just reuse it?

The answer is a very strong "No!" Can you think of why? What will be the impact if two users are using the same salt? At the very least, it means that it is instantly easy to recognize if two users are sharing the *same* password. Thus, best practice is to store the user name and salt along with the password hash.

If our friend smithj has the terribly chosen password, "password", at least it will be stored correctly on our system:

```
...
smithj,cei6LtJVQYSM+n6Cty0O2w==,
    bd51dac1e2fca8456069f38fcce933f1ff30a656320877b596a14a0e05db9567
...
```

We have now walked through the basics of password storage, but there are better algorithms. They are built on the same principle but do additional steps to make it even harder for an attacker to invert the password. One highly recommended algorithms for password storage is called **scrypt** by Colin Percival and described in RFC 7914 [16]. Other popular ones are the newer **bcrypt**[7] (https://pypi.org/project/bcrypt/) and the algorithm considered by some to be its successor: **Argon2** (https://pypi.org/project/argon2/).

Fortunately, using scrypt is easy using the cryptography module you set up in Chapter 1. Listing 2-7 is an example derived from the cryptography module's online documentation. The listing derives the key (hash) to be stored on the file system.

---

[7]The bcrypt algorithm is quite good and has only one "difficulty" parameter, making it easier to use correctly than approaches with many parameters.

Listing 2-7. Scrypt Generate

```
1    import os
2    from cryptography.hazmat.primitives.kdf.scrypt import Scrypt
3    from cryptography.hazmat.backends import default_backend
4
5    salt = os.urandom(16)
6
7    kdf = Scrypt(salt=salt, length=32,
8                     n=2**14, r=8, p=1,
9                     backend=default_backend())
10
11   key = kdf.derive (b"my great password")
```

Both the key and the salt must be stored to disk. The `scrypt` parameters must be fixed or must also be stored. We will walk through these parameters in a moment, but first, verification is depicted in Listing 2-8 (it is presumed that salt and key are restored from disk).

Listing 2-8. Scrypt Verify

```
1    kdf = Scrypt(salt =salt, length =32,
2                 n=2**14, r=8, p=1,
3                 backend=default_backend())
4    kdf.verify(b"my great password", key)
5    print("Success! (Exception if mismatch)")
```

Pick Perfect Parameters

With regard to the `scrypt` parameters, let's talk about backend first. The `cryptography` module is primarily a wrapper around a lower-level engine. For example, the module can make use of OpenSSL as such an engine. This makes the system faster (because computations aren't being done in Python) and more secure (because it relies on a robust, well-tested library). Throughout this book, we will always rely on `default_backend()`.

The other parameters are specific to `scrypt`. The `length` parameter is how long the key will be once the process is finished. In these examples, the password is processed into an output of 32 bytes. The parameters r, n, and p are tuning parameters that impact how long it will take to compute and how much memory is required. To better protect your password, you want the process to take longer and require more memory, preventing attackers from compromising large chunks of a database at once (every compromise should take a long time).

Fortunately for you, recommended parameters are available. The r parameter should be 8, and the p parameter should be 1. The n parameter can vary based on whether you are doing something like a web site that needs to give a relatively prompt response or something more securely stored that does not need quick responsiveness. Either way, it must be a power of 2. For the interactive logins, 2^{14} is recommended. For the more sensitive files, a number as high as 2^{20} is better.

This is actually an excellent segue into a more general discussion about parameters. A lot of the security in cryptography depends on how parameters are set. Unless you are a cryptography expert, know the exact details of the algorithm, and understand why they are what they are, it may be difficult to choose them properly. It is important that you familiarize yourself with what the parameters mean, at least at a high level, and how they should be used in different contexts. Refer to trusted sources, such as `https://cryptodoneright.org`, for advice and recommendations. Keep an eye on these sources too. What is presumed to be secure can change as new attacks and computational resources are unveiled.

Cracking Weak Passwords

Let's take a look at how attackers try to crack passwords. Unfortunately for smithj, choosing such a bad password means that he will most likely be compromised if the password file gets stolen, since attackers will try common words (including words in *other* stolen databases) against all the hashes anyway. But even less sophisticated methods would probably figure out the password as well.

In this section, we are going to practice cracking weak passwords using the least sophisticated method of all: brute force. This exercise is meant to reinforce why good passwords are so important.

The scenario is this: an attacker has a password file with usernames, salts, and password hashes. What can they do? Well, they could just try all lowercase letter combinations up to a certain length, starting, for example, with "a," "b," "c," and so on.

To make these exercises a little bit easier to start, Listing 2-9 shows some simple code for generating all possible combinations of an alphabet set up to a maximum length.

Listing 2-9. Alphabet Permutations

```
1    def generate(alphabet, max_len):
2        if max_len <= 0: return
3        for c in alphabet:
4            yield c
5        for c in alphabet:
6            for next in generate(alphabet, max_len-1):
7                yield c + next
```

Calling generate('ab', 2) will generate 'a', 'b', 'aa', 'ab', 'ba', 'bb'. Using helpful sets in the built-in string module, such as

- `string.ascii_lowercase`

- `string.ascii_uppercase`

- `string.ascii_letters`

makes the following exercises fairly easy. Recall that hashing algorithms require bytes as inputs, so don't forget to do an `encode` operation before passing these generated strings to the hashing function, like this:

`string.ascii_letters.encode('utf-8').`

ASCII letters encode correctly to bytes, so this will not lead to incorrect hashing or unexpected behaviors.

EXERCISE 2.5. THE POWER OF ONE

Write a program that does the following ten times (so, ten full loops with the time computed):

- Randomly select a single, lowercase letter. This is the "preimage seed."

- Use MD5 to compute the hash of this initial letter. This is the "test hash."

- In a loop, iterate through all possible lowercase one-letter inputs.

    – Hash each letter in the same way as before, and compare against the test hash.

    – When you find a match, stop.

- Compute the amount of time it took to find a match.

How long, on average, did it take to find a match for a random preimage seed?

EXERCISE 2.6. THE POWER OF ONE, BUT BIGGER!

Repeat the previous exercise, but use an increasingly bigger input alphabet set. Try the test with both lowercase and uppercase letters. Then try it with lowercase letters, uppercase letters, and numbers. Finally, try all printable characters (`string.printable`).

- How many total symbols are in each input set?

- How much longer does each run take?

EXERCISE 2.7. PASSWORD LENGTH'S EFFECTS ON ATTACK TIME

Repeat the previous exercise, but this time for two-symbol inputs. Then try it with three and four symbols at a time. How much longer does it take to invert the randomly chosen input?

You will notice that increasing the length of the password and increasing the size of the alphabet both increase the time it takes to invert the hash. Let's look at the math.

When using just lowercase letters, how many possible one-symbol inputs are there? Rather trivially, there are 26 lowercase letters in ASCII, so 26 one-symbol inputs. At worst, it will take 26 hash computations to invert a one-letter password. But, if we have both lowercase *and* uppercase letters, this increases the number of hashes needed to 52. Adding digits increases this to 62. There are 100 characters in `string.printable`. That's nearly a fourfold increase of the worst-case number of hashes required to do brute-force inversion.

What about when we increase the size to two input symbols? How many two-symbol passwords are there using just lowercase letters? If you can have 26 characters for the first symbol and 26 characters for the second symbol, then there are $26 * 26 = 676$ total combinations. That's quite a jump!

Now look what happens if you use two symbols drawn from the 52 uppercase and lowercase letters. The math works out to be 52 * 52 = 2704! Doubling the size of the input set quadrupled the complexity for two-symbol inputs! If we throw in digits, the worst-case computation is 3844 hashes, and for all printable ASCII characters, it is around 10,000 hashes.

Do the math for three, four, and five symbols, and you can easily see why longer passwords matter. Hackers with GPU-enabled rigs are able to invert anything smaller than six characters, and most passwords under eight, so *at a minimum*, passwords should be that long. And for the reasons demonstrated here, choosing from *all* printable letters greatly increases the complexity.

EXERCISE 2.8. MORE HASH, MORE TIME

Choosing a complex-to-invert password is the responsibility of the user, but the systems storing the passwords can also slow down attackers by using a more complicated *hashing function*. Repeat any of the preceding exercises that use MD5, but now use SHA-1 and SHA-256 instead. Record how much longer it takes to get through the brute-force operations. Finally, try out brute force using scrypt. You might not get very far!

One final note. Just because a password is *big* doesn't mean it is *secure*. Attackers will also use large dictionaries to look for known words and phrases, even with various common number or symbol substitutions. A password such as "chocolatecake" is pretty long, but still easily broken. Randomly chosen letters or words are still the best bet. The key is that they are "random," meaning you would never find them in any real writing or common transformations on real writing. Typically, choosing passphrases that are composed of common utterances reduces a successful attack to *seconds* instead of *years*.

Proof of Work

Another area where hashing is used extensively is so-called "proof-of-work" schemes in blockchain technologies. To introduce this, we need to do a very quick overview of how blockchains work.

The basic idea of a blockchain is a "distributed ledger." The system is a *ledger* because it records information related to transactions between participants. It can also store additional information, but the primary operations are transactions. It is a *distributed* ledger because its contents are stored across the set of participants and not in any central location.

The problem is that there is no central location to enforce the correctness of the system. How does the ledger not get corrupted (intentionally or otherwise) by the users? Note that we won't go into the ledger in detail here, but we do want to talk about the blocks that a ledger is composed of.

Every transaction must be stored in a block. There's nothing special about a "block"; it's just a collection of data. Each transaction within the block must be digitally signed by the transactor (we will discuss signatures more in Chapter 5, but for now, simply accept that it means nobody can create a transaction for somebody else without their private key). The overall block structure is protected by a hash. Blocks are copied to the entire set of participants; should anyone try to "lie" about the contents of a block, the data wouldn't verify correctly and their information would be rejected.

How does a new block get created, and how does it get the protective hash? For this part of the discussion, we will use the Bitcoin network blockchain to walk through these concepts. The designer (or designers, the source is actually unknown) of Bitcoin, who goes by "Satoshi Nakamoto," wanted to control how quickly new blocks could be created and also wanted the system to incentivize participation. The solution was to award bitcoins to the "miner" that produced a new block while making the production of the new block very difficult.

Basically, at any given time, various parties known as miners are searching for the next block in the blockchain. Any user of blockchain can request a transaction. They broadcast their desired transaction throughout the blockchain network and miners will pick them up. The miners take some set of requested transactions (there is a limited number per block) and create a candidate block. This candidate block has all the right pieces of information. It has the transactions, the metadata, and so forth. But it isn't the next block in the blockchain until the miner can solve a cryptographic puzzle.

That puzzle is to find a special kind of SHA-256 hash value, specifically a value smaller than a certain threshold. As we discussed earlier, finding an input that produces one particular output would take a really, *really* long time, but finding any output less than a certain value takes a lot *less* time. Making that threshold smaller reduces the number of valid hashes, requiring more work to find a suitable value, and that's how Bitcoin adjusts the difficulty to account for faster hardware or larger computational pools as time goes on. Ultimately, it takes about 10 minutes for the entire Bitcoin network to find a suitable hash. If it takes less than that on average over a period of weeks, the maximum allowed hash value is decreased. Figure 2-1 shows two different example blocks, one with a suitable nonce (a random value that miners are trying to find to produce an acceptable hash) and one without, where the maximum allowed hash value is $2^{236}-1$ (20 leading zeros required). For Bitcoin, the very *easiest* that a problem is allowed to be is determined by a maximum value of $2^{224}-1$, which would take our little program an average of 2^{12} times longer than before. That translates to 11.3 hours, and the difficulty is *much harder than that* today.

Invalid Block	Valid Block
Hello, Blockchain!	Hello, Blockchain!
:5	:1030399
b366873e9261b5a72b642d ad804bfbd00cd30e69fa85 a0a9ae4d4ca5f8889990	000008c8e96b7b13885b48 21a38082492278c2a7ae9a 2c33ec1a1e91b62be712

Figure 2-1. *Two block hashes with the same content but different nonce values. A nonce that produces a hash with 20 leading binary zeros (5 leading zeros in hexadecimal) is valid. Requiring 20 leading zeros is the same as requiring that the hash number be less than $2 * * 236$.*

Our program definitely won't be beating the network's 10-minute average expectation anytime soon.

Saying that the first few bits must be zero is the same, by the way, as saying the hash value number (the hash is just a number, just like any other string of bits) should be less than some threshold that happens to be a power of 2. Since good hash functions (like SHA-256) produce essentially random hash values, the more structure you impose on the hash, the longer it takes to find one that fits. You can get some intuition for this by thinking about the number of zeros as defining the size of the search space: if you must have a single leading zero, then it's basically a coin flip; it should only take two tries on average to find a suitable hash that starts with a zero bit. If, on the other hand, you need to find a hash with 8 leading zeros, that's a harder problem: 256 different numbers can be represented in 8 bits, so on average it will take 256 attempts to find a suitable value.

That's why this strategy is called "Proof of Work": if you found a suitable hash under the threshold, you had to have done some work (or you broke the hash function, which is deemed to be extremely unlikely, but potentially awesome for you).

This raises an interesting question: how do each of the network participants decide how hard the problem should be? It isn't like there is a central authority telling everyone that the difficulty just went from 11 to 12, for example. That would defeat the whole purpose of the network. The "authority" in the network is tacit agreement between participants to use the same *algorithms* for determining these things. When there is someone on the network doing things differently, their blocks are simply rejected by everyone else and they thus have no incentive to do it wrong. Majority rules.

In the specific case of hashing difficulty, each participant knows the standard algorithm for computing what the number of leading zeros should be and uses that to do mining (or to reject bad proposals from wayward participants looking to compute an easy hash).

You might be asking, however, how a different value of hash is computed when the input data really doesn't change. That's a great question, since hashes are deterministic: they always produce the same output given the same input (they wouldn't be very useful, otherwise!). The answer is that they change one little piece of the input, called the "nonce." It's just a number, and it isn't part of the actual block data: its sole purpose is to enable the proof-of-work concept. When searching for a suitable hash, the participant tries hashing the block with different values for the nonce, typically searching randomly or merely adding 1 to the last value at each attempt. Eventually a suitable hash value is found and the block is sent to all other participants for validation.

Every participant then verifies the block by performing the hash for themselves, checking the leading zeros against their algorithm, and making sure that their answer matches the submitted hash value. If it's good, they accept it and the chain lengthens.

EXERCISE 2.9. PROOF OF WORK

Write a program that feeds a counter into SHA-256, taking the output hash and converting it to an integer (we did this earlier before converting to binary). Have the program repeat until it finds a hash that is less than a target number. The target number should start out pretty big, like 2^{255}. To make this more like blockchain, include some arbitrary bytes to be combined with the counter.

Time to Rehash

We have covered a lot of information about what hashes are and how to use them, including why you should never use MD5 unless you are teaching people that it is broken, and how to use them for more secure password storage and even crypto currency. Hashing is a powerful and important part of cryptography, and we will be seeing it again and again as we move forward.

Now that we have learned a bit about how to digest a document into a safely representative value, it's time to back up a bit and revisit encryption.

CHAPTER 3

Symmetric Encryption: Two Sides, One Key

Symmetric encryption is at the foundation of all modern secure communications. It is what we use to "scramble" messages so that people can only decrypt them if they have access to the same key used to encrypt them. That's what "symmetric" means in this case: one key is used on both ends of the communication channel, to both encrypt and decrypt messages.

Let's Scramble!

Unsurprisingly, the villains[1] of East Antarctica are at it again, causing all kinds of trouble for their neighbors. This time, Alice and Bob are spying on the enemy troops to the west, doing reconnaissance on the size of their snowballs and the accuracy of their throws.

In earlier missions, Alice and Bob used the Caesar cipher from Chapter 1 to protect their messages. As you discovered, this cipher is easy to crack. As a result, the East Antarctica Truth-Spying Agency (EATSA) has equipped them with modern cryptography that uses a key to encode and decode secret messages. This new technology belongs to a class of encryption algorithms called **symmetric ciphers**, because both the encryption and decryption processes use the same shared key. The specific algorithm they are using in this post-et-tu-Brute world is the Advanced Encryption Standard (AES).[2]

---

[1]...or heroes, depending on your point of view, Padawan.

[2]The name "Advanced Encryption Standard" is actually more of a title. Many algorithms competed to become the "Advanced Encryption Standard" including many algorithms that are still available today. The original name of the algorithm was *Rijndael*, which is a composite of the last names of the two inventors.

53

Alice and Bob don't have a lot of information about the proper care and handling of AES. They have just enough documentation to get encryption and decryption working.

"The docs say we have to create AES keys," Alice says holding one of the manuals. "Apparently, it's fairly easy. We have sample code here."

```
import os
key = os.urandom(16)
```

"Wait... really?" Bob asks. "That's it?"

Alice is right: that's all it takes! An AES key is just random bits: 128 of them (16 bytes' worth) in this example. This will allow us to use AES-128.

With the random key created, how do we then encrypt and decrypt messages? Earlier, we used the Python `cryptography` module to create hashes. It does many other things as well. Let's see how Bob—encouraged by the ease of creating keys—uses it now to encrypt messages with AES.

Bob takes the documentation from Alice and looks at the next section, noting that there are many different *modes* of AES computation. Having to choose between them sounds a bit overwhelming, so Bob picks the one that looks easiest to use.

"Let's use ECB mode, Alice," he says, looking up from the docs.

"ECB mode? What is that?"

"I don't really know, but this is the *Advanced* Encryption Standard. It should all work fine, right?"

Warning: ECB: Not for You

We're going to find out later that ECB mode is *terrible* and should *never be used*. But we'll just follow along for now.

Listing 3-1 has the code they used to create an "encryptor" and "decryptor."

Listing 3-1. AES ECB Code

```
1   # NEVER USE: ECB is not secure!
2   from cryptography.hazmat.primitives.ciphers import Cipher,
    algorithms, modes
3   from cryptography.hazmat.backends import default_backend
4   import os
```

```
5
6    key = os.urandom(16)
7    aesCipher = Cipher(algorithms.AES(key),
8                            modes.ECB(),
9                            backend=default_backend())
10   aesEncryptor = aesCipher.encryptor()
11   aesDecryptor = aesCipher.decryptor()
```

"That's not so bad," Alice says. "What happens now?"

"Apparently, both the encryptor and decryptor have an update method. That's pretty much it. The encryptor's update returns the ciphertext."

EXERCISE 3.1. A SECRET MESSAGE

Without looking at additional documentation, try to figure out how the aesEncryptor.
update() and aesDecryptor.update() methods work. Hint: You are going to get some
unexpected behavior, so try lots of inputs. Consider starting with b"a secret message" and
then decrypting the result.

Alice and Bob start trying to figure out the update method. Perhaps inspired by the previous chapter on hashing, where they hashed their names, they try encrypting their names in an interactive Python shell. Alice goes first.

The AES example code here uses the key b"\x81\xff9\xa4\x1b\xbc\xe4\
x84\xec9\x0b\x9a\xdbu\xc1\x83" in case you want to get identical results.

```
>>> aesEncryptor.update(b'alice')
b''
```

"I didn't get any ciphertext," Alice grumbles. "What did I do wrong?"

"I don't know. Let me try," Bob responds.

```
>>> aesEncryptor.update(b'bob')
b''
```

"Me too," he says, confused. Out of frustration, he tries it several more times.

```
>>> aesEncryptor.update(b'bob')
b''
>>> aesEncryptor.update(b'bob')
b''
>>> aesEncryptor.update(b'bob')
b'\xe7\xf9\x19\xe3!\x1d\x17\x9f\x80\x9d\xf5\xa2\xbaTi\xb2'
```

"Wait!" Alice stops him. "You got something!"

"Weird!" Bob exclaims. "I didn't do anything different. What happened?"

"Now try decrypting it," Alice suggests.

```
>>> aesDecryptor.update(_)
b'alicebobbobbobbo'
```

Playing around a bit more, and re-reading docs, Alice and Bob learn what you already discovered from the exercise: the update functions for both encryption and decryption always work on 16 bytes at a time. Calling update with fewer than 16 bytes produces no immediate result. Instead, it accumulates data until it has at least 16 bytes to work with. Once 16 or more bytes are available, as many 16-byte blocks of ciphertext as possible are produced. This is illustrated in Figure 3-1.

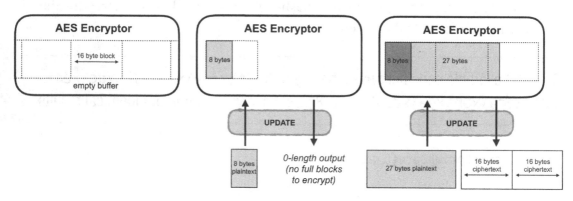

Figure 3-1. *Two calls to the update method. The first 8 bytes return nothing because there isn't a full block of data to encrypt yet.*

EXERCISE 3.2. UPDATED TECHNOLOGY

Upgrade the Caesar cipher application from Chapter 1 to use AES. Instead of specifying a *shift value*, figure out how to get *keys* in and out of the program. You will also have to deal with the 16-byte message size issue. Good luck!

What Is Encryption, Really?

For those who have heard of cryptography, encryption is probably what they have heard about most. Web sites and online services will often mention encryption to reassure you that your information is "secure." They will typically include phrases like "All data transmitted over the Internet is protected by 128-bit encryption, preventing theft."

Don't you feel better already?

Statements like that are really just marketing. They sound nice, but don't usually mean much. That's because "encryption" includes easy-to-break things like Caesar ciphers, it also *isn't enough by itself* to make communications secure. In cryptography, there are *several* properties that contribute to different aspects of security, and they need to work together [11, Chap. 1]. These properties are commonly viewed as the most critical:

1. Confidentiality

2. Integrity

3. Authentication

The encryption we explore in this chapter is all about *confidentiality*. **Confidentiality** means that only folks with the right key are able to read the data. We use encryption to protect messages so that outsiders cannot read them.

Equally important is *integrity*. **Integrity** means that the data cannot be *changed without you noticing*. It is critical to understand that just because something cannot be *read* does not mean it cannot be *usefully altered*. To drive that point home, we are going to do exactly that sort of mischief in this chapter.

Finally, *authentication* relates to knowing the identity of the party with whom you are communicating. **Authentication** typically includes some mechanism to establish *identity and presence,*[3] as well as the ability to tie communication to the established identity.

Hopefully it is obvious that all three of these properties are essential in many forms of communication. Confidentiality will do Alice and Bob little good if Eve can change what the messages *actually say* without them knowing: Eve doesn't need to *read* the messages to cause real problems. Likewise, Alice and Bob will have little success in their covert communications if they aren't sure they have the right person on the other end of the channel.

Keep these ideas in mind as you go through this chapter! Our focus on confidentiality is useful for presentation and it is indeed a critical component of security, but it is not enough. Spending some time with confidentiality by itself will help us to demonstrate how inadequate it is without its friends.

AES: A Symmetric Block Cipher

As mentioned before, the idea behind symmetric encryption is that the same key is used for both encryption and decryption. In the real world, almost all keys to physical locks can be thought of as "symmetric": the same key that locks your door also unlocks it. There are other extremely important approaches to encryption that use distinct keys for each operation, but we'll get to those in later chapters.

Symmetric key encryption algorithms are often divided into two subtypes: **block ciphers** and **stream ciphers**. A block cipher gets its name from the fact that it works on blocks of data: you have to give it a certain amount of data before it can do anything, and larger data must be broken down into block-sized chunks (also, every block must be full). Stream ciphers, on the other hand, can encrypt data one byte at a time.

---

[3]**Identity and presence** mean loosely "I know who this is, and I know that they consent to my knowing that right now." If you have ever had to dig out your credit card to provide the "CVV code" to a web site that *already has your card on file*, you have run into the concept of presence: the CVV code is meant to be an indication that your card is *there with you* and therefore that *you are around to consent to its use*. This assumes that you are the only one who can hold your own card, a *huge* and easily falsified assumption. Thus, the CVV is an extremely *weak* indication of presence, but ultimately establishment of presence is exactly what it's trying to accomplish.

AES is fundamentally a symmetric key, block cipher algorithm. It is not the only one by any stretch, but it is the only one that we will pay any attention to here. It is used in many common Internet protocols and operating system services, including TLS (used by HTTPS), IPSec, and file-level or full-disk encryption. Given its ubiquity, it is arguably the most important cipher to know how to use properly. More importantly, the principles of correct use of AES transfer easily to correct use of other ciphers.

Finally, even though AES is essentially a block cipher, it (like many other block ciphers) can be used in a way that makes it behave like a stream cipher, so we don't lose any teaching opportunities by excluding native stream ciphers from the discussion. In the past, RC4 was a commonly used stream cipher, but it has been found vulnerable to various attacks and is being replaced by stream modes of AES.

Also, as Bob says, "It's *advanced!*" That ought to be enough for anyone, right?

EXERCISE 3.3. HISTORY LESSON

Do some research online about **DES** and **3DES**. What is the block size for DES? What is its key size? How does 3DES strengthen DES?

EXERCISE 3.4. OTHER CIPHERS

Do a little research about RC4 and Twofish. Where are they used? What kinds of problems does RC4 have? What are some of Twofish's advantages over AES?

Since AES is a pretty good place to start, let's dig in with a little bit of background. We know it's a symmetric key block cipher. Given what we saw of Alice's and Bob's attempts to use it, can you guess the block size?

If you were thinking "16 bytes!" (128 bits), you get a gold star. Tell all your friends![4]

---

[4]...over an encrypted channel.

AES has several modes of operation that allow us to achieve different cryptographic properties:

1. Electronic code book (ECB) (***WARNING! DANGEROUS!***)

2. Cipher block chaining (CBC)

3. Counter mode (CTR)

These are not the only modes of operation for AES [11, Chap. 7]. In fact, while CBC and CTR are still used, a newer mode called GCM is now recommended to replace them in many circumstances, and we will examine GCM in detail later in this book. These three modes are, however, very instructive, and together they cover the most important concepts. They will provide a solid foundation on which to build greater understanding of block ciphers in general and AES in particular.

ECB Is Not for Me

Be warned, relying on ECB mode for security is *irresponsibly dangerous* and it should *never* be used. Think of it as being good for testing and educational purposes only. Please, don't ever use it in your applications or projects! Seriously. You have been warned. Don't make us come over there.

By the way, do you see a pattern developing here? Sometimes the best approaches for *explaining* a thing are not at all suitable for *using* it in practice. This seems to apply particularly well to cryptography, which is one reason that we urge people to always use a well established library instead of building their own. The basic principles are simple, but without all of the complex trappings that come with mature libraries and a solid understanding of how to use them, those principles alone will give you *very* poor security, not just "slightly imperfect" security. There is rarely much in the way of middle ground; once the safe is cracked, it doesn't matter how thick its walls are. Cryptographic *concepts* are often simple, but safe and correct *implementation* is usually complex.

With all of those warnings out of the way (not really, there will be more), what is ECB? In a way, ECB is "raw" AES: it treats every 16-byte block of data independently, encrypting each one in exactly the same way using the provided key. As we will see with counter mode and cipher block chaining mode, there are a lot of interesting ways to use that approach as a *building block* for a more advanced (and secure) cipher, but it's really not a good way to go about encryption *by itself*.

The name "electronic code book" hearkens back to earlier days of cryptographic code books, where you would take your (small) key, go to the right page in the book, and use the table on that page to look up the output (ciphertext) that corresponded to each part of your input (plaintext). AES ECB mode can be thought of in that way, but with a mind-bogglingly huge book. The key similarity (ha!) is that once you have the key, *every possible block's encrypted value is known*, and the same is true for decryption; it's like we're looking them up, as visualized in Figure 3-2.

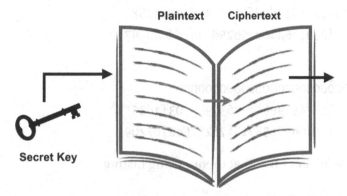

Figure 3-2. *ECB mode is analogous to having a big dictionary of plaintext to ciphertext. Every 16 bytes of plaintext has a corresponding 16-byte output.*

As we will see, the properties of determinism and independence are useful but not sufficient properties for message security. ECB mode is useful because it can be used for testing, for example, to make sure that the AES algorithm is behaving as expected. Some systems will pick a special key, say, all zeros, as a "test key." As part of a self-test, the system will run AES in ECB mode with the test key to see if it encrypts as expected. You will sometimes see tests of this kind called "KATs" (known answer tests).

The National Institute of Standards and Technology (NIST) in the United States publishes a list of KATs that are used for implementation validation. You can download a zip file with these KATs from https://csrc.nist.gov/CSRC/media/Projects/Cryptographic-Algorithm-Validation-Program/documents/aes/KAT_AES.zip. That archive contains response (.rsp) files that identify expected outputs for given inputs. For example, in the ECBGFSbox128.rsp file, the first four ENCRYPT entries are

```
COUNT = 0
KEY = 00000000000000000000000000000000
PLAINTEXT = f34481ec3cc627bacd5dc3fb08f273e6
CIPHERTEXT = 0336763e966d92595a567cc9ce537f5e

COUNT = 1
KEY = 00000000000000000000000000000000
PLAINTEXT = 9798c4640bad75c7c3227db910174e72
CIPHERTEXT = a9a1631bf4996954ebc093957b234589

COUNT = 2
KEY = 00000000000000000000000000000000
PLAINTEXT = 96ab5c2ff612d9dfaae8c31f30c42168
CIPHERTEXT = ff4f8391a6a40ca5b25d23bedd44a597

COUNT = 3
KEY = 00000000000000000000000000000000
PLAINTEXT = 6a118a874519e64e9963798a503f1d35
CIPHERTEXT = dc43be40be0e53712f7e2bf5ca707209
```

That seems useful. Let's test that theory using Listing 3-2.

Listing 3-2. AES ECB KATs

```
1    # NEVER USE: ECB is not secure!
2    from cryptography.hazmat.primitives.ciphers import Cipher, algorithms,
     modes
3    from cryptography.hazmat.backends import default_backend
4
5    # NIST AES ECBGFSbox128.rsp ENCRYPT Kats
6    # First value of each pair is plaintext
7    # Second value of each pair is ciphertext
8    nist_kats = [
9        ('f34481ec3cc627bacd5dc3fb08f273e6',
         '0336763e966d92595a567cc9ce537f5e'),
```

```
10        ('9798c4640bad75c7c3227db910174e72',
          'a9a1631bf4996954ebc093957b234589'),
11        ('96ab5c2ff612d9dfaae8c31f30c42168',
          'ff4f8391a6a40ca5b25d23bedd44a597'),
12        ('6a118a874519e64e9963798a503f1d35',
          'dc43be40be0e53712f7e2bf5ca707209')
13    ]
14
15    # 16-byte test key of all zeros.
16    test_key = bytes.fromhex('00000000000000000000000000000000')
17
18    aesCipher = Cipher(algorithms.AES(test_key),
19                        modes.ECB(),
20                        backend=default_backend())
21    aesEncryptor = aesCipher.encryptor()
22    aesDecryptor = aesCipher.decryptor()
23
24    # test each input
25    for index, kat in enumerate(nist_kats):
26        plaintext, want_ciphertext = kat
27        plaintext_bytes = bytes.fromhex(plaintext)
28        ciphertext_bytes = aesEncryptor.update(plaintext_bytes)
29        got_ciphertext = ciphertext_bytes.hex()
30
31        result = "[PASS]" if got_ciphertext == want_ciphertext else "[FAIL]"
32
33        print("Test {}. Expected {}, got {}. Result {}.".format(
34            index, want_ciphertext, got_ciphertext, result))
```

Assuming that your processor is working correctly, you should see a 4/4 passing score.

EXERCISE 3.5. ALL NIST KATS

Write a program that will read one of these NIST KAT "rsp" files, and parse out the encryption and decryption KATs. Test and validate your AES library on all vectors on a couple of ECB test files.

This all seems very reasonable. So, what's wrong with ECB? Unless you've been completely asleep, you've noticed our dire warnings about it. Why? In a nutshell, because of its independence properties.

Let's return to Alice, Bob, and their nemesis Eve down in Antarctica. Alice and Bob are on a covert mission within the West Antarctica borders. They will send secret messages to each other over radio channels that Eve can monitor. Before they leave, they generate a shared key for encrypting and decrypting their messages, and they keep that key safe during their travels.

We can do that too. We'll start by generating a key. Normally, the key would be random, but we'll just pick one that is easy to remember, then we can also perfectly reproduce the following results. Here is the key:

```
key = bytes.fromhex('00112233445566778899AABBCCDDEEFF')
```

Alice and Bob, being government agents, use a standardized EATSA form for sending each other messages. For example, to arrange a meeting:

```
FROM: FIELD AGENT<codename>
TO: FIELD AGENT<codename>
RE: Meeting
DATE: <date>

Meet me today at <location> at <time>
```

If Alice is telling Bob to meet her at the docks at 11 p.m., the message would be

```
FROM: FIELD AGENT ALICE
TO: FIELD AGENT BOB
RE: Meeting
DATE: 2001-1-1

Meet me today at the docks at 2300.
```

We'll encrypt this message under the key we set out previously. We need to *pad* the message to make sure it is a multiple of 16 bytes long. We can do that by adding extra characters to the end until its length is a multiple of 16, like so.[5]

---

[5]We take advantage of Python's convenient "negative modulus" behavior, where `-len(msg) % 16` is the same as `16 - (len(msg) % 16)`.

Listing 3-3. AES ECB Padding

```
1   # NEVER USE: ECB is not secure!
2   from cryptography.hazmat.primitives.ciphers import Cipher, algorithms, modes
3   from cryptography.hazmat.backends import default_backend
4
5   # Alice and Bob's Shared Key
6   test_key = bytes.fromhex('00112233445566778899AABBCCDDEEFF')
7
8   aesCipher = Cipher(algorithms.AES(test_key),
9                      modes.ECB(),
10                     backend=default_backend())
11  aesEncryptor = aesCipher.encryptor()
12  aesDecryptor = aesCipher.decryptor()
13
14  message = b"""
15  FROM: FIELD AGENT ALICE
16  TO: FIELD AGENT BOB
17  RE: Meeting
18  DATE: 2001-1-1
19
20  Meet me today at the docks at 2300."""
21
22  message += b"E" * (-len(message) % 16)
23  ciphertext = aesEncryptor.update(message)
```

Listing 3-3 shows a straightforward but perhaps not optimal padding. We'll use more standard approaches in the next section. It is, however, good enough for now. When Bob decodes his message, it will simply have a few extra "E" characters at the end.

EXERCISE 3.6. SENDING BOB A MESSAGE

Using either a modification of the preceding program or your AES encryptor from the beginning of the chapter, create a couple of meetup messages from Alice to Bob. Also create a few from Bob to Alice. Make sure that you can correctly encrypt and decrypt the messages.

With their new cryptographic technology at the ready, Alice and Bob begin surveillance in West Antarctica. They meet occasionally to share information and coordinate their activities.

Meanwhile, Eve and her counter-intelligence colleagues learn of the infiltration and soon begin to identify the coded messages. Take a look at several messages from Alice to Bob from Eve's perspective, where all she can see is the ciphertext. Do you notice anything?

Consider these two messages:

```
FROM: FIELD AGENT ALICE
TO: FIELD AGENT BOB
RE: Meeting
DATE: 2001-1-1

Meet me today at the docks at 2300.

FROM: FIELD AGENT ALICE
TO: FIELD AGENT BOB
RE: Meeting
DATE: 2001-1-2

Meet me today at the town square at 1130.
```

Look at the two ciphertext outputs of these messages side-by-side. Note: even spacing and newlines matter, so make sure to use the format exactly as shown.

Message 1, Block 1	a3a2390c0f2afb700959b3221a95319a
Message 2, Block 1	a3a2390c0f2afb700959b3221a95319a
Message 1, Block 2	0fd11a5dcfa115ba89630f93e09312b0
Message 2, Block 2	0fd11a5dcfa115ba89630f93e09312b0
Message 1, Block 3	87597bf7f98759410ae3e9a285912ee6
Message 2, Block 3	87597bf7f98759410ae3e9a285912ee6
Message 1, Block 4	8430e159229e4bf5c7b39fe1fb72cfab
Message 2, Block 4	8430e159229e4bf5c7b39fe1fb72cfab
Message 1, Block 5	a5c7412fda6ac67fe63093168f474913

Message 2, Block 5	c9b3ccefda71f286895b309d85245421
Message 1, Block 6	dbd386db053613be242c6059539f93da
Message 2, Block 6	699f1cd5adbeb94b80980a0860ead320
Message 1, Block 7	800d3ece3b12931be974f36ef5da4342
Message 2, Block 7	a8ff0ed2ca9b80908757f8c3ecbc9b0d

How many of the 16-byte blocks are identical? Why?

Remember that AES in its raw mode is like a code book. For every input and key, there is exactly one output, independent of any other inputs. Thus, because much of the message header is shared between messages, much of the output is *also* the same.

Eve and her colleagues notice the repeating elements of the messages they see day after day and soon start to figure out what they mean. How do they do this? They might make a good start by guessing. If you saw the same message being sent repeatedly, you could start to guess at some of its contents.

Another way to make progress might be to utilize a deserter or mole within the enemy organization. They could conceivably get Eve a copy of the form or a discarded decoded message. All told, there are many ways for an adversary to learn about the structure and organization of an encrypted message, and you should never assume otherwise. A common error made by those trying to protect information is to assume that the enemy cannot know some detail about how the system works.

Instead, always live by Kerckhoff's principle. This nineteenth-century (long before modern computers) cryptographer taught that a cryptographic system must be secure even if *everything* is known about it, except the key. That means we should find a way for our messages to be secure if the enemy knows just about everything about our system and merely lacks access to the key.

We made this silly example with an overly bureaucratic form, but even in real messages, there is often a significant amount of predictable structure. Consider HTML, XML, or email messages. Those often have huge amounts of predictably positioned, identical data. It would be a terrible thing for an eavesdropper to start learning what's in a message just because it shares protocol headers with every other message.

Even worse, imagine if Eve's team can figure out a way to do what is called a "chosen plaintext" attack. In this attack, they figure out a way to get Alice or Bob to encrypt something on their behalf. Imagine, for example, that they figure out that Alice always calls a meeting with Bob after the Prime Minister of Western Antarctica gives a public speech. Once they know this, they can use political speeches to trigger a message where much of the content is known. Or maybe they manage to slip Bob some false information to send to Alice, encrypted. Once they can control some or all of the plaintext, they can look at the encryption and begin to *create their own code book*.

Eve can also easily create new messages by putting together bits and pieces of old messages. If Eve knows that the first blocks of a ciphertext are the header with a current date, she can take an old message body that directs Bob to an old meeting site and attach it to the new header. Then Bob ends up in the wrong place at the wrong time.

EXERCISE 3.7. SENDING BOB A FAKE MESSAGE

Take two different ciphertexts from Alice to Bob with different meeting instructions on different dates. Splice the ciphertext from the body of the first message into the body of the second message. That is, start by replacing the last block of the newer message with the last block (or blocks if it was longer) of the previous message. Does the message decrypt? Did you change where Bob goes to meet Alice?

All of this may still seem just a bit hypothetical. Perhaps ECB mode isn't really all that bad. Perhaps it is only bad in extreme situations or something like that. Just in case there is a shadow of a doubt remaining, let's do one more test (a pretty fun one) to convince ourselves that ECB mode should never, *ever* be used for real message confidentiality.

In this experiment, you will build a very basic AES encrypting program. It doesn't matter what key is used; feel free to generate a random one, or use a fixed test key. Read in a binary file, encrypt everything *except the first 54 bytes*, and then write it out to a new file. It might look something like Listing 3-4.[6]

Listing 3-4. AES Exercise Example

```
1    # Partial Listing: Some Assembly Required
2
3    ifile, ofile = sys.argv[1:3]
4    with open(ifile, "rb") as reader:
```

---

[6]This code listing does not show all the necessary imports, but it requires nothing new over previous listings. In the interest of space, we will regularly leave out details that have been shown in previous examples.

```
5        with open(ofile, "wb+") as writer:
6            image_data = reader.read()
7            header, body = image_data[:54], image_data[54:]
8            body += b"\x00"*(16-(len(body)%16))
9            writer.write(header + aesEncryptor.update(body))
```

The reason we're not encrypting the first 54 bytes is because this program is going to encrypt the contents of a bit map file (BMP) and the header is 54 bytes in length.[7] Once you have this listing written, in the image editor of your choice, create a large image with text that takes up most of the space. In Figure 3-3, our image simply has the words "TOP SECRET." It is 800x600 pixels.

TOP
SECRET

Figure 3-3. *An image with the text "TOP SECRET." Encrypting it should make it unreadable, right?*

Take your newly created file and run it through your encryption program, saving the output to something like encrypted_image.bmp. When finished, open *the encrypted file* in an image viewer. What do you see?

Our encrypted image is shown in Figure 3-4.

---

[7]In real life, if the header were encrypted, you could just overwrite it with something reasonable based on the file size.

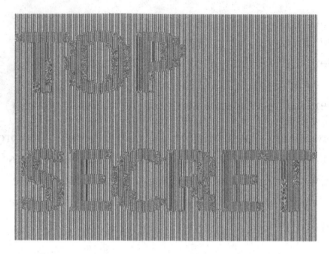

Figure 3-4. *This image was encrypted using ECB mode. This message is not very confidential.*

What happened here? Why is the text of the image still so readable?

AES is a block cipher that operates on 16 bytes at a time. In this image, many 16-byte chunks are the *same*. A chunk of black pixels is encoded with the same bits everywhere. Every time there's a 16-byte block of all black or all white, they encode to the same encrypted output. The *structure* of the image is thus still visible even once the individual 16-byte chunks are encrypted.

Really. Never use ECB. Leave that kind of thing to the "professionals" of the East Antarctica Truth-Spying Agency.

Wanted: Spontaneous Independence

To have an effective cipher, we need to

- Encrypt the same message differently each time.

- Eliminate predictable patterns between blocks.

To solve the first problem, we use a simple but effective trick to ensure that we never send the same *plaintext* twice, which means that we also never send the same *ciphertext* twice! We do this with an "initialization vector," or IV.

An IV is typically a random string that is used as a third input—in addition to the key and plaintext—into the encryption algorithm. Exactly how it is used depends on the mode, but the idea is to prevent a given plaintext from encrypting to a repeatable ciphertext.

Unlike the key, the IV is public. That is, one assumes that an attacker knows, or can obtain, the value of the IV. The presence of an IV doesn't help to keep things *secret* so much as it helps to keep them from being *repeated*, avoiding exposure of common patterns.

As for the second problem, that of being able to eliminate patterns between blocks, we will solve it by introducing new ways to encrypt the message *as a whole*, rather than treating each block as an individual, independent mini-message like ECB mode does.

The details of each solution are specific to the mode being used, but the principles generalize well.

Not That Blockchain

Recall from Chapter 2 that good hash algorithms are expected to have the *avalanche* property. That is, a single change in one input bit will cause approximately half of the output bits to change. Block ciphers should have a similar property, and thankfully, AES does. In ECB mode, however, the avalanche's impact is limited to the block size: if the plaintext is ten blocks long, a change in the very first bit will only change the output bits of the very first block. The remaining nine blocks will remain unchanged.

What if a change in the ciphertext of one block could affect all *subsequent* blocks? Well, it can, and it is quite easy to accomplish. When encrypting, for example, one can XOR the encrypted output of a block with the unencrypted input of the next block. To reverse this while decrypting, the ciphertext is decrypted and then the XOR operation is again applied to the previous ciphertext block to obtain the plaintext. This is called **cipher block chaining (CBC) mode**.

Let's pause here for just a quick moment to review an operation called XOR, often written symbolically as $\oplus$. We are going to use XOR constantly throughout the book so it's worthwhile to review it. XOR is a binary boolean operator with the following truth table (where we use 0 and 1 instead of "false" and "true').

Input 1	Input 2	Output
0	0	0
0	1	1
1	0	1
1	1	0

Truth tables are useful, showing precisely how functions like XOR behave for all combinations of inputs, but you actually don't need to think about XOR at this level. What is important is that XOR has an amazing inversion property: the XOR operation is its own inverse! That is, if you start with some binary number A and XOR it with B, you can recover A by XORing the output with B again. Mathematically, it looks like this: $(A \oplus B) \oplus B = A$.

Why does this work? If you look at "Input 1" as a control bit, when it is 0, what comes out is simply "Input 2." When "Input 1" is 1, on the other hand, what comes out is the inverse of "Input 2." If you take the outputs and apply XOR with "Input 1" again, it leaves the previously unchanged things unchanged (XOR with 0 again) while flipping the inverted things back to the way they were (XOR with 1 again).

Quite often we XOR not individual bits, but sequences of bits all at once. This is how we will use XOR throughout this book: as an operation between blocks of bits, like this:

$$
\begin{array}{r}
11011011 \\
\oplus \quad 10110001 \\
\hline
01101010 \\
\oplus \quad 10110001 \\
\hline
11011011
\end{array}
$$

You can see here how applying $\oplus$10110001 twice to 11011011 causes it to reappear.

EXERCISE 3.8. XOR EXERCISE

Because we will use XOR so much, it's a good idea to get comfortable with XOR operations. In a Python interpreter, XOR a few numbers together. Python supports XOR directly using ^ as the operator. So, for example, 5^9 results in 12. What do you get when you try 12^9? What do you get when you try 12^5? Try this out with several different numbers.

EXERCISE 3.9. THE MASK OF XOR-0?

Although this exercise will be even more important in counter mode, it's useful to understand how XOR can be used to *mask* data. Create 16 bytes of plaintext (a 16-character message) and 16 bytes of random data (e.g., using `os.urandom(16)`). XOR these two messages together. There's no built-in operation for XORing a series of bytes, so you'll have to XOR each byte individually using, for example, a loop. When you are done, take a look at the output. How "readable" is it? Now, XOR this output with the same random bytes again. What does the output look like now?

Returning from our XOR interruption to CBC, in this mode we XOR the output of one block of ciphertext with the next *plaintext* block. More precisely, if we call $P[n]$ block n of plaintext and $P'[n]$ block n of "munged, pre-encryption plaintext" (using the XOR operation to accomplish the very scientifically named "munging" process), we first create $P'[n]$ from the previous encrypted block $C[n-1]$, then we encrypt it to make $C[n]$. The formula for creating $P'[n]$ is this:

$$P'[n] = P[n] \oplus C[n-1],$$

From there we can apply AES encryption to $P'[n]$, which is the length of an AES block, to get $C[n]$. When decrypting, then, we don't get the plaintext, we get the "munged, pre-encryption plaintext" $P'[n]$. To get the actual plaintext, we need to reverse the preceding process, which we can do by running it through XOR with the previous encrypted block (recalling that XOR is its own inverse). You can see why this works by performing some basic algebraic manipulations:

$$P'[n] = P[n] \oplus C[n-1]$$
$$P'[n] \oplus P[n] = P[n] \oplus P[n] \oplus C[n-1]$$
$$P'[n] \oplus P[n] = C[n-1]$$
$$P'[n] \oplus P'[n] \oplus P[n] = P'[n] \oplus C[n-1]$$
$$P[n] = P'[n] \oplus C[n-1].$$

Thus, to get the original plaintext when decrypting, we need only XOR the decrypted block with the previous encrypted block. The very first block, which has no predecessor, is simply XORed with the initialization vector after decryption. That is the essence of

CBC mode: every block is dependent on the blocks that came before. This process is visualized, perhaps a little more intuitively, in Figure 3-5.

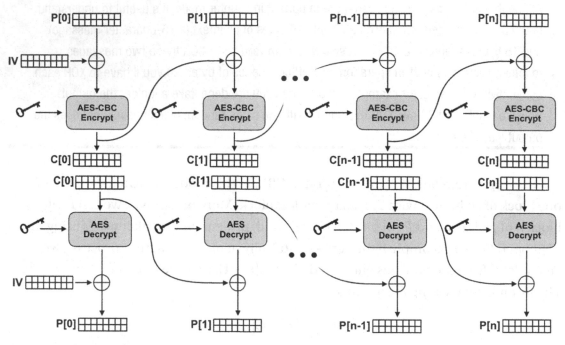

Figure 3-5. *Visual depictions of CBC encryption and decryption. Note that in encryption, the first block of plaintext is XORed with the IV before AES, while in decryption, the ciphertext goes through AES first and is then XORed with the IV to correctly reverse the encryption process.*

In CBC mode, changes to any input block thus affect the output block for all subsequent blocks. This doesn't produce a complete or perfect avalanche property because it does not affect any *preceding* blocks, but even having the avalanche effect moving forward prevents exposing the kinds of patterns that we observe in ECB mode.

Configuration of CBC mode is mostly familiar: we generate a key and then take the extra step of generating an initialization vector (IV). Because the IV is XORed with the first block, AES-CBC IVs[8] are *always* 128 bits long (16 bytes), even if the key size is larger (typically 196 or 256 bits). In the following example, the key is 256 bits and the IV is 128 bits, as it must be (Listing 3-5).

---

[8]We promise to use more initialisms next time.

Listing 3-5. AES-CBC

```
1   from cryptography.hazmat.primitives.ciphers import Cipher, algorithms,
    modes
2   from cryptography.hazmat.backends import default_backend
3   import os
4
5   key = os.urandom(32)
6   iv = os.urandom(16)
7
8   aesCipher = Cipher(algorithms.AES(key),
9                      modes.CBC(iv),
10                     backend=default_backend())
11  aesEncryptor = aesCipher.encryptor()
12  aesDecryptor = aesCipher.decryptor()
```

Notice that in this example, `algorithms.AES` takes the key as the parameter while `modes.CBC` takes the IV; AES *always* needs a key, but the use of an IV is dependent on the mode.

Proper Padding

While we are in the business of improving things, let's introduce a better padding mechanism. The `cryptography` module provides two schemes, one following what is known as the PKCS7 specification and the other following ANSI X.923. PKCS7 appends *n* bytes, with each padding byte holding the value *n*: if 3 bytes of padding are needed, it appends \x03\x03\x03. Similarly, if 2 bytes of padding are needed, it appends \x02\x02.

ANSI X.923 is slightly different. All appended bytes are 0, except for the last byte, which is the length of the total padding. In this example, 3 bytes of padding is \x00\x00\x03, and two bytes of padding is \x00\x02.

The `cryptography` module provides a padding context that is analogous to the AES cipher context. In the next code listing, `padder` and `unpadder` objects are created for adding and removing padding. Note that these objects also use `update` and `finalize`, since no padding is created from calling the `update()` method. It does, however, return full blocks, storing the rest of the bytes for either the next call to `update()` or the `finalize()` operation. When `finalize()` is called, all remaining bytes are returned along with enough bytes of padding to make a full block size.

Although the API seems straightforward, it doesn't necessarily behave as one might expect.

Listing 3-6. AES-CBC Padding

```
1   from cryptography.hazmat.primitives.ciphers import Cipher, algorithms,
    modes
2   from cryptography.hazmat.backends import default_backend
3   from cryptography.hazmat.primitives import padding
4   import os
5
6   key = os.urandom(32)
7   iv = os.urandom(16)
8
9   aesCipher = Cipher(algorithms.AES(key),
10                     modes.CBC(iv),
11                     backend=default_backend())
12  aesEncryptor = aesCipher.encryptor()
13  aesDecryptor = aesCipher.decryptor()
14
15  # Make a padder/unpadder pair for 128 bit block sizes.
16  padder = padding.PKCS7(128).padder()
17  unpadder = padding.PKCS7(128).unpadder()
18
19  plaintexts = [
20      b"SHORT",
21      b"MEDIUM MEDIUM MEDIUM",
22      b"LONG LONG LONG LONG LONG LONG",
23  ]
24
25  ciphertexts = []
26
27  for m in plaintexts:
28      padded_message = padder.update(m)
29      ciphertexts.append(aesEncryptor.update(padded_message))
30
```

```
31   ciphertexts.append(aesEncryptor.update(padder.finalize()))
32
33   for c in ciphertexts:
34       padded_message = aesDecryptor.update(c)
35       print("recovered", unpadder.update(padded_message))
36
37   print("recovered", unpadder.finalize())
```

Run the code in Listing 3-6 and observe the output. Is it what you expected? It should have looked like this:

```
recovered b''
recovered b''
recovered b'SHORTMEDIUM MEDIUM MEDIUMLONG LO'
recovered b'NG LONG LONG LON'
recovered b'G LONG '
```

Why did it not produce the original messages exactly as specified?

There is technically nothing incorrect with this code, but there is definitely a mismatch between the apparent *intention* of the code and the actual output. This code suggests that the author intended to encrypt each one of the three strings as an independent message. In other words, the probable intention of the code was to encrypt three distinct messages and get back three equivalent messages upon decryption.

That is not what we got. Listing 3-6 is reporting five outputs and two of them are empty.

Let's talk about the update() and finalize() API one more time. Because of how these methods behave for certain modes (e.g., ECB mode), it can be tempting to think about update() as a stand-alone encryptor wherein a plaintext block is provided as input and a ciphertext block is provided as output.

In reality, the API is designed such that the number of calls to update() is irrelevant. That is, what is being encrypted is not the input to \lstinline{update()}, but \emph{the concatenation of every input} to some number of \lstinline{update()} calls, and, of course, output (if any) from a finalize() call at the end.

Thus, the program in Listing 3-6 is not encrypting three inputs and producing five outputs, it is processing a single continuous output and producing a single continuous output.

Understanding the update() and finalize() API is especially important for the padding operations that we've introduced. Padding behavior can appear unusual if you try to think of update() as an independent operation. Figure 3-6 illustrates how padding processes the inputs from Listing 3-6. Note that individual calls to update() produce no padding. Only the finalize() operation will do that.

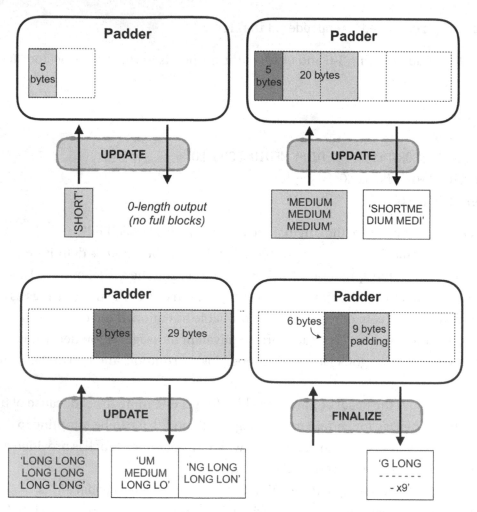

Figure 3-6. *PKCS7 padding does not add any padding until the finalize operation*

Unpadding can be even more jarring. Unlike the padding operations, you can submit a full block to the unpadder and still get *nothing* back. This is because the unpadder has to reserve the last block received in update() calls in case it is the last block. Because unpadding requires examining the last block, the unpadder has to be sure it has received all the blocks to know that it has the last one.

Walking through Listing 3-6 one more time illustrates how the effects of these operations are compounded when the padder and encryptor are used together. On the first pass through the loop for encrypting the messages, the input is SHORT. Five characters is less than of a block. The padder's update() method does not add any padding, so the *padder* buffers these five characters and the update() method returns an empty byte string. When this gets passed to the encryptor, there is obviously not a full block so the encryptor's update method also returns an empty byte string. This gets appended to the list of ciphertexts.

On our second pass through the loop, the input is MEDIUM MEDIUM MEDIUM. These 20 characters are passed into the padder's internal buffer and are added to the 5 that were there before. The UPDATE method now returns the first 16 of those 25 bytes (a full block), leaving the remaining 9 bytes in the internal buffer. The 16 bytes from the padder are encrypted and stored in the list of ciphertexts.

In the final pass, the LONG LONG LONG LONG LONG LONG input is added to the padder's internal buffer. These 29 bytes are added to the current 9 bytes in the buffer for a total of 38 bytes. The padder returns the 2 full blocks (of 16 bytes each) leaving the last 6 bytes in its buffer. The two blocks are encrypted, and the two-block output is stored in the list of ciphertexts.

Once the loop exits, the padder's finalize method is called. It takes the last bytes of input, appends the necessary padding, and passes it to the encryption operation. The ciphertext is appended to the list and encryption is over. There are now four ciphertext messages to decrypt. Reversing the process, the first message is, you may recall, the empty buffer. It just passes straight through everything and comes out as an empty message.

But the next recovered text is also empty. That's because the first full block to the unpadder is reserved for the reasons we explained. It produces an empty output fed into the AES decryptor's update() method. This generates our second empty output.

The remaining three are more straightforward.

Now that the walk-through is finished, did you notice that we were still using the incorrect terminology? We referred to individual outputs from update() methods as individual ciphertexts rather than a snippet of *the* ciphertext. Similarly, we called the output of the decryptor update methods recovered texts rather than part of a single recovered message.

This was intentional. The crucial principle is that *semantics* matter. How we think about our code can be different from how it operates, and this can result in unexpected, and often *insecure*, results. When you use a library (always better than creating your own!), you must understand the API's approach and design. It is critical that you *think* the way the API is designed to be used.

For the `cryptography` library, always think about everything submitted to a sequence of encryption `update()` calls and one `finalize()` call as a single input. Similarly, think about everything that is recovered from a series of decryption `update()` calls and one `finalize()` call as a single output.

And what is going on with the decryption? How did we get *five* outputs instead of four? The first ciphertext in the list was just the empty string so it makes sense that the first "recovered" plaintext was empty. But why was the second one empty too?

Let's look at another way to do this wrong.[9] Suppose we decide to create our own API that will actually work on a message level. That is, every message can be encrypted and decrypted individually and independently. The code is shown in Listing 3-7.

Listing 3-7. Broken AES-CBC Manager

```
1   from cryptography.hazmat.primitives.ciphers import Cipher, algorithms,
    modes
2   from cryptography.hazmat.backends import default_backend
3   from cryptography.hazmat.primitives import padding
4   import os
5
6   class EncryptionManager:
7       def __init__(self):
8           self.key = os.urandom(32)
9           self.iv = os.urandom(16)
10
11      def encrypt_message(self, message):
12          # WARNING: This code is not secure!!
13          encryptor = Cipher(algorithms.AES(self.key),
14                             modes.CBC(self.iv),
```

---

[9]Yes, this is a theme in the book. We have found that it is often when things are broken that they are best understood.

```
15                             backend=default_backend()).encryptor()
16             padder = padding.PKCS7(128).padder()
17
18             padded_message = padder.update(message)
19             padded_message += padder.finalize()
20             ciphertext = encryptor.update(padded_message)
21             ciphertext += encryptor.finalize()
22             return ciphertext
23
24     def decrypt_message(self, ciphertext):
25             # WARNING: This code is not secure!!
26             decryptor = Cipher(algorithms.AES(self.key),
27                             modes.CBC(self.iv),
28                             backend=default_backend()).decryptor()
29             unpadder = padding.PKCS7(128).unpadder()
30
31             padded_message = decryptor.update(ciphertext)
32             padded_message += decryptor.finalize()
33             message = unpadder.update(padded_message)
34             message += unpadder.finalize()
35             return message
36
37 # Automatically generate key/IV for encryption.
38 manager = EncryptionManager()
39
40 plaintexts = [
41     b"SHORT",
42     b"MEDIUM MEDIUM MEDIUM",
43     b"LONG LONG LONG LONG LONG LONG"
44 ]
45
46 ciphertexts = []
47
48 for m in plaintexts:
49     ciphertexts.append(manager.encrypt_message(m))
```

```
50
51   for c in ciphertexts:
52       print("Recovered", manager.decrypt_message(c))
```

Run the code and observe the output. Did you get each message individually this time? Good! You probably like this version a lot better!

The API might be more semantically aligned, this time, but the implementation is very broken and incredibly dangerous. Before we tell you what is wrong with it, can you try and see it yourself? Are there any security principles we've talked about in this chapter that we are violating? If it isn't obvious, read on!

A Key to Hygienic IVs

The problem with Listing 3-7 is that it is *reusing the same key and IV* for different messages. Take a look at the constructor where the key and IV are created. Using that single key/IV pair, the offending code re-creates encryptor and decryptor objects in every call to encrypt_message and decrypt_message. Remember, the IV is supposed to be *different* each time you encrypt, preventing the same data from being encrypted to the same ciphertext! **This is not optional.**

Once again, it is important to understand how an API is built and the security parameters associated with it. Go back and look at Figure 3-5. Remember that in CBC encryption, the algorithm combines the first plaintext block with the IV using the XOR operation before the AES operation is applied. Each subsequent plaintext block is combined with the previous ciphertext block using XOR before AES encryption. With the Python API, each call to update() adds blocks to this chain, leaving data less than a full block in an internal buffer for subsequent calls. The finalize() method does not actually do any more encrypting, but will raise an error if there is incomplete data still waiting to be encrypted.

Calling the update() method over and over is *not* reusing a key and IV because we are appending to the end of the CBC chain. On the other hand, if you create new encryptor and decryptor objects, as we did in Listing 3-7, you are re-creating the chain from the beginning. If you reuse a key and IV here, you will with the same key and IV! This results in *exactly the same output for the same input every time!*

Accordingly, when using the API of Python's cryptography module, never give the same key and IV pair to an encryptor more than once (obviously, you give the same key and IV to the corresponding decryptor). In fact, it's probably best to never reuse the same key again, period.

In Listing 3-8 we correct our previous error and only use a key/IV pair once. The encryptor and decryptor objects are moved to the constructor and, instead of having a single encrypt_message() or decrypt_message() call, we use the update/finalize pattern used by the cryptography module.

Listing 3-8. AES-CBC Manager

```
1   from cryptography.hazmat.primitives.ciphers import Cipher, algorithms,
    modes
2   from cryptography.hazmat.backends import default_backend
3   from cryptography.hazmat.primitives import padding
4   import os
5
6   class EncryptionManager:
7       def __init__(self):
8           key = os.urandom(32)
9           iv = os.urandom(16)
10          aesContext = Cipher(algorithms.AES(key),
11                              modes.CBC(iv),
12                              backend=default_backend())
13          self.encryptor = aesContext.encryptor()
14          self.decryptor = aesContext.decryptor()
15          self.padder = padding.PKCS7(128).padder()
16          self.unpadder = padding.PKCS7(128).unpadder()
17
18      def update_encryptor(self, plaintext):
19          return self.encryptor.update(self.padder.update(plaintext))
20
21      def finalize_encryptor(self):
22          return self.encryptor.update(self.padder.finalize()) + self.
            encryptor.finalize()
23
24      def update_decryptor(self, ciphertext):
25          return self.unpadder.update(self.decryptor.update(ciphertext))
26
27      def finalize_decryptor(self):
```

```
28              return self.unpadder.update(self.decryptor.finalize()) + self.
                unpadder.finalize()
29
30   # Auto generate key/IV for encryption
31   manager = EncryptionManager()
32
33   plaintexts = [
34       b"SHORT",
35       b"MEDIUM MEDIUM MEDIUM",
36       b"LONG LONG LONG LONG LONG LONG"
37   ]
38
39   ciphertexts = []
40
41   for m in plaintexts:
42       ciphertexts.append(manager.update_encryptor(m))
43   ciphertexts.append(manager.finalize_encryptor())
44
45   for c in ciphertexts:
46       print("Recovered", manager.update_decryptor(c))
47   print("Recovered", manager.finalize_decryptor())
```

Listing 3-8 does not reuse key/IV pairs, but you have probably noticed that we are no longer treating the individual messages as individual messages. Now that we're back to the update() finalize() pattern, we have to treat all the data passed to a single context as a single input. If we want each message treated separately, with a sequence of update() calls and finalize() call *per input*. Alternatively, we can submit all three messages as a single input from the perspective of the encryption and decryption and have an independent mechanism for splitting the single decryption output into messages.

In summary, it is important to carefully understand any cryptography APIs that you use, how they work, and what their requirements (especially security requirements) are. It is also important to understand how easy it can be to create an API that looks like it does the right thing but is actually leaving you vulnerable.

Remember, YANAC (You Are Not A Cryptographer... yet!). Don't roll your own crypto like we are doing in these educational examples.

So why does the `cryptography` module use the update/finalize pattern? Quite often, data needs to be processed in chunks in many practical cryptographic operations. Suppose that you are transmitting data over the network. Do you really want to wait until you have the entire content before you can encrypt it? Even if you were encrypting a local file on the hard drive, it might be impractically large for all-at-once encryption. The `update()` method allows you to feed data to an encryption engine as it becomes available.

The `finalize()` operation is useful for enforcing requirements such as the CBC operation did not leave an incomplete block unencrypted and that the session is over.

Of course, there's nothing wrong with a per-message API so long as a key and IV aren't reused. We will look at strategies for this later.

EXERCISE 3.10. DETERMINISTIC OUTPUT

Run the same inputs through AES-CBC using the same key and IV. You can use Listing 3-7 as a starting point. Change the inputs to be the same each time and print out the corresponding ciphertexts. What do you notice?

EXERCISE 3.11. ENCRYPTING AN IMAGE

Encrypt the image that you encrypted with ECB mode earlier. What does the encrypted image look like now? Don't forget to leave the first 54 bytes untouched!

EXERCISE 3.12. HAND-CRAFTED CBC

ECB mode is just raw AES. You can create your own CBC mode using ECB as the building block.[10] For this exercise, see if you can build a CBC encryption and decryption operation that is compatible with the `cryptography` library. For encryption, remember to take the output of each block and XOR it with the plaintext of the next block before encryption. Reverse the process for decryption.

---

[10]Never use this for production code! Always use well-tested libraries.

Cross the Streams

Counter mode has a number of advantages to CBC mode and, in our opinion, is significantly easier to understand than CBC mode. Also, while CTR is the traditional abbreviation, "CM" is a really nice set of initials.

Although simple, the concept behind this mode can be a little counter-intuitive at first (yup). In CTR mode, you actually *never use AES* for encryption or decryption of the data. Instead, this mode generates a *key stream* that is the same length as the plaintext and then uses XOR to combine them together.

Recall from earlier exercises in this chapter that XOR can be used to "mask" plaintext data by combining it with random data. The previous exercise masked 16 bytes of plaintext with 16 bytes of random data. This is a real form of encryption called a "one-time pad" (OTP) [11, Chap. 6]. It works great but requires that the *key is the same size as the plaintext*. We don't have the space here to explore the OTP further; the important concept is that using XOR to combine plaintext and random data is a great way to create ciphertext.

AES-CTR mimics this aspect of OTP. But instead of requiring the key to be the same size as the plaintext (a real pain when encrypting a 1TB file), it uses AES and a counter to generate a key stream of almost arbitrary length from an AES key as small as 128 bits.

To do this, CTR mode uses AES to encrypt a 16-byte counter, which generates 16 bytes of key stream. To get 16 more bytes of key stream, the mode increases the counter by one and encrypts the updated 16 bytes. By continually increasing the counter and encrypting the result, CTR mode can produce an almost arbitrary amount of key stream material.[11] Once a sufficient amount of key material is generated, the XOR operation is used to combine them together to produce the ciphertext.

Although the counter is changing by a small amount each time (often just changing by a single bit!), AES has good per-block avalanche properties. Thus, each output block appears completely different from the last, and the stream as a whole appears to be random data.

---

[11]There are limits but these are beyond the scope of this book.

Note: Random Thoughts

Randomness is actually a huge deal in cryptography. Many otherwise acceptable algorithms have been compromised in practice if they did not have sufficient sources of randomness for keys, among other things. The OTP algorithm we briefly mentioned requires a key that is the same size as the plaintext (no matter how large) and that the entire key be truly random data. AES-CTR mode only requires that the AES key be truly random. The key stream produced by AES-CTR *looks* random, but is actually *pseudo-random*. This means that if you know the AES key, you know the whole key stream no matter how random it appears to be.

Ensuring that you have a sufficiently random source of data is beyond the scope of this book. For our purposes, we will *assume* that os.urandom() can return acceptably random data for our needs. In production cryptography environments, you would need to analyze this far more carefully.

Randomness is so important that we will mention it more than once. In fact, we will return to it near the end of this very chapter.

Although AES-CTR is a stream cipher, we can still think about it one block at a time. To encrypt any given block of plaintext, generate the key stream for that block's index and XOR it with the (possibly partial) block. Expressed another way (where the subscript k indicates "encrypted with key k"):

$$C[n] = P[n] \oplus n_k.$$

That's mostly it! The only other slight twist is that we don't want to start with the same counter value every time. So, our IV, which we'll call our "nonce," is used as the starting counter value. To update our definition:

$$C[n] = P[n] \oplus (IV + n)_k.$$

XOR is a really versatile mathematical operation. You can think of it as "controlled bit-flipping": to compute $A \oplus B$, you march down their bits in tandem; when you encounter a 1 in B, you invert the corresponding bit in A, and when you encounter a 0 in

B, you leave that bit in A alone. Thinking of it that way, it's easy to see how doing that *twice* simply restores A to what it was before.

More formally, as discussed earlier, XOR is its own inverse: $(A \oplus B) \oplus B = A$. Since we created a stream of encrypted blocks by applying XOR to the appropriate value in the key stream, we simply do *exactly the same thing* to decrypt: apply XOR to the encrypted blocks and their corresponding keys:

$$P[n] = C[n] \oplus (IV + n)_k.$$

Of course, nothing happens if you merely XOR with 0 (since $A \oplus 0 = A$, which is where the inverse property comes from), so the keys in the stream need to be composed of random-looking bits, but that is exactly the type of key stream that AES produces.

Figure 3-7 provides a visual representation of AES-CTR operations.

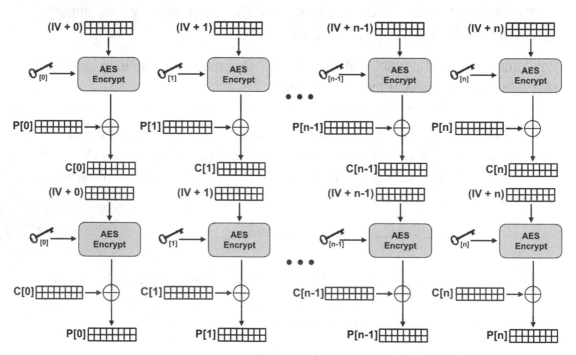

Figure 3-7. *Visual depictions of CTR encryption and decryption. Note that encryption and decryption are the same process!*

Happily, stream ciphers do not require padding! It is quite simple to only XOR a partial block, discarding the later parts of the key that aren't needed.

In general, this approach is much simpler. Padding goes away and blocks can again be encrypted independent of one another.

Let's see it in action in the cryptography module (Listing 3-9).

Listing 3-9. AES-CTR

```
1  from cryptography.hazmat.primitives.ciphers import Cipher, algorithms,
   modes
2  from cryptography.hazmat.backends import default_backend
3  import os
4
5  class EncryptionManager:
6      def __init__(self):
7          key = os.urandom(32)
8          nonce = os.urandom(16)
9          aes_context = Cipher(algorithms.AES(key),
10                              modes.CTR(nonce),
11                              backend=default_backend())
12         self.encryptor = aes_context.encryptor()
13         self.decryptor = aes_context.decryptor()
14
15     def updateEncryptor(self, plaintext):
16         return self.encryptor.update(plaintext)
17
18     def finalizeEncryptor(self):
19         return self.encryptor.finalize()
20
21     def updateDecryptor(self, ciphertext):
22         return self.decryptor.update(ciphertext)
23
24     def finalizeDecryptor(self):
25         return self.decryptor.finalize()
26
27  # Auto generate key/IV for encryption
28  manager = EncryptionManager()
29
```

```
30   plaintexts = [
31       b"SHORT",
32       b"MEDIUM MEDIUM MEDIUM",
33       b"LONG LONG LONG LONG LONG LONG"
34   ]
35
36   ciphertexts = []
37
38   for m in plaintexts:
39       ciphertexts.append(manager.updateEncryptor(m))
40   ciphertexts.append(manager.finalizeEncryptor())
41
42   for c in ciphertexts:
43       print("Recovered", manager.updateDecryptor(c))
44   print("Recovered", manager.finalizeDecryptor())
```

Because no padding is needed, the finalize methods are actually unnecessary except for "closing" the object. They are kept for symmetry and pedagogy.

How do you choose between CTR and CBC modes? In almost all circumstances, counter mode (CTR) is recommended.[12] Not only is it easier, but in some circumstances it is also more secure. As if that wasn't enough, counter mode is also easier to parallelize because keys in the key stream are computed from their index, not from a preceding computation.

---

[12]You can remember it because it also stands for "choose the right." You can even buy "CTR" rings as a friendly, constant, and, when twisted a bit to our purposes, *cryptographic* reminder.

Why even talk about CBC, then? At the very least it is still in wide use, so you will benefit from understanding it when you encounter it in the wild.

We will introduce other modes later in the book that build on counter mode to make something even better. For now, it is enough to understand the basic characteristics of CBC and CTR modes and how each one works to build a better algorithm from an underlying block cipher.

EXERCISE 3.13. WRITE A SIMPLE COUNTER MODE

As you did with CBC, create counter mode encryption from ECB mode. This should be even easier than it was with CBC. Generate the key stream by taking the IV block and encrypting it, then increasing the value of the IV block by one to generate the next block of key stream material. When finished, XOR the key stream with the plaintext. Decrypt in the same manner.

EXERCISE 3.14. PARALLEL COUNTER MODE

Extend your counter mode implementation to use a thread pool to generate the key stream in parallel. Remember that to generate a block of key stream, all that is required is the starting IV and which block of key stream is being generated (e.g., 0 for the first 16-byte block, 1 for the second 16-byte block, etc.). Start by creating a function that can generate *any* particular block of key stream, perhaps something like keystream(IV, i). Next, parallelize the generation of a key stream up to *n* by dividing the counter sequence among independent processes any way you please, and have them all work on generating their key stream blocks independently.

Key and IV Management

As you have seen, having a library such as cryptography makes all kinds of encryption convenient and simple to use. Unfortunately, this simplicity can be deceptive and lead to mistakes; there are many ways to get it wrong. We have already touched briefly on one of them: reuse of keys or IVs.

That kind of mistake falls under the broader category of "Key and IV Management," and doing it incorrectly is a common source of problems.

Important   You must *never* reuse key and IV pairs. Doing so seriously compromises security and disappoints cryptography book authors. Just don't do it. Always use a new key/IV pair when encrypting anything.

Why don't you want to reuse a key and IV pair? For CBC, we already mentioned one of the potential problems: if you reuse a key and IV pair, you will get *predictable output for predictable headers*. Parts of your messages that you might be inclined not to think about at all, because they are boilerplate or contain hidden structure, will become a liability; adversaries can use predictable ciphertext to learn about your keys.

Think about an HTML page, for example. The first characters are often the same across multiple pages (e.g., `"<!DOCTYPE html>\n"`). If the first 16 bytes (an AES block) of HTML pages are the same and you encrypt them under the same key/IV pair, the ciphertext will be the same for each one. You have just leaked data to your enemy, and they can start to analyze your encrypted data for patterns.

If your web site has a large amount of static content or dynamic results that are identically generated, each encrypted page becomes uniquely identifiable. The enemy may not know what each page says, but they can determine the frequency of use and track which parties receive the same pages.

Reusing a key and IV in CBC mode is *bad*.

Reusing a key and IV in counter mode, on the other hand, is *much worse*. Because counter mode is a stream cipher, the plaintext is simply XORed with the key stream. If you happen to know the plaintext, you can *recover the key*: $K \oplus P \oplus P = K$!

"So what?" you might be thinking. "Who cares if they can get the key stream? If they already know the plaintext, why do we care?"

The problem is, under many circumstances an attacker might know some or all of the contents of one of your plaintext messages. If *other* messages are encrypted *with the same key stream*, the attacker can recover *those* messages too!

Bad, bad, bad.

Let's explore this idea a little further. Suppose that you buy something for $100.00 with a credit card at a store. Let's assume a simplified version of the world where the card reader sends a message to your bank to authorize the purchase protected by only AES-CTR encryption.

Imagine that the message to the bank from the credit card reader is XML that looks like this:

```
1    <XML>
2      <CreditCardPurchase>
3        <Merchant>Acme Inc</Merchant>
4        <Buyer>John Smith</Buyer>
5        <Date>01/01/2001</Date>
6        <Amount>$100.00</Amount>
7        <CCNumber>555-555-555-555</CCNumber>
8      </CreditCardPurchase>
9    </XML>
```

The store creates this message, encrypts it, and sends it to the bank. In order to communicate, the store and the bank must share a key. If the programmers who wrote the code were lazy and negligent, they may have created a system with a constant key and IV that are reused on every message, like what we find in Listing 3-10.

Listing 3-10. AES-CTR for a Store

```
1    # ACME generates a purchase message in their storefront.
2    from cryptography.hazmat.primitives.ciphers import Cipher, algorithms,
     modes
3    from cryptography.hazmat.backends import default_backend
4
5    # WARNING! Never do this. Reusing a key/IV is irresponsible!
6    preshared_key = bytes.fromhex('00112233445566778899AABBCCDDEEFF')
7    preshared_iv = bytes.fromhex('000000000000000000000000000000000')
8
9    purchase_message = b"""
10   <XML>
11     <CreditCardPurchase>
12       <Merchant>Acme Inc</Merchant>
13       <Buyer>John Smith</Buyer>
14       <Date>01/01/2001</Date>
15       <Amount>$100.00</Amount>
16       <CCNumber>555-555-555-555</CCNumber>
```

```
17      </CreditCardPurchase>
18    </XML>
19    """
20
21    aesContext = Cipher(algorithms.AES(preshared_key),
22                        modes.CTR(preshared_iv),
23                        backend=default_backend())
24    encryptor = aesContext.encryptor()
25    encrypted_message = encryptor.update(purchase_message)
```

For simplicity, the purchase message was included in the preceding code. Feel free to change it to accept a file or command-line flags that set the buyer's name, purchase price, and so forth. You probably ought to also write the encrypted message to a file.

Back to our scenario, if you are trying to crack this system, you can spend $100.00 at this store, then tap the line and intercept the purchase message transmitted to the bank. If you do this, how much of the plaintext message do you know? You know *all* of it! You know who made the purchase, you know the amount of the purchase, you know the date, and you know your own credit card number.

That means that you can recreate the plaintext message, XOR it with the ciphertext, and recover keystream material. Because the merchant is reusing the same key and IV for the next customer, you can trivially decrypt the message and read the contents. Oops. We feel a news story about a data breach coming on.

EXERCISE 3.15. RIDING THE KEYSTREAM

Put into practice this keystream-stealing attack. That is, encrypt two different purchase messages using the same key and IV. "Intercept" one of the two messages and XOR the ciphertext contents with the known plaintext. This will give you a keystream. Next, XOR the keystream with the other message to recover that message's plaintext. The message sizes may be a little different, but if you're short some keystream bytes, recover what you can.

Even if the attacker does not know *any* of the plaintext and cannot recover a keystream, he or she can still take advantage of messages encrypted with the same key and IV pair. If you have two messages encrypted with the same keystream, you can do the following trick (where K is the key stream):

$$c_1 = m_1 \oplus K$$
$$c_2 = m_2 \oplus K$$
$$c_1 \oplus c_2 = (m_1 \oplus K) \oplus (m_2 \oplus K)$$
$$c_1 \oplus c_2 = m_1 \oplus m_2 \oplus K \oplus K$$
$$c_1 \oplus c_2 = m_1 \oplus m_2$$

What do you get out of having the XOR of the two plaintext messages? Is that readable? It depends. Because plaintext messages often have structure, private data is often extractable or guessable. Take these made-up purchase messages from our example. If you XORed two such messages together, what could you learn?

First of all, any parts that overlap exactly simply reduce to 0. Instantly, you know where the messages are the same and where they diverge. If the attacker were lucky enough that two messages had the same length of name for the buyer, the amount fields would line up as well. This field yields a lot of information when the two are XORed together because there are so few legal characters for this field ("0"–"9" and "."). The XOR of the ASCII characters for the digits leaves open only a few possibilities.

For example, there are only two pairs of digits for which the XOR of their ASCII values is 15. These are "7" and "8" (ASCII values 55 and 56) and "6" and "9" (ASCII values 54 and 57). So, if we know that we have the XOR of two purchase amount field digits and the XOR value is 15, then the two messages each have one of these two pairs of numbers. That's only four possibilities, which will not be very difficult for an attacker to figure out under most circumstances.

You might be surprised how often this vulnerability can show up if you're not careful. One simple example is full-duplex messages. If you have two parties that want to send encrypted messages to each other, they must not use the same key and IV to encrypt each side of the connection. Each side's encryption must be independent of the other. If you think about how CBC and CTR mode work, this will be pretty obvious. If you are going to write messages in both directions, each side needs a separate read key and write key.[13] The read key of the first party will be the write key of the second and vice versa. This way, different messages will not be written under the same key and IV pair.

EXERCISE 3.16. SIFTING THROUGH XOR

XOR together some plaintext messages and look around for patterns and readable data. There's no need to use any encryption for this, just take some regular, human-readable messages and XOR the bytes. Try human-readable strings, XML, JSON, and other formats. You may not find a lot that is instantly decipherable, but it's a fun exercise.

Exploiting Malleability

Some aspects of cryptography are unintuitive at first. For example, an enemy can fail to *read* a confidential message while still being able to *change* it in meaningful, deceptive ways. In this section, we will experiment with altering encrypted messages while not being able to read them.

Counter mode is a really good encryption mode for all of the reasons described earlier. At the risk of being too repetitive, however, it only guarantees *confidentiality*. In fact, because it is a stream cipher, it is trivial to change a small part of the message without changing the rest of it. In counter mode, for example, if an attacker modifies one byte of the ciphertext, it only affects the corresponding byte of plaintext. While that one byte of plaintext will not decrypt correctly, the remaining bytes will remain intact.

Cipher block chaining mode is different because a change to a single byte of ciphertext will affect all subsequent blocks.

---

[13]Technically, they could use the same key, provided the IVs were different. However, there are a number of ways in practice that IVs might intentionally or accidentally overlap, so it is typically recommended to use different keys and not rely on having different IVs.

EXERCISE 3.17. VISUALIZING CIPHERTEXT CHANGES

To better understand the difference between counter mode and cipher block chaining mode, go back to the image encryption utility you wrote previously. Modify it to first encrypt and then decrypt the image, using either AES-CBC or AES-CTR as the mode. After decryption, the original image should be completely restored.

Now introduce an error into the ciphertext and decrypt the modified bytes. Try, for example, picking the byte right in the middle of the encrypted image data and setting it to 0. After corrupting the data, call the decryption function and view the restored image. How much of a difference did the edit make with CTR? How much of a difference did the edit make with CBC?

HINT: If you can't see anything, try an all-white image. If you still can't see it, change 50 bytes or so to figure out where the changes are happening. Once you find where the changes are happening, go back to changing a single byte to view the differences between CTR and CBC. Can you explain what's happening?

To illustrate this concept of malleability, we are going to let our attacker know some of the plaintext of an encrypted message. This knowledge is going to allow them to change the message en route. What's different this time around is that this vulnerability is *not* dependent on a reused keystream.

If an attacker knows the plaintext behind a keystream-enciphered message, it is easy to extract the keystream from the ciphertext. If the keystream is reused, the attacker can decrypt all messages that used it. Even if it is *not* reused, the attacker can *alter* a message with known plaintext.

Let's revisit our encrypted purchase messages. Suppose that Acme's competitor, Evil LLC, wants to redirect this payment to themselves. They have a tap on the network connection coming out of Acme's store and can intercept and modify the message. When an encrypted form of this message comes along, even though they don't have the key and cannot decrypt it, they can strip out the original message parts that are known and replace them with their own chosen parts.

The part that Evil LLC wants to change is this part:

```
1    <XML>
2      <CreditCardPurchase>
3        <Merchant>Acme Inc</Merchant>
```

That data is known and fixed in every payment message. To obtain the keystream, all Evil LLC has to do is XOR this data with the ciphertext. Once this part is XORed, they have the keystream for this many bytes. Then, they create their modified message:

```
1    <XML>
2        <CreditCardPurchase>
3            <Merchant>Evil LLC</Merchant>
```

This message has the exact same size as the true message. Because AES-CTR is so malleable, it is easy to XOR this partial message with the extracted keystream and join it to the rest of the still-encrypted message. This process is illustrated in Figure 3-8.

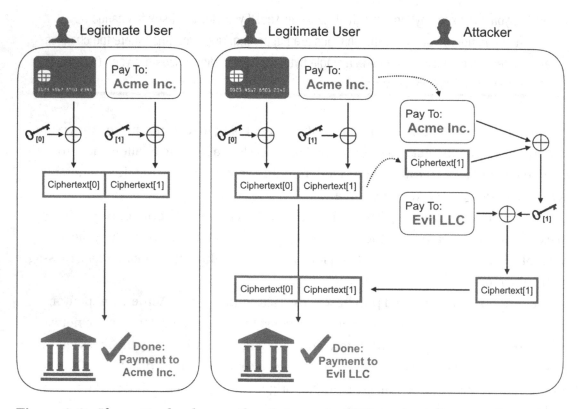

Figure 3-8. *If an attacker knows the plaintext in CTR mode ciphertext, she can extract the keystream to encrypt her own evil message!*

EXERCISE 3.18. EMBRACING EVIL

You work for (or own!) Evil LLC. Time to steal some payments from Acme. Start with one of
the encrypted payment messages you created in the earlier exercises. Calculate the size of
the header up through the identification of the merchant and extract that many bytes of
the encrypted data. XOR the plaintext header with the ciphertext header to get the *keystream*.
Once you have this, XOR the extracted keystream with a header identifying Evil LLC as the
merchant. This is the "evil" ciphertext. Copy it over the bytes of the encrypted file to create
a new payment message identifying your company as the recipient. Prove that it works by
decrypting the modified file.

The key lesson here is that encryption is insufficient to protect data by itself.
In subsequent chapters, we will use message authentication codes, authenticated
encryption, and digital signatures to ensure that data cannot be altered without
disrupting communications.

Gaze into the Padding

While CBC mode is less susceptible to alteration than counter mode, it is by no means
perfect in that regard. In fact, it is CBC's malleability that made one of the early versions of
SSL vulnerable. Remember that CBC mode is a block-based mode and requires padding.
An interesting error in the padding specification and the malleability of AES-CBC enabled
attackers to execute a "padding oracle attack" and decrypt confidential data.

Let's create that attack right now. It's extremely interesting and educational.

For this little exercise, you will need to write your own padding functions; the ones
in the cryptography module are too secure. Your functions will follow the very broken
SSL 3.0 specification (we'll talk about SSL/TLS more in the last chapter). Basically, *N*–1
bytes of *anything* followed by a single byte that indicates the total length of the padding.
Because padding was always required in that specification, it would be added even if the
plaintext was a multiple of the block size. This will be important later.

Listing 3-11. SSLv3 Padding

```
1    def sslv3Pad(msg):
2        padNeeded = (16 - (len(msg) % 16)) - 1
3        padding = padNeeded.to_bytes(padNeeded+1, "big")
4        return msg+padding
5
6    def sslv3Unpad(padded_msg):
7        paddingLen = padded_msg[-1] + 1
8        return padded_msg[:-paddingLen]
```

Let's talk about what we have so far (Listing 3-11). The padding bytes in this scheme are completely ignored *except for the last byte*. It doesn't matter what the bytes are, so long as the last byte is correct. Padding goes at the end of a message, right? Guess which part of a CBC message is the most malleable.

The reason that the last part of the CBC message is more malleable is that it has no impact on any subsequent blocks. It can be changed without messing up anything else. Recall that CBC decryption starts out the same for every single block no matter where it is. The ciphertext block is decrypted by AES with the key. It's only after decryption that it is XORed with the ciphertext from the previous block.

This means that you could substitute *any* block from the CBC chain at the very end of the chain. It will get decrypted at the end just like it would in the middle or the beginning. After decryption, it is XORed with the ciphertext from the previous block.

How is this helpful? Well, suppose that we are fortunate enough to have the original plaintext message be a multiple of 16 bytes long, the AES block length. Because we're using a padding scheme that *always* uses padding, there will be a full block of padding at the end. Since we don't care what bytes are in the padding except for the last one, we can correctly recover the entire message, even if we replace the last block, so long as the very last byte decodes to *15* (the padding length when there is a full block of padding).

Explained another way, when there is a full block of padding at the end, 15 of the 16 bytes are completely ignored. It doesn't matter what they are. If we're going to try to "fool" the decryption, this is a great place to do it, because we only have to get *one* byte correct!

This small change, only caring about the value of the last byte, changes everything! It reduces brute-force guessing to something reasonable. Normally, if you wanted to "guess" a correct AES block, you would have to try all possible combinations of all 16 bytes. You might recall from previous discussion that this works out to a very big number and it is impossible to try every combination for all practical purposes.

But now that we only care about the last byte, we only need to correctly guess *one* byte of data. To repeat, so long as the last byte decrypts to 15, our padding will be "correct." One byte of data has 256 possible values, so if our last byte is randomly selected, then 1 out of 256 times it will correctly decrypt to 15!

You might protest that the data *isn't* random. We are trying to decrypt a specific byte. Very true! But remember that in CBC we XOR the real plaintext with the ciphertext of the previous block! The ciphertext, at least for our purposes here, behaves like random data. For any given key/IV pair, the last byte of ciphertext that will be XORed with our plaintext byte has an equal chance of being any of the 256 possible 1-byte values. If we are lucky, the "random" byte of ciphertext XORed with our plaintext byte will be 15!

If the padding is accepted and decrypts to 15, we can use our knowledge of the previous ciphertext block to get the true plaintext byte.

Actually, recovering the plaintext byte is a little trick and requires that we think through CBC decryption carefully. Remember that the last block of plaintext (e.g., the true padding in the original message) was XORed with the ciphertext from the second-to-last block. This intermediate data was encrypted by the AES algorithm. So, working backward, if we overwrite the final ciphertext block, the CBC operation will first run this block through the AES decryption operation to produce an intermediate value that is then XORed with the preceding ciphertext. If this is difficult to follow, refer back to Figure 3-5.

If the padding is accepted (e.g., the last byte is 15), we know that the *last byte* of the intermediate value decrypted by AES is the XOR of 15 and the last byte of the *previous ciphertext block*. We, of course, have the ciphertext. Now, even without the AES key, we can simply compute the intermediate byte directly (e.g., by taking the XOR of 15 and the last byte of the second-to-last ciphertext block).

But the intermediate value isn't the plaintext byte. Remember, we are decrypting an earlier ciphertext block. That ciphertext block is the AES encryption of the real plaintext XORed with the actual preceding ciphertext (or the IV if it's the first plaintext block). So, when we recover the intermediate last byte, we still have to remove that mixed-in data with an appropriate XOR.

Let's work on putting this into code. First, we need to define our "oracle." In real life, the oracle was the SSLv3 server. If you sent it a message with bad padding, it would send you an error message that the padding was bad. That knowledge is all that is necessary to pull off this attack. For our code in Listing 3-12, we will just have an accept() method in an Oracle class that indicates whether the padding is valid, performing the same purpose as the server.

Listing 3-12. SSLv3 Padding Oracle

```
1    from cryptography.hazmat.primitives.ciphers import Cipher, algorithms,
     modes
2    from cryptography.hazmat.backends import default_backend
3
4    class Oracle:
5        def __init__(self, key, iv):
6            self.key = key
7            self.iv = iv
8
9        def accept(self, ciphertext):
10           aesCipher = Cipher(algorithms.AES(self.key),
11                              modes.CBC(self.iv),
12                              backend=default_backend())
13           decryptor = aesCipher.decryptor()
14           plaintext = decryptor.update(ciphertext)
15           plaintext += decryptor.finalize()
16           return plaintext[-1] == 15
```

This might seem a little weird: we have the key and are using it to create the oracle. Just remember: we're simulating a vulnerable remote server, which *would* have its own key. The attack we write below will proceed without knowledge of the key used here.

Once we have the oracle, it's a pretty easy function to see if we can get lucky and decode the last byte of an arbitrary block in the ciphertext, as in Listing 3-13.

Listing 3-13. Lucky SSLv3 Padding Byte

```
1    # Partial Listing: Some Assembly Required
2
3    # This function assumes that the last ciphertext block is a full
4    # block of SSLV3 padding
5    def lucky_get_one_byte(iv, ciphertext, block_number, oracle):
6        block_start = block_number * 16
7        block_end = block_start + 16
8        block = ciphertext[block_start: block_end]
9
10       # Copy the block over the last block.
11       mod_ciphertext = ciphertext[:-16] + block
12       if not oracle.accept(mod_ciphertext):
13           return False, None
14
15       # This is valid! Let's get the byte!
16       # We first need the byte decrypted from the block.
17       # It was XORed with second to last block, so
18       # byte = 15 XOR (last byte of second-to-last block).
19       second_to_last = ciphertext[-32:-16]
20       intermediate = second_to_last[-1]^15
21
22       # We still have to XOR it with its *real*
23       # preceding block in order to get the true value.
24       if block_number == 0:
25           prev_block = iv
26       else:
27           prev_block = ciphertext[block_start-16: block_start]
28
29       return True, intermediate ^ prev_block[-1]
```

To repeat: we are counting on the penultimate (second-to-last) block being lucky! As shown in Figure 3-9, we have to be lucky enough that the last byte of the penultimate block will just happen to XOR with our intermediate byte to be 15. This luck that we are counting on is dependent on the key and IV chosen. Once again, for any given key/IV pair, there is a 1-in-256 chance that the penultimate block will "accidentally" XOR with our intermediate plaintext block to give us 15.

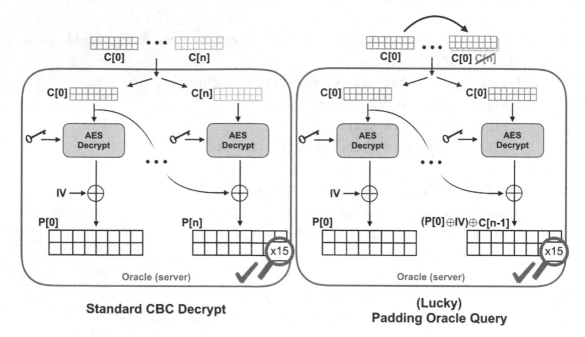

Standard CBC Decrypt   **(Lucky)**
                                                           Padding Oracle Query

Figure 3-9. *If the first 15 bytes of the padding block are ignored, we can substitute in the second to last block and see if the oracle tells us the padding is correct. If so, we can figure out the last byte in the previous block.*

Is that really all that useful? In the first place, we have to be lucky enough to have a full block of padding. In the second place, we only have a 1-in-256 chance of decoding *a single byte*. That doesn't seem terribly helpful.

Or does it?

Again, cryptography can be very counter-intuitive. Computers don't behave like we would expect them to, and that's where we get into trouble.

While SSLV3 was busy protecting web traffic, it turned out there were a number of ways that a malicious advertisement could generate traffic to an SSL-encrypted web site. But because that advertisement was generating the traffic, its authors could control how long the encrypted message was. Thus, if the attacker was trying to decrypt an encrypted cookie, triggering a GET request of various lengths could control how long the overall message was.

Getting the full block of padding in this case really isn't very difficult as the malicious requester could put arbitrary data in the GET request.

And it is nothing for a computer to make 256 requests over a network. Note that, in the SSLV3 context, the client and server are going to use different keys with every connection (for good reason, as we have seen!). This means that on each connection, the ciphertext will be different! So, if the attacker sends 256 requests, the penultimate block will be different each time, providing a new opportunity to be lucky and have the right "random" number that will provide the needed 15.

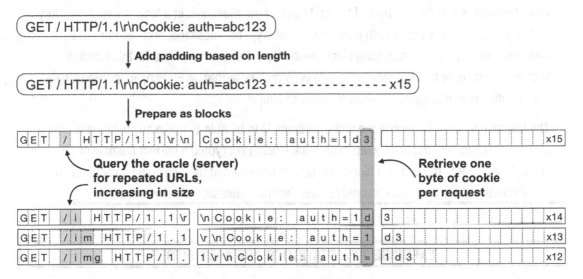

Figure 3-10. In order to decrypt a byte that matters, an attacker controls the GET request size so that the cookie is in the right spot. This requires the ability to insert arbitrary requests such as an advertiser within a TLS-secured context.

It's still just one byte, right? As illustrated in Figure 3-10, the attacker can control the length of the message. Once one byte is decoded, it's pretty straightforward to increase the message length by 1 by inserting a byte earlier in the message, pushing the new byte into the last slot of the arbitrary block. Another 256 tries and that second byte will be decoded too! Wash, rinse, and repeat!

EXERCISE 3.19. RESISTANCE IS FUTILE

Finish the code for the padding oracle attack. We've given you the major pieces, but it will still take some work to put everything together. We will do a few things to try and simplify as much as possible. First, pick a message that is exactly a multiple of 16 bytes in length (the AES block size) and create a fixed padding to append. The fixed padding can be any 16 bytes as long as the last byte is 15 (that's the whole point of the exercise, right?). Encrypt this message and pass it to the oracle to make sure that code is working.

Next, test recovering the last byte of the first block of the message. In a loop, create a new key and IV pair (and a new oracle with these values), encrypt the message, and call the `lucky_get_one_byte()` function, setting block number to 0. Repeat the loop until this function succeeds and verify that the recovered byte is correct. Note that, in Python, an individual byte isn't treated as a byte type but is converted to an integer.

The last step in order to decode the entire message is to be able to make any byte the last byte of a block. Again, for simplicity, keep the message being encrypted a perfect multiple of 16. To push any byte to the end of a block, add some extra bytes at the beginning and cut off an equal number at the end. You can now recover the entire message one byte at a time!

EXERCISE 3.20. STATISTICS ARE ALSO FUTILE

Instrument your padding oracle attack in the previous exercise to calculate how many guesses it took to fully decrypt the entire message and calculate an average number of tries per byte. In theory, it should work out to about 256 tries per byte. But you're probably working with such small numbers that it will vary widely. In our tests on a 96-byte message, our averages varied between about 220 guesses per byte and 290 guesses per byte.

Once again, encryption is about confidentiality, and confidentiality is simply not enough to solve all security problems. In subsequent chapters we will learn how to combine confidentiality and integrity to solve a larger class of problems.

Weak Keys, Bad Management

To conclude this chapter, let's briefly discuss *keys*. Hopefully, it has already become very clear to you how important keys are.

In almost all cryptographic systems, key management is the hardest part. It can be difficult to generate good keys, to share keys, and to manage keys afterward (e.g., keeping them secret, updating them, or revoking them). For now, we'll focus on key generation.

Keys must be drawn from good sources of randomness. We mentioned randomness once already in this chapter in a brief aside, but let's take a second look. For example, the following code is *really wrong*.

```
import random
key = random.getrandbits(16, "big")
```

The random package is a *pseudo-random* number generator and not even a good one at that. Pseudo-random generators are *deterministic*, generating numbers that appear random to humans, but are always the same given a known seed value. Default seeds used to be based on the system time. This may seem reasonable, but it means that if the attacker can guess when the random number generator was seeded, they can completely predict all the random numbers produced. About the only way to make this worse is to hard-code the key or the seed (which is effectively the same thing).

```
import random

# Set the random number generator seed to 0.
r = random.Random(0)
key = r.getrandbits(16, "big")
```

This code will produce the same "random" numbers on every run of the program. This can sometimes be useful for testing, but you must not leave it in production code!

Although Python's default seeding is no longer quite so predictable, it is not suitable for generating secrets like passwords. Instead, always pull from `os.urandom()` or, if using Python 3.6 or later, `secrets.SystemRandom()`. Under most circumstances, this is enough randomness. If you need something stronger, you might need to use different hardware and should consult an expert cryptographer.

In some deployments, a key is not pulled from random numbers. Instead, it is derived from a password. If you are going to derive a key from a password, the password needs to be very secure! In the previous chapter, you learned about brute-force attacks and all of those lessons apply here.

Let's get a feel for the difference in difficulty of guessing a key in these scenarios. How long would it take to try every possible 128-bit (random) key? How many tries is that?

There are 2^{128} different 128-bit keys. That's this many different keys:

340,282,366,920,938,463,463,374,607,431,768,211,456.

If your key is derived from a five-digit pin number, though, you have reduced it to 99,999! It's true that very few passwords will be as hard to brute force as a truly random 128-bit key. After all, you'd need to have a password composed of about 20 random characters to require the same kind of brute-force effort as a 128-bit key. But still, 99,999 is just begging a computer to accept your challenge. You can do better than that!

As a reminder, there are proven algorithms for deriving a key from a password. Make sure you use a good one. In the previous chapter, we used scrypt. There are others that some people feel are even better (such as bcrypt or Argon2). What makes a good derivation function? One characteristic is how long it takes. If someone picks a weak password (e.g., "puppy1"), it won't take the attacker long to figure it out. It might be possible, however, to make it take too long if the derivation function is slow.

In short, don't bother using a good cipher with a bad key. Make sure that your keys are securely generated and adequately resistant to abuse by a determined adversary.

EXERCISE 3.21. PREDICTING TIME-BASED RANDOMNESS

Write an AES encryption program (or modify one of the others you've written for this chapter) that uses the Python random number generator to generate keys. Use the seed method to explicitly configure the generator based on the current time using `time.time()` rounded to the nearest second. Then use this generator to create a key and encrypt some data. Write a separate program that takes the encrypted data as input and tries to guess the key. It should take a minimum time and a maximum time as a range and try iterating between these two points as seed values for random.

Other Encryption Algorithms

In this chapter, we have focused exclusively on AES encryption. There are good reasons for this. AES is the most popular symmetric cipher currently in use. It's used in network communications as well as storing data on disk. And as we will see in Chapter 7, it is the basis for several advanced AEAD (authenticated encryption with associated data).

However, there are other symmetric key ciphers that can be used. Here are a few that are supported by the `cryptography` library:

- Camellia

- ChaCha20

- TripleDES

- CAST5

- SEED

Even though we are always encouraging you to use a well-tested, well-respected third-party library, be aware that libraries often include support for less desirable algorithms for legacy support. In this list of algorithms supported by `cryptography`, a few ciphers are already known to be insecure and are being phased out. For example, while DES is not included in the `cryptography` library's ciphers (GOOD! DES is VERY BAD!), the module does include 3DES (TripleDES). While 3DES is not as broken as DES, it should be retired ASAP. CAST5 fits in this same category.

Another cipher supported by `cryptography` is Blowfish. This algorithm is also not recommended for use, and its stronger successor, Twofish, is not available in the current `cryptography` implementation.

finalize()

This chapter covered a *lot* of material, and we barely scratched the surface. Perhaps the most important principle that you can take away from this chapter is that cryptography is usually far more complicated than perhaps it first seems. The different modes of operation we reviewed have different strengths and weaknesses, some of which we explored by example. We found that even how we approach the APIs to cryptographic operations can have a significant impact on security.

Hopefully, this lesson reinforced the YANAC principle (You Are Not A Cryptographer... yet!). Please remember that these exercises are introductory and educational. Please do not go copying this code into production and don't use the introductory knowledge you have gained to write security-critical operations. Do you really want to risk people's personal information, financial information, or other sensitive data on your newly developed skills?

At the same time, after just one chapter on encryption, you have a broader view of what that word even means. The next time you hear "protected by AES 128-bit encryption," you might wonder whether they're using CTR, CBC, or (heaven forbid!) ECB mode. You might also wonder if they are using their encryption correctly because you already have experienced some of the ways (often unexpected) that symmetric encryption can be broken.

Yes, you've taken your first steps into a cryptography world. Are you ready to take a few more? Then let's talk about *asymmetric* encryption!

Asymmetric Encryption: Public/Private Keys

Asymmetric encryption is one of the most important advances in cryptographic security ever made. It underpins all of the security on the Web, in your Wi-Fi connections, and in secure email and other communication of all kinds. It is ubiquitous, but it is also subtle and easy to implement or use incorrectly, and a lack of correctness means a sometimes drastic reduction in security.

Perhaps you've heard of "public keys," "public key infrastructure," and/or "public key encryption." There are actually multiple operations within asymmetric cryptography and a number of different algorithms. Within this chapter, we are going to focus exclusively on *asymmetric encryption* and specifically using an algorithm known as *RSA*. We are going to leave other asymmetric operations, such as signatures and key exchange, for later chapters.

RSA encryption is, in fact, almost completely obsolete. Why study it? Because RSA is one of the classic asymmetric algorithms and does a good job, in our opinion anyway, of introducing some core concepts that will be helpful when learning about more modern approaches.

A Tale of Two Keys

The East Antarctica Truth-Spying Agency (EATSA) has a new mission for Alice and Bob. Bob is to remain behind in East Antarctica (EA) as Alice's handler and Alice is to get an undercover position in the West Antarctica Government Greasy Spoon (WAGGS). Alice will report back to Bob what the West Antarctica (WA) politicians are eating. EATSA plans to blackmail these politicians over how much hot food they are eating, while their constituents are stuck eating frozen dinners.

111

© Seth James Nielson, Christopher K. Monson 2019
S. J. Nielson and C. K. Monson, *Practical Cryptography in Python*,
https://doi.org/10.1007/978-1-4842-4900-0_4

EATSA, however, is concerned about compromised communications. If Alice is captured with a *symmetric* key, the West Antarctica Central Knights Office (WACKO) will be able to use it to decrypt any messages they have intercepted from her to EATSA. That would ruin the entire plan!

EATSA decides to implement a new technology they've been hearing about: asymmetric encryption. Their collective minds are blown when they find out that there are encryption schemes with *two* keys: what is encrypted with one key *can only be decrypted by the other*!

Using this new technology, Bob can send Alice into the field with just one of the two keys (the "public" key). Alice will be able to encrypt messages back to Bob that *not even she can decrypt*! Only Bob, safe within EA territory and in possession of the corresponding "private" key, can decrypt the messages. That sounds perfect—if her key is compromised, it will at least not allow her captors to decrypt what she has written, which is strictly better than before.[1] What could go wrong?

To finish cooking up this scheme, EATSA chooses to use RSA encryption, an asymmetric algorithm that uses very large integers as both keys and messages, and the "modular exponentiation" as the primary mathematical operator for encryption and decryption. The algorithm is simple to understand and, with modern programming languages, relatively easy to implement. It looks in all ways to be the perfect recipe for culinary subterfuge.

Getting Keyed Up

Generating keys in RSA is a little bit tricky, as it requires finding two very large integers with a high likelihood of being *co-prime*. That looked like a lot of math to the agents of EATSA, so they opted to just use existing libraries to do that part. Listing 4-1 shows the package they pulled into Python 3 and the code they wrote that makes use of it.

---

[1] They can still send fake messages pretending to be her, but that was possible with symmetric encryption as well.

Listing 4-1. RSA Key Generation

```
1   from cryptography.hazmat.backends import default_backend
2   from cryptography.hazmat.primitives.asymmetric import rsa
3   from cryptography.hazmat.primitives import serialization
4
5   # Generate a private key.
6   private_key = rsa.generate_private_key(
7       public_exponent=65537,
8       key_size=2048,
9       backend=default_backend()
10  )
11
12  # Extract the public key from the private key.
13  public_key = private_key.public_key()
14
15  # Convert the private key into bytes. We won't encrypt it this time.
16  private_key_bytes = private_key.private_bytes(
17      encoding=serialization.Encoding.PEM,
18      format=serialization.PrivateFormat.TraditionalOpenSSL,
19      encryption_algorithm=serialization.NoEncryption()
20  )
21
22  # Convert the public key into bytes.
23  public_key_bytes = public_key.public_bytes(
24      encoding=serialization.Encoding.PEM,
25      format=serialization.PublicFormat.SubjectPublicKeyInfo
26  )
27
28  # Convert the private key bytes back to a key.
29  # Because there is no encryption of the key, there is no password.
30  private_key = serialization.load_pem_private_key(
31      private_key_bytes,
32      backend=default_backend(),
33      password=None)
34
```

```
35   public_key = serialization.load_pem_public_key(
36       public_key_bytes,
37       backend=default_backend())
```

That's not too bad, once you know how it's used. This pattern is the same for any private/public key generation, so even though there are a few constants in there with long names, it definitely seemed like the library was making this easier for EATSA.

See how everything hinges on the private key in RSA? The public key is derived from it. While either key can be used to encrypt (and the other can be used to decrypt), the private key is special because of this property. RSA keys are not only asymmetric because one encrypts and the other decrypts, they are also asymmetric because you can derive an RSA public key from the private key, but not the other way around.

The `private_bytes` and `public_bytes` methods convert large integer keys into bytes that are in a standard network- and disk-ready encoding called a PEM. The corresponding serialization "load" methods can be used to decode these after reading those bytes from disk so that they look like keys again to the encryption and decryption algorithms.

It is possible (and a very good idea) to encrypt the *private key itself*, but we opted not to do that here, which is why no password is used.

RSA Done Wrong: Part One

Alice and Bob are going to help us learn about RSA largely by exploring all the ways to use RSA incorrectly.

The actual encryption and decryption parts looked pretty simple to EATSA, and every library they looked at seemed to have a lot of unnecessary extra stuff making it harder to understand and even (gasp) slowing it down. Not having been taught the YANAC principle, they decided to implement encryption and decryption on their own. Rather than using the third-party library as written, they opted to omit *padding*. This results in a very "raw" or basic form of RSA that will be useful to us in learning about internals even though the results will be very broken.

Warning: Do Not Roll Your Own Encryption

Once again, implementing your own RSA encryption/decryption, rather than using a library, is not a good idea *at all*. Using RSA without padding is especially unsafe and insecure for numerous reasons, just a few of which we'll explore in this section. Although we will be writing our own RSA functions here for educational purposes, **do not under any circumstances use this code for real communication**.

Here is the math for encryption, where c is the ciphertext, m is the message, and the remaining parameters form the public and private keys, to be explained later:

$$c \equiv m^e \pmod{n} \tag{4.1}$$

Similarly, here it is for decryption:

$$m \equiv c^d \pmod{n} \tag{4.2}$$

That doesn't seem too bad, right? Modular exponentiation is a pretty standard operation in large integer math libraries,[2] so there really isn't much to this.

If you're new to this, don't be thrown off by $\equiv$. For simplicity, you can usually just think about it as an equal sign.

The operations in (4.1) and (4.2) can be written concisely in Python using gmpy2, a large number math library. The powmod function performs the necessary modular exponentiation operation, as shown in Listing 4-2.

Listing 4-2. GMPY2

```
1  #### DANGER ####
2  # The following RSA encryption and decryption is
3  # completely unsafe and terribly broken. DO NOT USE
```

---

[2]It certainly became popular after PKI was invented.

```
4    # for anything other than the practice exercise
5    ################
6    def simple_rsa_encrypt(m, publickey):
7        # Public_numbers returns a data structure with the 'e' and 'n'
         parameters.
8        numbers = publickey.public_numbers()
9
10       # Encryption is(m^e) % n.
11       return gmpy2.powmod(m, numbers.e, numbers.n)
12
13   def simple_rsa_decrypt(c, privatekey):
14       # Private_numbers returns a data structure with the 'd' and 'n'
         parameters.
15       numbers = privatekey.private_numbers()
16
17       # Decryption is(c^d) % n.
18       return gmpy2.powmod(c, numbers.d, numbers.public_numbers.n)
19   #### DANGER ####
```

As mentioned before, and perhaps more obvious now, RSA operates on integers, not message bytes. How do we convert messages into integers? Python makes this convenient because its int type has to_bytes and from_bytes methods. Let's make them a little nicer to use in Listing 4-3.

Listing 4-3. Integer/Byte Conversion

```
1    def int_to_bytes(i):
2        # i might be a gmpy2 big integer; convert back to a Python int
3        i = int(i)
4        return i.to_bytes((i.bit_length()+7)//8, byteorder='big')
5
6    def bytes_to_int(b):
7        return int.from_bytes(b, byteorder='big')
```

> **Important**   Because RSA works on integers, not bytes, the default
> implementation loses leading zeros. As far as integers are concerned, 01 and 1
> are the same number. If your byte sequence begins with any number of zeros, they
> will not survive encryption/decryption. For our example, we are sending text, so it
> won't ever be a problem. For binary data transmissions, however, it could be. This
> problem will be solved with padding.

EATSA now has all of the necessary pieces to create a simple RSA encryption/
decryption application. Before looking at their code in Listing 4-4, try creating your own
version.

Listing 4-4. RSA Done Simply

```
1   # FOR TRAINING USE ONLY! DO NOT USE THIS FOR REAL CRYPTOGRAPHY
2
3   import gmpy2, os, binascii
4   from cryptography.hazmat.backends import default_backend
5   from cryptography.hazmat.primitives.asymmetric import rsa
6   from cryptography.hazmat.primitives import serialization
7
8   #### DANGER ####
9   # The following RSA encryption and decryption is
10  # completely unsafe and terribly broken. DO NOT USE
11  # for anything other than the practice exercise
12  ################
13  def simple_rsa_encrypt(m, publickey):
14      numbers = publickey.public_numbers()
15      return gmpy2.powmod(m, numbers.e, numbers.n)
16
17  def simple_rsa_decrypt(c, privatekey):
18      numbers = privatekey.private_numbers()
19      return gmpy2.powmod(c, numbers.d, numbers.public_numbers.n)
20  #### DANGER ####
21
```

```
22   def int_to_bytes(i):
23       # i might be a gmpy2 big integer; convert back to a Python int
24       i = int(i)
25       return i.to_bytes((i.bit_length()+7)//8, byteorder='big')
26
27   def bytes_to_int(b):
28       return int.from_bytes(b, byteorder='big')
29
30   def main():
31       public_key_file = None
32       private_key_file = None
33       public_key = None
34       private_key = None
35       while True:
36           print("Simple RSA Crypto")
37           print("--------------------")
38           print("\tprviate key file: {}".format(private_key_file))
39           print("\tpublic key file: {}".format(public_key_file))
40           print("\t1. Encrypt Message.")
41           print("\t2. Decrypt Message.")
42           print("\t3. Load public key file.")
43           print("\t4. Load private key file.")
44           print("\t5. Create and load new public and private key files.")
45           print("\t6. Quit.\n")
46           choice = input(" >> ")
47           if choice == '1':
48               if not public_key:
49                   print("\nNo public key loaded\n")
50               else:
51                   message = input("\nPlaintext: ").encode()
52                   message_as_int = bytes_to_int(message)
53                   cipher_as_int = simple_rsa_encrypt(message_as_int,
                         public_key)
54                   cipher = int_to_bytes(cipher_as_int)
```

```
55          print("\nCiphertext (hexlified): {}\n".
                format(binascii.hexlify(cipher)))
56      elif choice == '2':
57          if not private_key:
58          print("\nNo private key loaded\n")
59          else:
60              cipher_hex = input("\nCiphertext (hexlified): ").encode()
61              cipher = binascii.unhexlify(cipher_hex)
62              cipher_as_int = bytes_to_int(cipher)
63              message_as_int = simple_rsa_decrypt(cipher_as_int,
                    private_key)
64              message = int_to_bytes(message_as_int)
65              print("\nPlaintext: {}\n".format(message))
66      elif choice == '3':
67          public_key_file_temp = input("\nEnter public key file: ")
68          if not os.path.exists(public_key_file_temp):
69              print("File {} does not exist.")
70          else:
71              with open(public_key_file_temp, "rb") as public_key_
                    file_object:
72                  public_key = serialization.load_pem_public_key(
73                                  public_key_file_object.read(),
74                                  backend=default_backend())
75                  public_key_file = public_key_file_temp
76                  print("\nPublic Key file loaded.\n")
77
78                  # unload private key if any
79                  private_key_file = None
80                  private_key = None
81      elif choice == '4':
82          private_key_file_temp = input("\nEnter private key file: ")
83          if not os.path.exists(private_key_file_temp):
84              print("File {} does not exist.")
85          else:
```

```python
86                      with open(private_key_file_temp, "rb") as private_
                        key_file_object:
87                          private_key = serialization.load_pem_private_key(
88                                          private_key_file_object.read(),
89                                          backend = default_backend(),
90                                          password = None)
91                          private_key_file = private_key_file_temp
92                          print("\nPrivate Key file loaded.\n")
93
94                          # load public key for private key
95                          # (unload previous public key if any)
96                          public_key = private_key.public_key()
97                          public_key_file = None
98          elif choice == '5':
99              private_key_file_temp = input("\nEnter a file name for
                new private key: ")
100             public_key_file_temp = input("\nEnter a file name for a
                new public key: ")
101             if os.path.exists(private_key_file_temp) or os.path.
                exists(public_key_file_temp):
102                 print("File already exists.")
103             else:
104                 with open(private_key_file_temp, "wb+") as private_
                    key_file_obj:
105                     with open(public_key_file_temp, "wb+") as public_
                        key_file_obj:
106
107                         private_key = rsa.generate_private_key(
108                                         public_exponent =65537,
109                                         key_size =2048,
110                                         backend = default_backend()
111                                         )
112                         public_key = private_key.public_key()
113
```

```
114                        private_key_bytes = private_key.private_
                           bytes(
115                            encoding=serialization.Encoding.PEM,
116                            format=serialization.PrivateFormat.
                               TraditionalOpenSSL,
117                            encryption_algorithm=serialization.
                               NoEncryption()
118                        )
119                        private_key_file_obj.write(private_key_bytes)
120                        public_key_bytes = public_key.public_bytes(
121                            encoding=serialization.Encoding.PEM,
122                            format=serialization.PublicFormat.
                               SubjectPublicKeyInfo
123                        )
124                        public_key_file_obj.write(public_key_bytes)
125
126                        public_key_file = None
127                        private_key_file = private_key_file_temp
128            elif choice == '6':
129                print("\n\nTerminating. This program will self destruct
                   in 5 seconds.\n")
130                break
131            else:
132                print("\n\nUnknown option {}.\n".format(choice))
133
134    if __name__ == '__main__':
135        main()
```

Take a few minutes to try this exercise on your own before we walk through it together. Note, by the way, that because a public key can be derived from a private key, loading the private key also loads the public key.

When you are ready, continue reading! You may want to refer back to Listing 4-4 from time to time. Many of our subsequent listings will reuse these imports and function definitions. To save space, we will generally not reprint them so this listing is also useful as a template.

EXERCISE 4.1. SIMPLE RSA ENCRYPTION

Using the preceding application, set up communication from Alice to Bob and then send a few encrypted messages from Alice to Bob for decryption.

Stuffing the Outbox

Once EATSA has built the RSA encryption application, they hand it off to Alice and Bob and order them to begin the mission. Alice will infiltrate WAGGS and send updates to Bob. What do Alice and Bob need to do first?

What's amazing about public/private key pairs is that they don't have to agree on much of anything before they split up in order for Alice to send secure messages to Bob![3] As long as Alice knows where to look, Bob can publish a public key to her *anywhere*. He could send it in a newspaper, recite it to her over the phone, or publicize it on a Goodyear blimp flying around West Antarctica. The key is *public*. It does not matter if the West Antarctica Counter Intelligence sees it: they won't be able to decrypt Alice's messages.

Right?

Alice departs from EATSA headquarters, crosses the border, and makes her way to West Antarctica City where she infiltrates WAGGS. While she's thus engaged in her covert culinary caper, Bob generates a public/private key pair. He hangs onto the private key and publishes the public key for Alice to see.

Let's follow along. Start up an instance of the application that represents Bob's version and select option 5, which generates new paired keys and saves them to disk. Once that's done, you will have two files you can inspect in an editor.

Take a look at the public key file (you chose the name for it when prompted). Its contents should look something like this:

```
-----BEGIN PUBLIC KEY-----
MIIBIjANBgkqhkiG9w0BAQEFAAOCAQ8AMIIBCgKCAQEAuGFr+NV3cMu2pdl+i52J
XkYwwSHgZvAOFyIPsZ/rp6Ts5iBTkpymt7cf+cQCQro4FSw+udVt4A8wvZcppnBZ
h+17ZZ6ZZfjOLCr/3sJw8QfZwuaX5TZxFbJDxWWwsR4jLHsiGsPNf7nzExn7yCSQ
```

---

[3]Bob won't necessarily know who they're coming from, but that's a separate (and very interesting) problem. At least he'll know he's the only one who can read them.

```
sXLNqc+mLKP3Ud9ta14bTQ59dZIKKDHVGlQ1iLlhjcE1dhOAjWlsdCVfE+L/bSQk
Ld9dWKCM57y5tiMsoqnVjl28XcsSuiOd4QPGITprsXOjb7/p/rzXc9OQHHGyAQzs
WTAbZNaQxf9AY1AhE4wgMVwhnrxJA2g+DpY1yXUapOIH/hpDOsMH56IGcMx9oV/y
SwIDAQAB
-----END PUBLIC KEY-----
```

That's a PEM-formatted public key. Congratulations! Bob can take this key and publish it to a West Antarctica newspaper in the classifieds.

Meanwhile, Alice has been carefully observing what the West Antarctica politicians like to eat. *How un-Antarctican!* she thinks to herself as she watches them eat *hot* dogs and *hot* chocolate. Then, glancing back to the newspaper in her hands, she finds the classified ad she's been looking for! The public key has arrived! She copies it down carefully into a file and now has the ability to encrypt messages for Bob's eyes only.

Following along, let's copy the public key we just generated into a new file. This represents the file that Alice creates after copying the text out of the classified ads. Now launch a new instance of the application that represents Alice's copy of the program. Choose option 3 to load her public key.

Alice needs to send a message back to Bob. That's option 1 in our program. Run it, select option 1, and enter the text "hot dogs" into the plaintext field. Out pops the encrypted message.[4] If you used the preceding public key, you would get the following output:

```
Plaintext: hot dogs

Ciphertext (hexlified): b'56d5586cab1764fae575bc5815115f1c5d759
daddccbd6c9cb4a077026e2616dfca756ffa7733538e66997f06ebbbb853028
3926383a6bb80b7145990a29236d042048eed8eb7607bd35fcafe3dadd5d60a
1f8694192bddedac5728061234ffbb7a407155844a7e79b3dbc9704df0de818
d24acad32ccd6d2afe2d0734199c76e5c5c770fa8c3c208eceae00554aa2f29
9a8510121d388d85f35fa49c08f3e9d7540f22fe5eb4ea15da5f387dbdd0e00
6710aa9031b885094773ef3329cde91dbede53ed77b96483d34daa4fedbf5bc
d95e95b6b482a7decbf47fe2df0e309d706ab9c73ce73a2bdef33b786dd12e9
8a9ce34bbc1847f36e13ae9eea4007b616'
```

---

[4]The message is displayed as the hex representation of its bytes to make it easy to select and paste elsewhere.

Let's do it again, but this time for "hot chocolate." If you do so using the preceding public key we showed you, you would get this output (but go ahead and use your own generated public key):

Plaintext: hot chocolate

Ciphertext (hexlified): b'4d1e544e71c4cb15636ef4b0d629294538a05
979db762952cc5f0fc494f71535dff326dbb8543d0f2ace51a2279f65c2a76b
2a5ca5a3ee151e65e516afcb1d4da9ca9871dc7ce1dd4361a3b49def05c5089
99f5fab81b869b251ba8694fb171ab56ca1cde7cef0ac3934da4c28f7bfbb65
b03afa9cff30db974f0bd4fb8dee7fac75c99cd4def94ca8de83d46fffa092a
90642c9cfbfbf07c371f5aa3a62dc997d20e9959fcbec7dd0b434709b679619
ea195008a9a12eaa7462ffdbe8e6f765dd86b21f0f1d9b8b2b523ca7f11785e
fc6da84ec717bd1f0e2191e5a3bef74e489b5e396c49bd8f222ccd89984dbec
8b5e4cbb23ba739637d3307bca4e9f57e7'

Again, Alice cannot decrypt these messages, even though she encrypted them herself: she doesn't have the private key. At least, that's what the theory tells them.

Confident in her edible espionage, she takes these messages and sends them to Bob via an insecure carrier penguin [15]. Bob receives the message and reloads his application. First, he loads the private key file using option 4 and then chooses option 2 to attempt a decryption. Sure enough, when he copies in the message for Alice, it decrypts correctly:

Ciphertext (hexlified): 56 d5586cab1764fae575bc5815115f1c5d759da
ddccbd6c9cb4a077026e2616dfca756ffa7733538e66997f06ebbbb85302839
26383a6bb80b7145990a29236d042048eed8eb760735fcafe3dadd5d60a1f86
94192bddedac5728061234ffbb7a407155844a7e79b3dbc9704df0de818d24a
cad32ccd6d2afe2d0734199c76e5c5c770fa8c3c208eceae00554aa2f299a85
10121d388d85f35fa49c08f3e9d7540f22fe5eb4ea15da5f387dbdd0e006710
aa9031b885094773ef3329cde91dbede53ed77b96483d34daa4fedbf5bcd95e
95b6b482a7decbf47fe2df0e309d706ab9c73ce73a2bdef33b786dd12e98a9c
e34bbc1847f36e13ae9eea4007b616

Plaintext: b'hot dogs'

"Hot dogs!" Bob exclaims. "Disgraceful!"

Ciphertext (hexlified): 4d1e544e71c4cb15636ef4b0d629294538a05979
db762952cc5f0fc494f71535dff326dbb8543d0f2ace51a2279f65c2a76b2a5c
a5a3ee151e65e516afcb1d4da9ca9871dc7ce1dd4361a3b49def05c508999f5f
ab81b869b251ba8694fb171ab56ca1cde7cef0ac3934da4c28f7bfbb65b03afa
9cff30db974f0bd4fb8dee7fac75c99cd4def94ca8de83d46fffa092a90642c9
cfbfbf07c371f5aa3a62dc997d20e9959fcbec7dd0b434709b679619ea195008
a9a12eaa7462ffdbe8e6f765dd86b21f0f1d9b8b2b523ca7f11785efc6da84ec
717bd1f0e2191e5a3bef74e489b5e396c49bd8f222ccd89984dbec8b5e4cbb23
ba739637d3307bca4e9f57e7

Plaintext: b'hot chocolate'

Bob's eyes narrow. "Hot chocolate?! Have they no shame?!"

So far, so good! Alice's messages got to Bob. They were intercepted by agent Eve of
WACKO, but she shouldn't be able to read them, even though she also has the public
key. If Alice can't read her own messages, why should Eve be able to?

What Alice and Bob don't know is that Eve is about to wreak all kinds of havoc.
In the rest of this chapter, we'll be walking through some of the ways that RSA can be
compromised and how to do it right. But first, exercises!

EXERCISE 4.2. WHO GOES THERE? BOB? IS THAT YOU?

Assume the role of Eve and imagine that you know everything about Alice's and Bob's
operation *except* the private key. That is, suppose you know about the classified ads, the
carrier penguins, and even the encryption program.[5] Their scheme is strengthened by using
asymmetric encryption, but is still vulnerable to an MITM (man-in-the-middle) attack. How can
Eve position herself such that she can trick Alice into sending messages that Eve can decrypt,
and Bob into receiving *only* false messages from Eve instead of Alice?

---

[5]Remember Kerckhoff's principle? Here it is again!

EXERCISE 4.3. WHAT'S THE ANSWER TO LIFE, THE UNIVERSE, AND EVERYTHING?

We have already talked about chosen plaintext attacks in the previous chapter. The same attack can be used here. Again assume the role of Eve, the WACKO agent. You've intercepted Bob's public key in the newspaper, and you have access to the RSA encryption program. If you suspect you know what Alice is sending in her encrypted messages, explain or demonstrate how you would verify your guesses.

What Makes Asymmetric Encryption Different?

As you learned already in this section, RSA is an example of *asymmetric encryption*. If you haven't heard of asymmetric encryption before now, hopefully the exercises you just walked through have exposed you to the key concepts. Now let's make a few things explicit.

In symmetric encryption, there is a single, shared key that works to both encrypt and decrypt the message. This means that anyone with the power to create an encrypted message has the same ability to decrypt the same message. It is impossible to give somebody the power to decrypt a symmetrically encrypted message without also giving them the ability to encrypt the same kind of messages and vice versa.

In asymmetric cryptography, there is always a private key that must never be disclosed and a public key that can be disclosed widely. Exactly what can be done with the key pair depends on the algorithm. In this chapter we have been focusing on RSA encryption. We'll review RSA's operations in this section as a concrete example but keep in mind that they may not apply to other asymmetric algorithms and operations.

Specifically, RSA supports an asymmetric encryption scheme in which you can use one key to encrypt the message and a different key to decrypt a message. Typically, either key can act in either role: a private key can encrypt messages that can be decrypted by the public key and vice versa. With RSA, of course, one key is clearly the *private* key because the public key can be *derived* from the private key, but not the other way around. It is impossible to have an RSA private key and not *also* have the matching public key. Thus, one key is unambiguously designated as "private" and the other is "public."

The possessor of a properly protected RSA private key and an adequately robust protocol can use asymmetric encryption for two purposes:

1. **Cryptographic dropbox**: Anyone with the public key can encrypt a message and send it to the owner of the private key. Only someone with the private key can decrypt the message.

2. **Signatures**: Anyone with the public key can decrypt a message encrypted by the private key. This obviously is not helpful for confidentiality (anyone can decrypt the message) but it helps to prove *the identity of the sender*, or at least that the sender is in possession of the private key; they wouldn't be able to encrypt a public-key-decryptable message otherwise. This is an example of a cryptographic *signatures*, which we will talk about later.

Note: RSA Encrypts Small Things

The cryptographic dropbox operation we are learning about right now is almost never used to send complete messages in this way. The most common way RSA encryption was used (again, it is being phased out) was to encrypt a symmetric key for transport from one party to another. This is another concept we'll save for a later chapter.

What is really fantastic about the asymmetric nature of RSA encryption is that the two parties do not need to have met each other to begin exchanging messages. In our example, Alice and Bob did not need to create any shared keys together. Alice did not even need to meet or know Bob. So long as Alice had Bob's public key, she can encrypt messages that only Bob can read.

Unfortunately, the ability to encrypt something for only one person is not the only important thing in real life. As demonstrated in the exercises, the advantage of asymmetric encryption is also its weakness. The ability to communicate without any previous interactions also means that, absent additional information, there is no way to know that you are communicating with the *right person*.

If you worked through the earlier exercises, you will have also learned that it is quite simple for WACKO to *both read and alter* the communications between Alice and Bob by deceiving both parties by intercepting messages and keys.

1. They can deceive Alice by intercepting and modifying the public key published in the newspaper. By inserting *their own* public key—which Alice now wrongly assumes is Bob's—they can read all messages sent by Alice intended for Bob. Alice, without additional information, cannot know that the public key has been compromised.

2. They can then deceive Bob by preventing Alice's incorrectly encrypted messages from reaching him and sending him false messages encrypted under the correct public key, which they intercepted. Bob, without additional information, has no way of knowing who is sending the messages.

This is a critical difference between symmetric keys and asymmetric keys. In fact, some cryptographers distinguish between a "secret" symmetric key and a "private" asymmetric key. Two people can share a secret, but only one person knows their own private key. What this means in practice is that a symmetric key, provided that it *remains secret to both parties*, can be used to establish that you are talking to the right person (i.e., the person you created the shared secret key with) while asymmetric keys cannot.[6]

Let's sidestep that problem for now and save it for later, since there is indeed a solution to it that is discussed in the context of *certificates*.

Pass the Padding

Recall from earlier that the EATSA chose to implement RSA without any padding. They really shouldn't have done that; it's a pretty serious mistake. In fact, it's so serious that the `cryptography` module does not even *allow* you to encrypt with RSA without padding!

What, then, is padding, and why is padding such a big deal?

---

[6]Unless the public key is *also* guaranteed to be secret, but then we've just defeated the purpose of asymmetric keys, in a way, by requiring a secure shared channel for key exchange.

The best way to explain this is to demonstrate how to read messages encrypted with the public key *even if you don't have the private key*, so long as those messages are not padded. Another great exercise is to search the Internet for RSA padding attacks. There are *many* problems with using unpadded plaintext.

Deterministic Outputs

Let's start with the most basic problem. RSA by itself is a *deterministic* algorithm. That means that, given the same key and message, you will always get the same ciphertext, byte for byte. Recall that we had the same problem with symmetric key ciphers like AES. It was essential to use the *initialization vector (IV)* to prevent deterministic outputs. Do you remember why deterministic outputs are so bad?

The problem with deterministic outputs is that they enable passive eavesdroppers, such as Eve, to do some cryptographic reverse engineering. Because the encryption is deterministic, if Eve knows that m encrypts to c then any time Eve sees c she knows what the plaintext is.

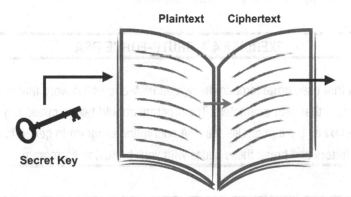

***Figure 4-1.** If RSA's outputs are deterministic, an adversary that discovers the mapping between a plaintext and the corresponding ciphertext can record it into a lookup table for later use. Does this figure look familiar?*

Eve has both the public key *and the algorithm* (you can never assume that a cryptographic algorithm is secret). She can encrypt any number of potential messages and store a lookup table of pre-encrypted values. Does Figure 4-1 look familiar? We showed this same image in Chapter 3 to talk about ECB mode for symmetric ciphers and the problems with it.

But a deterministic asymmetric encryption would be worse. Unlike symmetric encryption we have to assume that the adversary *has* the (public) key. In our hypothetical Antarctican conflict, Eve could discover, or simply guess, that Alice is sending messages based on her surveillance of the cafeteria. If she tries encrypting a few hundred words by making a list of things found within the room (e.g., the names of the politicians eating in the cafeteria, topics of conversation, and the food being eaten), as soon as she encrypted "hot dogs" or "hot chocolate," the encrypted values would match up perfectly with what is intercepted in the message back to Bob. For short messages such as these, especially if EA Intelligence always writes words in lowercase, there are less than 300 million messages to try that are 8 characters long. It's not too much trouble to create a table of that many messages to their ciphertext. Using this lookup table, Eve could identify "hot dogs" relatively quickly.

Even if Eve cannot guess the message, there is still all kinds of analysis that can be done. Suppose that Alice continues to send the same message day after day. While Eve may not be able to decrypt the message, she would still be able to confidently state that it was the *same* message. We have considered numerous examples wherein this kind of "information leak" is exploited in previous chapters.

EXERCISE 4.4. BRUTE-FORCE RSA

Write a program that uses brute force to decrypt an RSA-encrypted word that is all lowercase (no spaces) and less than four characters. The program should take a public key and the RSA-encrypted ciphertext as the inputs. Use the RSA encryption program to generate a few words of four or fewer letters and break these codes with your brute-force program.

EXERCISE 4.5. WAITING IS THE HARDEST PART

Modify the brute-force program to try all possible words of five or fewer letters. Measure the time it takes (worst cast) to brute force a four-letter word vs. a five-letter word. About how many times longer does it take and why? How long would it take to try all possible six-letter words?

EXERCISE 4.6. DICTIONARY ATTACKS

It should be pretty clear that it will take longer than your probable attention span to try all possible lowercase ASCII words of length much greater than four or five. But we already saw this same problem in previous chapters. Let's try the same solutions. Modify your brute-force program to take a dictionary as input for trying arbitrary English words.

Chosen Ciphertext Attack

RSA without padding is also vulnerable to something called a "chosen ciphertext attack."[7] This type of attack works when you can get the victim to decrypt *some* ciphertexts of your choosing on your behalf. That may sound counter-intuitive. Why would anyone decrypt anything for you? For example, why would Bob decrypt anything for Eve?

Remember that a lot of computer security is all about psychology, trickery, and human thinking [1, Chap. 2]. What is Bob looking for? Bob is assuming that he is decrypting human-readable messages from Alice. What if he got a message that was not human readable? Suppose, for example, that upon decrypting a message (supposedly from Alice) he got the following output:

```
b'\xe8\xca\xe6\xe8'
```

It's entirely possible that this is just assumed to be due to a transmission error. Those things happen in real life all the time. It could be bit error, or a carrier penguin might have smudged the ink. Bob probably sees a lot of messages that do not decrypt correctly.

What does Bob do? If he does not have very good security controls in place, he might just throw it away. But if Alice can infiltrate the enemy, it can work the other way as well. Which do you think is easier for Eve to get into her hands? Top-secret messages that are being sent up the chain of command for analysis, or "incorrect" messages that get thrown away in the trash? If Eve has a covert agent of her own on the janitorial staff, it might be very possible to get discarded paper or inadequately destroyed data.

---

[7]Chosen ciphertext attacks (CCA) are way more complicated than we have space to discuss here. Please consider our CCA discussion to be hyper-simplistic. If you want to know more about CCA and indistinguishability under CCA, Dr. Matthew Green has some great blog posts [7].

CHAPTER 4   ASYMMETRIC ENCRYPTION: PUBLIC/PRIVATE KEYS

Let's assume this scenario then: Eve can send arbitrary ciphertext to Bob. For our purposes, Eve cannot see any of the human-readable messages but can recover the supposedly erroneous messages discarded by Bob because they seem to make no sense.

Unfortunately for Alice and Bob, Eve can use this trick to decrypt almost any message Alice sends back to her home base. The mathematics behind this trick are really cool and are used in multiple examples throughout the chapter. So let's pause a minute to talk about *homomorphisms* in encryption.

The basic concept of an encryption homomorphism is that if you perform some kind of computation on the ciphertext, the result is reflected in the plaintext. Not all crypto systems have homomorphic properties, but RSA does to some extent. In RSA we will see that there are ways to do multiplication on the ciphertext that results in multiplications on the plaintext. There are other special homomorphic encryption technologies that exist and are being developed right now that enable third parties to provide services on data *without being able to read it*. You may have heard of some of these; if not, try searching for "homomorphic encryption" online. It's pretty interesting stuff.

While RSA is not a homomorphic encryption scheme, this multiplication property is very interesting (and also powers a number of vulnerabilities). Do you remember from algebra class that $(a^c)(b^c) = (ab^c)$? The same is true for modular exponentiation as shown in the following equation:

$$(m_1)^e (m_2)^e \pmod{n} = (m_1 m_2)^e \pmod{n} \tag{4.3}$$

Does any part of this equation look familiar? Take a look back at (4.1). Do you see it now?

Any time we encrypt a value (m) in RSA, we end up with $m^e \bmod n$. On the left-hand side of the (4.3), we have *two* encryptions, one of m_1 and one of m_2, both using the same public exponent e and both modulo the same modulus n.

On the right-hand side, we have a *single* encryption of the value m_1 times m_2. What this equation tells us is that if you take each of these individually encrypted values and multiply them together (mod n), you get the encrypted result of the multiplication!

Restated another way, the product of two ciphertexts (encrypted under the same public key) decrypts to the product of the two plaintexts. Try to do the following exercise on your own before we walk through it.

```
┌──────────────────────────────────────────────────────────────────┐
│         EXERCISE 4.7. HOMOMORPHIC PROPERTY OF UNPADDED RSA         │
└──────────────────────────────────────────────────────────────────┘
```

Use (4.3) to multiply two RSA-encrypted numbers together and decrypt the result to verify the equation.

___

The code for this exercise is very simple, so definitely try it yourself first. When you're ready, our solution is in Listing 4-5.

Listing 4-5. Solution

```
1    # FOR TRAINING USE ONLY! DO NOT USE THIS FOR REAL CRYPTOGRAPHY
2
3    import gmpy2, sys, binascii, string, time
4    from cryptography.hazmat.backends import default_backend
5    from cryptography.hazmat.primitives import serialization
6    from cryptography.hazmat.primitives.asymmetric import rsa
7
8    #### DANGER ####
9    # The following RSA encryption and decryption is
10   # completely unsafe and terribly broken. DO NOT USE
11   # for anything other than the practice exercise
12   ################
13   def simple_rsa_encrypt(m, publickey):
14       numbers = publickey.public_numbers()
15       return gmpy2.powmod(m, numbers.e, numbers.n)
16
17   def simple_rsa_decrypt(c, privatekey):
18       numbers = privatekey.private_numbers()
19       return gmpy2.powmod(c, numbers.d, numbers.public_numbers.n)
20
21   private_key = rsa.generate_private_key(
22       public_exponent=65537,
23       key_size=2048,
24       backend=default_backend()
25   )
26   public_key = private_key.public_key()
```

```
27
28   n = public_key.public_numbers().n
29   a = 5
30   b = 10
31
32   encrypted_a = simple_rsa_encrypt(a, public_key)
33   encrypted_b = simple_rsa_encrypt(b, public_key)
34
35   encrypted_product = (encrypted_a * encrypted_b) % n
36
37   product = simple_rsa_decrypt(encrypted_product, private_key)
38   print("{} x {} = {}".format(a,b, product))
```

If this kind of math doesn't make a lot of sense, don't worry too much about it at this point. Just try to grasp how it is *used* even if you aren't fully sure how it works.

Returning to our current example, suppose that Eve has a ciphertext c obtained by the RSA public key encryption of m. Without the private key, Eve should not be able to decrypt it. And presumably Bob won't decrypt it for her either. If he will decrypt a *multiple* of it, however, Eve can recover the original.

For our example, let's choose our multiple to just be 2. Eve starts by encrypting 2 using (4.1) and the public key to get c_r.

For clarity, let's call the original ciphertext c_0. If we multiply c_0 and c_r (modulo n), we'll get a new ciphertext that we'll call c_1.

$$c_1 = c_0 c_r \pmod{n}.$$

From (4.3), this works out to be

$$\begin{aligned} c_1 &= c_0 c_r \pmod{n} \\ &= m^e r^e \pmod{n} \\ &= (mr)^e \pmod{n}. \end{aligned}$$

So how does Eve use this? Suppose that Eve has intercepted one of Alice's ciphertexts c. Eve takes her computed c_r (again, this is just the value of 2 encrypted under the public key) and then multiplies the two encrypted values together (modulo n). Eve sends this new ciphertext c_1 to Bob.

Bob receives c_1 and decrypts it to *mr* and converts the integers to bytes. He finds that it does not decrypt to anything legible and assumes that something was damaged in transport. Shrugging his shoulders, he crumples up the paper and throws it in the waste basket. Later that night, Eve's agent goes through the trash and finds the crumpled up paper. Creating a quick copy, she sends it by secret carrier back to Eve.

Eve now has *mr* and needs to extract *m*. No problem. She chose *r* to be 2. In familiar arithmetic you would divide by *r* to extract *m*. But when doing this arithmetic with modulo operations, you have to use a different inverse operation: $r-1$ (mod *n*). Fortunately, there are libraries that compute these kinds of numbers for us, like gmpy2.

```
r_inv_modulo_n = gmpy2.powmod(r, -1, n)
```

EXERCISE 4.8. EVE'S PROTEGE

Recreate Eve's chosen ciphertext attack. Create a sample message in Python, as you have done previously, using the public key to encrypt it. Then, encrypt a value of *r* (such as 2). Multiply the two *numeric* versions of the ciphertext together and don't forget to take the answer modulo *n*. Decrypt this new ciphertext and try to convert it to bytes. It shouldn't be anything human readable. Take the numeric version of this decryption and multiply it by the inverse of *r* (mod *n*). You should be back to the original number. Convert it to bytes to see the original message.

Common Modulus Attack

Another problem for RSA without padding is the "common modulus" attack. Recall that the *n* parameter is the modulus and is included in both the public key and private key. For mathematical reasons beyond the scope of this book, if the same RSA message is encrypted by two different public keys with the same *n* modulus, the message can be decrypted without the private key.

In the chosen ciphertext example, we walked through the math in some detail both because it can be described relatively easily and because it is critical to multiple attacks. For this example, in the interests of simplicity and conserving space, we won't get into the mathematical details. Instead, use the code in Listing 4-6 to test and explore the attack. If you're interested in the details of the math, you can read "Common Modulus Attacks on Small Private Exponent RSA and Some Fast Variants (in Practice)" by Hinek and Lam.

Listing 4-6. Common Modulus

```
1    # Partial Listing: Some Assembly Required
2
3    # Derived From: https://github.com/a0xnirudh/Exploits-and-Scripts/
     tree/master/RSA At tacks
4    def common_modulus_decrypt(c1, c2, key1, key2):
5        key1_numbers = key1.public_numbers()
6        key2_numbers = key2.public_numbers()
7
8        if key1_numbers.n != key2_numbers.n:
9            raise ValueError("Common modulus attack requires a common
             modulus")
10       n = key1_numbers.n
11
12       if key1_numbers.e == key2_numbers.e:
13           raise ValueError("Common modulus attack requires different
             public exponents")
14
15       e1, e2 = key1_numbers.e, key2_numbers.e
16       num1, num2 = min(e1, e2), max(e1, e2)
17
18       while num2 != 0:
19           num1, num2 = num2, num1 % num2
20       gcd = num1
21
22       a = gmpy2.invert(key1_numbers.e, key2_numbers.e)
23       b = float(gcd - (a*e1))/float(e2)
24
25       i = gmpy2.invert(c2, n)
26       mx = pow(c1, a, n)
27       my = pow(i, int(-b), n)
28       return mx * my % n
```

Note that in order to test this attack, you will need two public keys with the same modulus (*n* value) and different public exponents (*e* values). Recall that *e* is recommended to always be 65537. But obviously you won't use that for both keys in this example.

How does one create a public key? In all of our examples so far, we either generated new keys or loaded them from disk.

Recall that the *n* and *e* values *define* the public key. Everything else is just wrappers for convenience. The `cryptography` module provides an API for creating a key directly from these values. The RSA private key objects have a method called `private_numbers`, and the RSA public key objects have a method called `public_numbers`. These methods return data structures with data elements such as *n*, *d*, or *e*. These "numbers" objects can also be used to create the key objects.

In Listing 4-7, we generate a private key and then manually create another key with the same modulus and different public exponent.

Listing 4-7. Common Modulus Key Generation

```
1   # Partial Listing: Some Assembly Required
2
3   private_key1 = rsa.generate_private_key(
4       public_exponent =65537,
5       key_size=2048,
6       backend = default_backend()
7   )
8   public_key1 = private_key1.public_key()
9
10  n = public_key1.public_numbers().n
11  public_key2 = rsa.RSAPublicNumbers(3, n).public_key(default_backend())
```

Now you should have all the Python code you need to test out this attack.

At this point you might be asking yourself, "how practical is this attack?" In order to carry it out, you have to have *the same message* encrypted under *two keys with the same modulus*. Why would the same message ever be encrypted twice under two different keys and why would two different keys ever have the same modulus?

When dealing with cryptography, you should never rely on this kind of thinking. If there is a way for the cryptography to be exploited, the bad guy will figure out a way to exploit it. Let's start by thinking about how to get the same message encrypted by two different keys.

One possibility is to convince Alice that a new public key has been created and that she needs to switch. If we control the new public key, we can give her a key with n and e values of our choosing.

But if we can control her key, why would we need to use the common modulus attack? Why not just give her a public key that we created and for which we have the paired private key?

It is true that a new private key/public key pair will allow Eve to decrypt any messages Alice sends in the future. But the common modulus attack will allow Eve to potentially determine some messages sent *in the past*. In our example with Alice infiltrating the cafeteria, the food service probably repeats with some regularity. In fact, as we discussed previously, Eve can already tell if the same message is being resent even if she cannot decrypt it. If Eve observes that the same messages are being sent over and over, the common modulus attack provides a much greater view into the history of what is sent as well as information about messages sent in the future.

EXERCISE 4.9. COMMON MODULUS ATTACK

Test out the code in this section by creating a common modulus attack demo.

EXERCISE 4.10. COMMON MODULUS USE CASES

Write out an additional scenario when the use of the common modulus attack might be useful to an attacker.

The Proof Is in the Padding

As we have just demonstrated, this very raw form of RSA, sometimes referred to as "textbook RSA," is relatively easy to break. There are two critical problems. As we have already seen, one problem with textbook RSA is that the outputs are deterministic. This makes attacks like the common modulus attack, which require encrypting the same message twice, much easier.

Perhaps the bigger problem is how malleable the messages are. We talked about malleability with symmetric encryption in the previous chapter. With RSA we have similar problems, for example, multiplying the RSA ciphertext and getting a decryptable value.

There are also potential problems with trying to encrypt tiny messages, such as some of the small messages we have encrypted in our exercises. In addition to the brute-force methods in the exercises, there are ways to break smaller messages especially with smaller public exponents (e.g., $e = 3$).

To reduce or eliminate these problems, practical uses of RSA always utilizes padding with *random elements*. RSA padding is applied to the plaintext message before encryption by the raw RSA computations we have been working with. The padding ensures that messages are not too small and provide a certain amount of structure that reduces malleability. Also, the randomized elements operate not unlike an IV for symmetric encryption: good randomized padding ensures that each ciphertext produced by the RSA encryption operation, even for the same plaintext, is (with very high probability) unique.

RSA without padding is dangerous enough that the cryptography module does not even have a padding-free RSA operation. It should be absolutely clear to you that you must not use RSA for encryption without padding. While the cryptography module does not allow this, other libraries do. Significantly, this includes OpenSSL.

At the time of this writing, there are two padding schemes that are typically used. The older scheme is called PKCS #1 v1.5 and the other is OAEP, which stands for Optimal Asymmetric Encryption Padding. Either of these padding schemes can be used with the cryptography module as shown in Listing 4-8.

Listing 4-8. RSA Padding

```
1   from cryptography.hazmat.backends import default_backend
2   from cryptography.hazmat.primitives.asymmetric import rsa
3   from cryptography.hazmat.primitives import serialization
4   from cryptography.hazmat.primitives import hashes
5   from cryptography.hazmat.primitives.asymmetric import padding
6
7   def main():
8       message = b'test'
9
```

```
10      private_key = rsa.generate_private_key(
11          public_exponent =65537,
12          key_size=2048,
13          backend=default_backend()
14      )
15      public_key = private_key.public_key()
16
17      ciphertext1 = public_key.encrypt(
18          message,
19          padding.OAEP(
20              mgf = padding.MGF1(algorithm = hashes.SHA256()),
21              algorithm = hashes.SHA256(),
22              label = None # rarely used. Just leave it 'None'
23          )
24      )
25
26      ###
27      # WARNING: PKCS #1 v1.5 is obsolete and has vulnerabilities
28      # DO NOT USE EXCEPT WITH LEGACY PROTOCOLS
29      ciphertext2 = public_key.encrypt(
30          message,
31          padding.PKCS1v15()
32      )
33
34      recovered1 = private_key.decrypt(
35      ciphertext1,
36      padding.OAEP(
37          mgf=padding.MGF1(algorithm=hashes.SHA256()),
38          algorithm=hashes.SHA256(),
39          label=None # rarely used.Just leave it 'None'
40      ))
41
```

```
42        recovered2 = private_key.decrypt(
43        ciphertext2,
44         padding.PKCS1v15()
45      )
46
47      print("Plaintext: {}".format(message))
48      print("Ciphertext with PKCS #1 v1.5 padding(hexlified): {}".
        format(ciphertext1.hex()))
49      print("Ciphertext with OAEP padding (hexlified): {}".
        format(ciphertext2.hex()))
50      print("Recovered 1: {}".format(recovered1))
51      print("Recovered 2: {}".format(recovered2))
52
53  if __name__=="__main__":
54      main()
```

If you run this demonstration script repeatedly, you will observe that the ciphertext for both padding schemes causes the output to change *every time*. Consequently, adversaries like Eve cannot execute the chosen ciphertext attack nor the common modulus attack demonstrated earlier in this chapter. She is also unable to use RSA's deterministic encryption to analyze message patterns, frequency, and so forth.

Padding also solves the problem of losing leading zeros during encryption. Padding ensures that the input is always a fixed size: the bit size of the modulus. So, for example, with padding, the input to RSA encryption with a modulus size of 2048 will always be 256 bytes (2048 bits). Because the size of the output is known, it also allows the plaintext to start with leading zeros. Regardless of whether the combined message starts with 0, the known size means that zeros can be affixed until the correct size is reached.

So everything is fine now, right? Alice and Bob will switch to using padding and Eve will be shut out of their communications?

First of all, please note that padding does not solve either of the man-in-the-middle or authentication problems. Eve can still intercept and change the public key, enabling complete decryption of Alice's messages. Bob still cannot tell who is sending him messages. These are problems for another chapter.

Second, the astute reader probably noticed the warning in the source code listing. Just in case you glanced over it without paying attention, we will emphasize it again.

Warning: Say "No" to PKCS #1 v1.5

Do *not* use PKCS #1 v1.5 unless you must do so to be compatible with legacy protocols. It is obsolete and has vulnerabilities (including one we will test in the next section)! For encryption, always use OAEP when possible.

Before moving on from this section, two other comments are in order regarding the use of OAEP:

1. You may have noticed the "label" parameter to OAEP. This is rarely used and can typically be left as None. Using a label does not increase security, so ignore it for now.

2. OAEP requires the use of a hashing algorithm. In the example we used SHA-256. Why not SHA-1? Is this related to known weaknesses in SHA-1? No. Actually, there are no known attacks against OAEP that depend on SHA-1's weaknesses. Because SHA-1 is considered obsolete, it is best to not use it when writing your own code, but if you have to use OAEP with SHA-1 for compatibility reasons or to maintain someone else's code, it is not known to be less secure than SHA-256 *as of the time of this writing*.

EXERCISE 4.11. GETTING AN UPGRADE

Help Alice and Bob out. Rewrite the RSA encryption/decryption program to use the `cryptography` module instead of gmpy2 operations.

Exploiting RSA Encryption with PKCS #1 v1.5 Padding

This section is going to be exciting and fun! Eve is not a cryptographer and you—because you are reading this book—are probably not a master cryptographer either. However, you and Eve are going to implement an attack designed by a brilliant cryptographer and use it to break Alice and Bob's cipher.

This attack is not only *fun*, but it is very real. Not only has it been a real attack in the past, but it even continues to be used today against poorly configured TLS servers. It's both historical and contemporary at the same time.

The paper in question is "Chosen Ciphertext Attacks Against Protocols Based on the RSA Encryption Standard PKCS #1" by Daniel Bleichenbacher [2]. You can find this paper online, and some readers may be interested in the mathematics behind the attack. In the sections that follow, we are going to walk through this paper creating an implementation of the attack. At the same time, we will try to give some intuition behind certain key concepts. If you find the in-depth details frustrating or uninteresting, you should be able to ignore most of the explanation and just put together a working RSA cracker from the source code listings. We won't be offended.

There are going to be a lot of code snippets for this example. You should start with Listing 4-9 that initializes a few imports. Don't forget about the dependencies on other functions we've already seen in this chapter. As we work through new snippets, add them to this skeleton.

Listing 4-9. RSA Padding Oracle Attack

```
1    from cryptography.hazmat.primitives.asymmetric import rsa, padding
2    from cryptography.hazmat.primitives import serialization
3    from cryptography.hazmat.primitives import hashes
4    from cryptography.hazmat.backends import default_backend
5
6    import gmpy2
7    from collections import namedtuple
8
9    Interval = namedtuple('Interval', ['a','b'])
10   # Imports and dependencies for RSA Oracle Attack
11   # Dependencies: simple_rsa_encrypt(), simple_rsa_decypt()
12   #                  bytes_to_int()
```

Alice and Bob are at it again. This time, though, they're using RSA with padding. But EATSA is still making bad decisions. They decide to use PKCS #1 v1.5 simply because it requires no parameters. Originally they were going to use OAEP, but the East Antarctica Taskforce for Modern Operational RSA Employment and Better Encryption, Especially in the Field (EATMOREBEEF) apparently argued for weeks about the task force *name*. Pressing up against a deadline, and unable to agree about which hashing algorithm should be used for OAEP, and whether "EATMOREBEEF" should be used for the label, they threw up their hands and said, "We're pretty sure PKCS #1 v1.5 is good enough."

143

Once again, we find Alice in the West Antarctica spying on her neighbors. This time, however, Alice is posing as a CEO for an ice-making company meeting other executives in the ice industry at a conference in West Antarctica City. Sales of ice have melted in the last few years, and the government, facing its own problems with frozen assets and decreased liquidity, has been either unable or unwilling to offer subsidies. Alice's mission is to continue crystallizing the dissent against the current party in power, in an attempt to solidify influence in the next election.

After the conference, Alice needs to send Bob a report of CEOs that she has convinced to donate significantly to the opposition party. Alice transmits the following message using RSA with PKCS #1 v1.5: "Jane Winters, F. Roe Zen, and John White."

Alice whips out a mobile flip phone (they are slowly catching up in technology... no smart phones yet, but they finally did away with carrier penguins). She keys in the message to Bob and it automatically converts it to a number, encrypts it, and transmits it. A few seconds later, her phone vibrates with a new message:

Received: OK

Elsewhere in the city, Eve watches this communication. She has been tracking Alice since crossing the border. But she cannot decrypt the messages. Alice even came with the public key already installed in the phone so Eve can't give her a fake key either. What can she do?

Fortunately for Eve, she finds out through her own intelligence agency that Alice and Bob are using PKCS #1 v1.5 for the RSA padding. Eve is surprised. After all of the events of the earlier part of this chapter, Eve has been reading up on RSA quite a bit, and she knows that this padding scheme has known vulnerabilities. Why are they using it, she wonders. Did they not get the memo?

Eve has a copy of the Bleichenbacher paper and begins reading. The paper explains that the PKCS #1 v1.5 padding can be broken with an oracle attack similar to the one we saw in the previous chapter.

In this case, Eve needs an oracle to tell her whether or not a given ciphertext (a number) decrypts to something with proper padding. The oracle will not, of course, tell her what the ciphertext decrypted to; all it needs to say is "yes" or "no" with regard to the padding.

Fortunately, Eve has been monitoring EA communications, and it appears that they built an error-reporting system into their technologies. When Alice sends a valid message, she gets back

Received: OK

But when Eve sends a random number (ciphertext), she almost always gets back
`Failed: Padding`

After sending a thousands of random numbers, she did eventually get back one that answered with the OK message. As far as she could tell, it was not a "real" message (human readable, or one that Bob understood), but it did have the correct padding as reported by the automated processing system.

This is Eve's oracle. It is all she needs to completely decrypt a ciphertext message.

For convenience in writing her attack program, Eve will start by breaking a message encrypted locally with a self-generated private key. Eve will use a pluggable oracle configuration so that when it's time to attack Bob, she can simply switch out the oracle used to power the attack. The test oracle uses the real private key to decrypt the message and check whether the message has the proper formatting.

Eve starts reading up on PKCS v1.5 and starts playing around with her own experiments. Creating her own key pair, she encrypts messages with the padding and then examines the output. She encrypts the message "test" and then decrypts the message *without removing the padding*. Listing 4-10 shows the key snippet of the code that she used.

Listing 4-10. Encrypt with Padding

```
1    # Partial Listing: Some Assembly Required
2
3    from cryptography.hazmat.primitives.asymmetric import rsa, padding
4    from cryptography.hazmat.primitives import hashes
5    from cryptography.hazmat.backends import default_backend
6    import gmpy2
7
8    # Dependencies: int_to_bytes(), bytes_to_int(), and simple_rsa_decrypt()
9
10   private_key = rsa.generate_private_key(
11        public_exponent=65537,
12        key_size=2048,
13        backend=default_backend()
14   )
15   public_key = private_key.public_key()
16
17   message = b'test'
18
```

```
19    ###
20    # WARNING: PKCS #1 v1.5 is obsolete and has vulnerabilities
21    # DO NOT USE EXCEPT WITH LEGACY PROTOCOLS
22    ciphertext = public_key.encrypt(
23        message,
24        padding.PKCS1v15()
25    )
26
27    ciphertext_as_int = bytes_to_int(ciphertext)
28    recovered_as_int = simple_rsa_decrypt(ciphertext_as_int, private_key)
29    recovered = int_to_bytes(recovered_as_int)
30
31    print("Plaintext: {}".format(message))
32    print("Recovered: {}".format(recovered))
```

You can see that she is using the cryptography module to create the encryption. But she is using her own simple_rsa_decrypt operation for the decryption in order to preserve the padding.

This is what she sees:

```
Plaintext: b'test'
Recovered: b'\x02@&\x1cC\xb1\xe4\x0f\x14\xd9\x93oU
\x07\x1b\xfdC\xe1\xe2K\xeeP\xdd\x8b\x10\xf9cZJ\x0c
42\x8e\xbblZ\xfb\x80\x8b\xfcA?p\xac\xba\xf7I\x9e\x
11\x1cn&t\xb8\x15\xbfo\xfe\xcc\xdf\xe7=\xc2\x9e\x
ca<v\xcd\x9ep\xd8\x1c\xf6b2"\x8c\xc0\x1e\xb8\xdb\x
97\x89\xfauj\x8f``\x99m~,\x18h\xc2k6d~qr-\x0c\xb9\
xfe?\xf9\xf9\xa6o\x05\\ZV\xfd4?\x0e;y\xf3\xd3q\xb2
\x94\xf6\xf8~a\xc1eA\xe4\x14\xce\x82\xdcc\xbf4e\xa
e\xa3<"\xcb,L\xd8\xed\xca}\xeb\x82\xa67\x1a\xd1\xc
7)\x13\xc1D)\xe8\x05h\xbe/\x97\xdf>\xf0\xef\xeb\xe
4Q\xc2\x85(*\xdcE\x9ct\x08c0\xb1\x80la\x94_/2\xd4y
\xc7\x95\x01\x90@\xea\x92\xaa\xb8\x18!\xc7\xff\xab
\x03\xea\x8b\xa3\xb4\xf6\xf2\xd6GH\x98-fM\x1c\x99\
x84\x8d4\xaf"\x95\xa7XR(M\x836\xd4\x17\x99m\xa8\x1
a\xb3\x00test'
```

Eve notices that the actual message is at the end of the padding, consistent with the PKCS #1 v1.5 standard. (From the rest of this section, we will just say "PKCS.")

She does notice that the first byte of the recovered text is 2. That seems weird to her because the standard says that the padding should start with a 0 and a 2. Where did the initial 0 go?

Then Eve remembers! Of course! Because RSA works with *integers* instead of bytes, any leading zeros are wiped out. Fortunately, when RSA padding is used, the size of the bytes is fixed to the key size. Eve decides to update her conversion function with an optional parameter for minimum size,[8] shown in Listing 4-11.

Listing 4-11. Integer to Bytes

```
1    # Partial Listing: Some Assembly Required
2
3    # RSA Oracle Attack Component
4    def int_to_bytes(i, min_size = None):
5        # i might be a gmpy2 big integer; convert back to a Python int
6        i = int(i)
7        b = i.to_bytes((i.bit_length()+7)//8, byteorder='big')
8        if min_size != None and len(b) < min_size:
9            b = b'\x00'*(min_size-len(b)) + b
10       return b
```

Now properly updated, Eve writes her "fake" oracle that she will use just for testing. The code in Listing 4-12 performs a simple RSA decryption, converts the result to bytes (using the minimum size parameter we just implemented), and checks if the first and second bytes are 0 and 2, respectively. Make sure that the new int_to_bytes is working correctly. The old version will always drop the leading zero and the oracle will always report false.

---

[8]In most sources, because the size is fixed, it is specified as the expected size and the code checks to make sure it isn't too big.

Listing 4-12. Fake Oracle

```
1    # Partial Listing: Some Assembly Required
2
3    # RSA Oracle Attack Component
4    class FakeOracle:
5        def __init__(self, private_key):
6            self.private_key = private_key
7
8        def __call__(self, cipher_text):
9            recovered_as_int = simple_rsa_decrypt(cipher_text, self.
             private_key)
10           recovered = int_to_bytes(recovered_as_int, self.private_key.
             key_size //8)
11           return recovered [0:2] == bytes([0, 2])
```

With an oracle in place, Eve prepares to attack the algorithm described in the paper. The algorithm is described in four steps. We will review each one individually and develop the code incrementally.

Step 1: Blinding

Bleichenbacher's algorithm requires the blinding step both for setup and for "blinding" the message. However, the remarks section at the end of the algorithm explains that most of this is not necessary for our situation:

> Step 1 can be skipped if c is already PKCS-conforming (i.e., when c is an encrypted message). In that case, we set $s_0 \leftarrow 1$.

There are three values that get configured in this step. Because we are dealing with an already PKCS-padded encrypted message, we only need to set these values to the prescribed defaults:

$$c_0 \leftarrow c(s_0)^e \pmod{n}$$
$$M_0 \leftarrow [2B, 3B-1]$$
$$i \leftarrow 1.$$

Because $s_0 = 1$, we can reduce the first assignment to

$$c_0 \leftarrow c$$

Obviously, 1 to any power is still just 1, so neither the power nor the modulus has any effect.

The M parameter is going to be a list of lists of intervals (more on intervals in a second). This algorithm consists of repeated steps identified by i. M_0 records a list of intervals identified in the step identified by $i = 1$. In this case, there is only the single interval $[2B, 3B - 1]$.

What is B? As explained earlier in the paper, B is the number of legal values that have the proper padding. It is defined as

$$B = 2^{8(k-2)}.$$

Basically, k is the key size in bytes. So, if we're using a 2048-bit key, k = 256. But why subtract 2?

Let's break it down this way. For RSA with padding, our plaintext size in bytes is always supposed to be the same as the key size. If we're using a 2048-bit key, our padded plaintext must be 2048 bits (256 bytes) as well. That means that there are 2^{2048} possible plaintext values.

That isn't really true, though, is it? We know that the first two bytes must be 0 and 2, and that reduces the number of legal values by $2 \times 8 = 16$ bits. Thus, B is the maximum number of values for this key size when you account for the first two fixed bytes.

Returning to the intervals, what is $2B$ and $3B$? The intervals in this data structure represent legal values of PKCS numbers in which the actual plaintext message resides. Because the bytes at the beginning are the most significant bytes, the 0 has no impact on the integer number (e.g., 0020 = 20). But the 2 means that any legal number must be at a minimum $2B$ but must be less than $3B$.

Think about it this way. If I told you that a two-digit number must fall between 20 and 30, you would know that there are ten possible values that it could be. Moreover, you know that the minimum value is 2×10. This is the same idea.

The way this algorithm works is by narrowing down the legal interval until it is just a single number. That number is the plaintext message!

Eve decides to create a function for each of the steps of the algorithm. Given that there is state data that needs to be shared between these functions (e.g., B, M, etc.), she decides to use a class for storing state. The constructor takes a public key and an oracle.

Remember, the oracle simply takes a ciphertext as input and returns true if the ciphertext decrypts to a proper PKCS-padded plaintext.

Now, Eve writes the code for this step (step 1) of the algorithm. This step requires a ciphertext as input (c) and initializes the values of c_0, B, s, and M. Eve also copies n out of the public key in a convenience function called _step1_blinding, as in Listing 4-13.

Listing 4-13. RSA Oracle Attack: Step 1

```
1    # Partial Listing: Some Assembly Required
2
3    class RSAOracleAttacker:
4        def __init__(self, public_key, oracle):
5            self.public_key = public_key
6            self.oracle = oracle
7
8        def _step1_blinding(self, c):
9            self.c0 = c
10
11           self.B = 2**(self.public_key.key_size-16)
12           self.s = [1]
13           self.M = [ [Interval(2*self.B, (3*self.B)-1)] ]
14
15           self.i = 1
16           self.n = self.public_key.public_numbers().n
```

The value of B is computed directly from bits rather than converting from bytes. Everything else is computed exactly as described in the paper.

The Interval data structure in this code is created using the collections. namedtuple factory. Its two values are a (for lower bounds) and b (for upper bounds).

Step 2: Searching for PKCS-Conforming Messages

For this section, we need to dust off our mathematics from about multiplying RSA ciphertexts. Take a quick minute to review (4.3).

Conceptually, step 2 is about searching within the M_{i-1} intervals for new PKCS-conforming messages that are a multiples of the original plaintext message m and some other integer s_i.

Figure 4-2 depicts a (simplified) view of the PKCS-conformant space within all possible RSA ciphertext values. An RSA encryption ranges in output from 0 up to 2^k-1 where k is the key size in bits. Regardless of the key size, every number (in hexadecimal) begins with 1 of 16 digits 0 through f. The highlighted slice between 2 and 3 represents RSA ciphertext values that have proper PKCS padding. (This view is overly simplified because, in reality, the correct slice should be from 02 up to 03 out of a range from 00 to ff, so it would actually just be 1 slice out of 256.)

The reason the message space is shown as a ring is because we are dealing with modular (wrap-around) arithmetic. If you take two numbers within this space and multiply them together (modulo n), if the product is greater than n, it just wraps around.

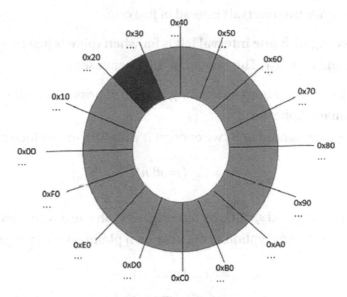

Figure 4-2. *Simplified view of PKCS-conformant space*

This brings us back to multiplying the plaintext message m by another number. In our simplified view in Figure 4-2, m must be inside the highlighted region somewhere. If we use modular multiplication, multiplying m by certain numbers (modulo n) will produce other numbers that have wrapped around that are also within the same region.

Of course, we don't know *exactly* where m is located because all we have is the encrypted version c. All we know is that, because it is PKCS-conformant, it is *somewhere* within the region. Similarly, because we don't know where m is, we also have no idea where a multiple of m will land in the ring. The exception, of course, is that using our oracle, we can determine if the multiple landed back inside the PKCS-conformant region!

Using the oracle, then, we will search for an s_i value that, when multiplied by m (modulo n), is PKCS-conformant and thus within the PKCS-conformant region of the RSA message space. We still won't know where m is, but knowing that it has a multiple that falls within a certain region introduces additional constraints on the interval that contains it. We'll talk more about those constraints and how to use them in step 3. But for now, let's find s_i!

Bleichenbacher breaks up finding s_i into three sub-steps:

1. 2a **Starting the search** is for the very first time we do this operation (i.e., when $i = 1$).

2. 2b **Searching with more than one interval left** is for rare cases when we have two intervals instead of just one.

3. 2c **Searching with one interval left** is for when there is just one interval and i is not 1. This should be all other cases.

Each of these sub-steps requires searching a range of possible s_i values to see if it produces a conformant ciphertext.

Specifically, for each candidate s_i, we encrypt it with RSA to produce c_i.

$$c_i = s_i^e \pmod{n}.$$

We multiply the encrypted s_i value by our original ciphertext c_0 to create a test cipher c_t. Because c_0 is the encryption of the unknown plaintext m_0[9], we get

$$s_t = c_i c_0 \pmod{n}$$
$$= s_i^e m_0^e \pmod{n}.$$

We send c_t to the oracle to test if it is conformant. For our fake oracle, it simply uses the private key to decrypt the c_t and check if the plaintext starts with bytes 0 and 2. (Remember, to break Alice's messages, we won't have a private-key-enabled oracle. Instead, we will send the ciphertext to Bob and check for padding error message responses.)

---

[9]We were just calling this m, but to tie it to the c_0 value, we will refer to it as m_0.

Because each sub-step needs to be able to check a range of s_i values in this way, Eve decides to create a helper function for performing the search. It takes a starting value and an optional inclusive upper bound (as in Listing 4-14).

Listing 4-14. Find "s"

```
1    # Partial Listing: Some Assembly Required
2
3    # RSA Oracle Attack Component, part of class RSAOracleAttacker
4        def _find_s(self, start_s, s_max = None):
5            si = start_s
6            ci = simple_rsa_encrypt(si, self.public_key)
7        while not self.oracle((self.c0 * ci) % self.n):
8            si += 1
9            if s_max and (si > s_max):
10                return None
11            ci = simple_rsa_encrypt(si, self.public_key)
12        return si
```

Using this helper function, the first two sub-steps are very straightforward. Step 2a requires testing all values of $s_i \geq n/(3B)$ until one of them is conformant. Eve encodes this step as shown in Listing 4-15.

Listing 4-15. Step 2a

```
1    # Partial Listing: Some Assembly Required
2
3    # RSA Oracle Attack Component, part of class RSAOracleAttacker
4        def _step2a_start_the_searching(self):
5            si = self._find_s(start_s=gmpy2.c_div(self.n, 3*self.B))
6            return si
```

Notice that the starting s value is computed as $n/(3B)$ using the c_div function from the gmpy2 module. Because we are working with such big numbers, we cannot trust Python's built-in floating point. Many of the values we are computing are just ranges and are not guaranteed to be integers, so fractional values are possible. The gmpy2 module provides us with fast operations on very large numbers, including floating point.

The c_div function itself provides division rounding up toward the ceiling. So, for example, c_div(3,4) computes 3/4 and rounds up, returning 1.

Using these RSA concepts, this step searches for values of s_i that multiply c to *another* PKCS-conformant value. Specifically, for a candidate value of s_i, we RSA encrypt it, then multiply it by the original ciphertext. We use the ceiling because s_i must be an integer and must be greater than or equal to the starting value. Whether the starting value is a whole number or not, the next integer (i.e., ceiling) is the starting point for s_i.

Sub-step 2*b* is also quite easy to do. This sub-step deals with rare occurrences where the interval for m_0 gets split in two. When this happens, we iterate s_i forward until we find another conforming value (Listing 4-16).

Listing 4-16. Step 2b

```
1    # Partial Listing: Some Assembly Required
2
3    # RSA Oracle Attack Component, part of class RSAOracleAttacker
4        def _step2b_searching_with_more_than_one_interval(self):
5        si = self._find_s(start_s=self.s[-1]+1)
6        return si
```

We will save every s value we find in the self.s array for being able to access these values. In truth, we only ever need the previous value, but we use this idiom to match the way the paper is written.

Finally, the last sub-step, 2*c*, is a bit more complicated. It requires searching for s across a range of possible values. Recall that there is only one interval found in the previous step and we take the lower bound as a and the upper bound as b. Next, we must iterate through r_i values:

$$r_i \geq 2 \frac{bs_{i-1} - 2B}{n}.$$

We use these r_i values to bound both sides of the s_i search:

$$\frac{2B + r_i n}{b} \geq s_i < \frac{3B + r_i n}{a}.$$

What we are doing here is picking s_i values within a particular range that will help us continue to narrow down the solution. Bleichenbacher explains in his paper why these bounds work, and we will not repeat his comments here. When we talk about step 3, we will give some further intuition on the entire algorithm that will help to clarify what is happening.

In the meantime, Eve encodes this algorithm as Listing 4-17.

Listing 4-17. Step 2c

```
1    # Partial Listing: Some Assembly Required
2
3    # RSA Oracle Attack Component, part of class RSAOracleAttacker
4        def _step2c_searching_with_one_interval_left(self):
5            a,b = self.M[-1][0]
6            ri = gmpy2.c_div(2*(b*self.s[-1] - 2*self.B),self.n)
7            si = None
8
9        while si == None:
10            si = gmpy2.c_div((2*self.B+ri*self.n),b)
11
12            s_max = gmpy2.c_div((3*self.B+ri*self.n),a)
13            si = self._find_s(start_s=si, s_max=s_max)
14            ri += 1
15        return si
```

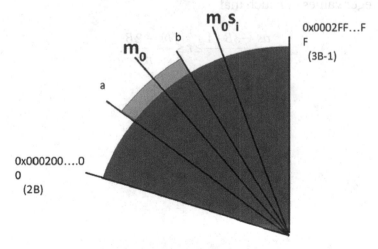

Figure 4-3. *Depiction of Bleichenbacher's attack*

As with previous computations, division is handled using gmpy2.c_div. This is very important. If you just use Python's division operators, you are likely to get incomplete results.

Step 3: Narrowing the Set of Solutions

Once an s_i value has been found from step 2, we update our bounds on the location of m. Before walking through the math, let's talk about what is going on in this algorithm.

In Figure 4-3 we are again visualizing the slice of the RSA message space ring that contains legitimate PKCS-padded values. The lower bound of this space is numbers beginning with 000200...00 and the inclusive upper bound is 0002FF...FF. The plaintext message m_0 is *somewhere* in here. At the start of the algorithm, we have no idea where.

However, for each s_i value we find that is conformant, we learn of a new value $m_0 s_i$ that is within this region as well (wrapping around because of modulo arithmetic). The fact that we know that $m_0 s_i$ (modulo n) falls within a particular range introduces new constraints on where m_0 can be. We are able to use these constraints to calculate a new interval a to b within which m_0 *must* be.

Once we update the bounds, we can repeat the process using *new* values of s_i that further tighten the bounds. Eventually, the bounds will restrict m_0 to being a single value. *That* is the plaintext we're looking for!

Hopefully this intuition will help even if the following formulas don't make much sense. Or, it will be helpful if you do try to tackle Bleichenbacher's paper. In any event, we compute the new upper and lower bounds as follows.

For each a, b interval in the previous M_0 (there will usually be one, but sometimes two), find all integer values of r such that

$$\frac{as_i - 3B + 1}{n} \geq r \leq \frac{bs_i - 2B}{n}.$$

For each of these values of *a*, *b*, and *r*, we calculate a new interval. First, we calculate a lower-bound candidate as follows:

$$a_i = \frac{2B + rn}{si}.$$

and an upper-bound candidate

$$b_i = \frac{3B - 1 + rn}{si}.$$

We define a new interval as [$max(a, a_i)$, $min(b, b_i)$].

The set of all intervals is inserted into M_i. Again, there is typically only one interval. Eve encodes this step of the algorithm as in Listing 4-18.

Listing 4-18. Step 3

```
1    # Partial Listing: Some Assembly Required
2
3    # RSA Oracle Attack Component, part of class RSAOracleAttacker
4        def _step3_narrowing_set_of_solutions(self, si):
5            new_intervals = set()
6            for a,b in self.M[-1]:
7                r_min = gmpy2.c_div((a*si - 3*self.B + 1),self.n)
8                r_max = gmpy2.f_div((b*si - 2*self.B),self.n)
9
10               for r in range(r_min, r_max+1):
11                   a_candidate = gmpy2.c_div((2*self.B+r*self.n),si)
12                   b_candidate = gmpy2.f_div((3*self.B-1+r*self.n),si)
13
14                   new_interval = Interval(max(a, a_candidate), min(b,
                     b_candidate))
15                   new_intervals.add(new_interval)
16           new_intervals = list(new_intervals)
17           self.M.append(new_intervals)
18           self.s.append(si)
19
```

```
20              if len(new_intervals) == 1 and new_intervals[0].a == new_
                intervals[0].b:
21                  return True
22              return False
```

In this code, note that r_max is calculated using f_div. This computes division rounding to the floor instead of the ceiling. We use this value because r is an integer and must be less than or equal to the value.

Once the intervals are computed, the code adds them to the self.M data structure and adds the s_i value to self.s.

Finally, it checks to see if we've found a solution. Eve is getting ahead of herself here. This is part of step 4, but it was simply more convenient to put it here.

Step 4: Computing the Solution

As hinted at in previous sections, this algorithm has termination criteria. Hopefully, it is fairly obvious considering the previous discussion. Either

- M_i contains only one interval, or

- The upper and lower bound in the interval of M_i are the same.

In short, we terminate when the interval that bounds the location of m is reduced to a single number.

We have already seen Eve's code for checking this condition at the end of step 3. Bleichenbacher's step 4 also deals with a more general problem than ours and includes steps that are unnecessary for when s_0 is 1. Recall that for processing RSA encryption messages where the plaintext was already PKCS-padded, s_0 was set to 1.

Although it's somewhat unnecessary, for sake of completeness and consistency, Eve does create a method for step 4 (Listing 4-19).

Listing 4-19. Step 4

```
1   # Partial Listing: Some Assembly Required
2
3   # RSA Oracle Attack Component, part of class RSAOracleAttacker
4       def _step4_computing_the_solution(self):
5           interval = self.M[-1][0]
6           return interval.a
```

That's it! That's the entire algorithm! Eve combines these steps into Listing 4-20's attack method.

Listing 4-20. Attack!

```
1    # Partial Listing: Some Assembly Required
2
3    # RSA Oracle Attack Component, part of class RSAOracleAttacker
4        def attack(self, c):
5            self._step1_blinding(c)
6
7            # do this until there is one interval left
8            finished = False
9            while not finished:
10               if self.i == 1:
11                   si = self._step2a_start_the_searching()
12               elif len(self.M[ -1]) > 1:
13                   si = self._step2b_searching_with_more_than_one_
                         interval()
14               elif len(self.M[-1]) == 1:
15                   interval = self.M[-1][0]
16                   si = self._step2c_searching_with_one_interval_left()
17
18               finished = self._step3_narrowing_set_of_solutions(si)
19               self.i += 1
20
21           m = self._step4_computing_the_solution()
22           return m
```

Please note that the attack() method's input is the ciphertext, but it must already be in integer form. Don't forget to call bytes_to_int() on the ciphertext first!

EXERCISE 4.12. RUN THE ATTACK!

Take the preceding code and run some experiments with breaking RSA encryption with PKCS padding. You should use the `cryptography` module to create the encrypted message, convert the encrypted message to an integer, and then use your attack program (and fake oracle) to break the encryption. To begin with, test your program on RSA keys of size 512. This breaks faster and will enable you to validate your code sooner.

EXERCISE 4.13. TAKING THE TIME

How long does the attack take? Instrument your code with timing checks and a count of how many times the oracle function is called. Run the attack on a suite of inputs and determine the average amount of time required to break keys of sizes 512, 1024, and 2048.

EXERCISE 4.14. STAYING UP TO DATE

Despite the fact that this attack is over 20 years old, it continues to haunt the Internet. Do a little Google searching and find out about the current state of this attack both in terms of prevention and updated variants. Make sure to find out about the ROBOT attack. We'll talk about this one again when we discuss TLS.

Additional Notes About RSA

We've spent a lot of time on RSA in this chapter, and we haven't even gotten into much of how it is actually used in practice. RSA, like most asymmetric ciphers, is almost never used to encrypt messages like we had Alice and Bob do throughout the chapter. When it is used, it is typically used to encrypt a session key for a *symmetric* cipher, or for signatures.

It is, however, critical to understand how asymmetric ciphers work and how they can be broken. Despite all of its weaknesses, RSA is still widely used, often incorrectly. Walking through the exploits and vulnerabilities in this chapter should help put you on the right path.

Here are a few other items for consideration.

Key Management

As with all ciphers, much of their security comes down to correctly creating and safeguarding keys.

When creating an RSA key, make sure to use a library. Do not try to generate the public and private keys yourself. At the same time, keep tabs on any bug reports for the library you do use. For example, some libraries have been found to generate RSA private keys without sufficient randomness, thus producing private keys that were vulnerable to various attacks. You can't possibly anticipate all of the things that will go wrong, or when the library or algorithm you use will be exposed as vulnerable, so you must "maintain" your cryptography by keeping up to date on known vulnerabilities.

Vulnerabilities can be system-specific. The ROCA vulnerability, for example, was largely confined to certain hardware chips.

It is also important to use the proper parameters when creating an RSA key. The key size should typically be at least 2048 bits unless legacy constraints force you to choose something smaller. And the value of the public exponent e should always be 65537.

You must also be careful to guard and protect private keys and their secrets. Obviously the private key itself should be stored securely and with appropriate permissions. Your private key should, at the very least, be stored with absolutely minimal permissions on the file system. A very sensitive key might need to be stored offline.

You should also consider storing the private key in encrypted form. This will require a password to decrypt the key which can have its own set of difficulties in a fully automated system. However, properly used, it can reduce the risk of a private key being compromised if an attacker gains access to the host system.

Moreover, the private key is made up of a number of component values. In our examples, we could think of d as the private key because that is the value we use to actually decrypt. But in addition to d, care must also be taken not to expose the secrets used to generate it. For example, the modulus n is not, itself, secret, but the two large primes, p and q, that generated it are.

There are additional values generated when creating a private key that will compromise security if disclosed. Along with p and q, these values are not strictly necessary after the key is generated, as everything can be computed from e, d, and n. However, most libraries do keep them as part of the private key both in memory and on disk. You should read your library's documentation about private key generation and follow recommended handling procedures.

One of the weaknesses of asymmetric cryptography is the inability to "revoke" a private key. If Bob's private key is compromised, how does Alice know to stop sending data encrypted under the associated public key? In practice, your RSA keys will probably be used in conjunction with certificates, which can include a hierarchy of certificates and keys allowing some keys to be less sensitive than others and also include an expiration date to limit the exposure of a compromised key. More is said on that elsewhere.

EXERCISE 4.15. FACTORING RSA KEYS

In this section, we recommended using 2048-bit keys. For this exercise, do an Internet search to find out the current size of keys that can easily be factored. For example, do a search for "factoring as a service" and see how much it costs to factor a 512-bit key.

EXERCISE 4.16. ROCA VULNERABLE KEYS

Unless your RSA keys are being generated by certain RSA hardware modules, the keys you have generated for the exercises in this chapter should not be vulnerable to ROCA, but it never hurts to check. For this exercise, visit the online ROCA vulnerability checking site at `https://keychest.net/roca#/` and test a couple of keys.

Algorithm Parameters

If there is one thing that you should take away from this chapter, it is this: *pay special attention to RSA's padding parameter*. As of the time of this writing, you should use the OAEP padding scheme for encryption operations and the PSS padding scheme for signatures. Do *not* use PKCS #1 v1.5 unless it is absolutely necessary for legacy applications.

Quantum Cryptography

We don't have the space to delve into quantum cryptography in this book, but we can't close out our discussion of RSA without mentioning it. When quantum computing arrives, most of our current asymmetric algorithms will become breakable. RSA is already vulnerable to a number of contemporary attacks, but when quantum computing becomes viable, it will be thoroughly broken. Thus, within the next decade or so, RSA will be completely useless.

Really Short Addendum

If there is one thing to get out of this chapter, it is this: parameters matter, and correct implementations are subtle and evolve over time. The intuition for how asymmetric encryption works and can be used is simple to explain, but there are numerous details that can make one implementation safe and another highly vulnerable.

Choose the right tool for the job, and choose the right parameters for the tool.

Oh, and breaking stuff is fun!

CHAPTER 5

Message Integrity, Signatures, and Certificates

In this chapter, we will be talking about "keyed hashes" and how asymmetric cryptography can be used to provide not only message privacy but also message *integrity* and *authenticity* via digital signatures. We will also be talking about how certificates differ from keys and why that distinction is important. Let's dive right into an example and some code!

An Overly Simplistic Message Authentication Code (MAC)

Checking in with Alice and Bob, our East Antarctic espionage duo has had some trouble on their most recent adventure in adversarial territory to the west. Apparently, Eve managed to intercept a few communications sent between them. The messages, encrypted with symmetric encryption, were unreadable, but Eve figured out how to *alter* them, inserting some false instructions and information. Alice and Bob, acting on false information, were almost trapped in an ambush. Fortunately for them, a bunch of ice melted due to global warming, and they managed to swim home to safety!

Quick to learn from their close call, they spent a little time at headquarters drying off and devising new communication mechanisms to prevent the unauthorized modification of their encrypted data.

Eventually, the East Antarctica Truth-Spying Agency (EATSA) discovered a new concept: "message authentication codes" or "MACs."

A MAC, Alice and Bob are told, is any "code" or data transmitted along with a message that can be evaluated to determine if the message has been altered. This is an informal definition for intuition purposes. Be patient while Alice and Bob work through

© Seth James Nielson, Christopher K. Monson 2019
S. J. Nielson and C. K. Monson, *Practical Cryptography in Python*,
https://doi.org/10.1007/978-1-4842-4900-0_5

this introductory and incorrect starting point. The basic idea for this overly simplistic MAC is this:

1. The sender computes a code C_1 using a function $f(M_1)$ for a given message M_1.

2. The sender transmits M_1 and C_1 to the recipient.

3. The recipient receives the data as M and C, but does not know if they have been modified.

4. The recipient recomputes $f(M)$ and compares the output to C to verify that the message is unaltered.

Suppose that Eve intercepts M_1 and C_1 sent by Alice to Bob. If Eve wants to change the message M_1 to M_2, she must *also* recompute $C_2 = f(M_2)$ and send both M_2 and C_2 to Bob. Otherwise, Bob will detect that something has been changed because $f(M)$ and C will not match.

If you are asking, "So what? Eve can just recompute the MAC, right?" then you are seeing the problem with our overly simplistic setup. We have to assume that Eve has everything *except the key*, but this example also assumes she does not have *f*. We will fix that shortly. Stay tuned!

For now, Alice and Bob are just going to assume that Eve can't compute, or easily compute, the function *f*. If this assumption is true (which it isn't in reality), then just about any mechanism for creating a fingerprint will work. The East Antarctican spying agency decides to send the message *hash* as an attachment to the message. Thus, the MAC is a hash in this case.

Let's dive into some code to see how this simple idea comes together. While we're at it, we can combine our new fake MAC technology with some symmetric encryption from Chapter 3. This is demonstrated in Listing 5-1.

Listing 5-1. Fake MAC with Symmetric Encryption

```
1    # THIS IS NOT SECURE. DO NOT USE THIS!!!
2    from cryptography.hazmat.primitives.ciphers import Cipher, algorithms, modes
3    from cryptography.hazmat.backends import default_backend
4    import os, hashlib
```

```
5
6   class Encryptor:
7       def __init__ (self, key, nonce):
8           aesContext = Cipher(algorithms.AES(key),
9                                     modes.CTR(nonce),
10                                    backend=default_backend())
11          self.encryptor = aesContext.encryptor()
12          self.hasher = hashlib.sha256()
13
14      def update_encryptor(self, plaintext):
15          ciphertext = self.encryptor.update(plaintext)
16          self.hasher.update(ciphertext)
17          return ciphertext
18
19      def finalize_encryptor(self):
20          return self.encryptor.finalize() + self.hasher.digest()
21
22  key = os.urandom(32)
23  nonce = os.urandom(16)
24  manager = Encryptor(key, nonce)
25  ciphertext = manager.update_encryptor(b"Hi Bob, this is Alice !")
26  ciphertext += manager.finalize_encryptor()
```

Recall that "counter mode" requires no padding and that in our previous examples the "finalize" functions really didn't do much. But now, when we finalize our manager, it not only finalizes encryption, it also returns the computed hash as the last few bytes to be appended to the encrypted data. Thus, the final encrypted message has our simple MAC tacked onto the end of it.

EXERCISE 5.1. TRUST BUT VERIFY

Finish out the code of the simple encryption plus hash system and add a decryption operation. The decryption operation should, upon finalization, recompute the hash of the ciphertext and compare it to the hash that was sent over. If the hashes don't match, it should raise an exception. Be careful! The MAC is not encrypted and should not be decrypted! If you don't think carefully about this, you might decrypt data that doesn't exist!

EXERCISE 5.2. EVER EVIL EVE

Go ahead and "intercept" some of the messages encrypted by the code you wrote in this section. Modify the intercepted messages and verify that your decryption mechanism correctly reports an error.

MAC, HMAC, and CBC-MAC

Alice and Bob were told by their support people that any mechanism for authenticating a message is a message authentication code (MAC). As we hinted, this is not a complete definition. A real MAC also requires a *key*.[1]

We've used keys for encryption, but so far we haven't used them for much else. A MAC key, as you might have guessed, isn't really related to encryption at all. Rather, it ensures that the message authentication code can *only* be computed by parties that know the key.

In our example, Alice and Bob had to assume that Eve couldn't compute the function $f(M)$. That, of course, isn't reasonable. Alice and Bob used SHA-256 to derive a fingerprint, so obviously Eve can use it to compute her own authentication code as well. Assuming that she can deterministically alter the ciphertext, as we saw in the previous chapter that she could under certain circumstances, she could insert a new message *and* a new fake MAC.

A real MAC, however, which depends on a key, *cannot* be generated by Eve unless she has compromised the key! Remember, good security means that *everything* can be known *except the key* and it still works right.[2]

A MAC protects the *integrity* of the message. An attacker without a key cannot undetectably alter the data. Furthermore, if the key remains secret, the MAC also provides *authenticity*: the receiver knows that only the other person sharing the key could have sent the MAC because only a person with a key could have generated a legal MAC at all.

While there are many MAC algorithms, we will look at two easy-to-understand approaches: HMAC and CBC-MAC. These algorithms do a good job of teaching how and why a MAC works. They are useful in practice as well.

---

[1]This is still just an informal definition. Formal definitions exist for the persnickety [11, Chap. 9].
[2]Kerckhoff's principle strikes again!

HMAC

An HMAC is a "hash-based message authentication code." In fact, you already know the most complicated characteristic of an HMAC: hashing. An HMAC is mostly just a hash that is *keyed*.

What does it mean to be "keyed"? To illustrate, let's first review standard cryptographic hashes that are not keyed. For such hashes, if the input doesn't change, neither does the output. They are fully deterministic based only on a single input: the message contents. If you revisit the exercise "GOOGLE KNOWS!" in Chapter 2, you will recall that we can actually enter some hash values into Google and find matching inputs.

Pull up a Python shell and test this one or two more times:

```
>>> import hashlib
>>> hashlib.sha256(b"hello world").hexdigest()
'b94d27b9934d3e08a52e52d7da7dabfac484efe37a5380ee9088f7ace2efcde9'
>>> hashlib.sha256(b"happy birthday").hexdigest()
'd7469a66c4bb97c09aa84e8536a85f1795761f5fe01ddc8139922b6236f4397d'
```

The SHA-256 outputs for "hello world" and "happy birthday" are *always* these values on every computer for the rest of eternity. They will *never change*. You can verify this by running the code yourself. The SHA-256 definition demands it. You can also try searching for the hashes online.

To repeat, with an unkeyed algorithm the same input *always* produces the same output.

When an algorithm is *keyed*, it means that the output is dependent on both the input and a key. But how can a hashing algorithm be keyed?

Conceptually, it is actually pretty easy. Because even a minor change to the input of a hashing algorithm completely changes the output, we can have the key be part of the input itself!

While the following example is *not* a real HMAC and is *not* considered sufficiently secure, it illustrates the idea:

```
>>> import hashlib
>>>
>>> password1 = b"CorrectHorseBatteryStaple" # See XKCD 936
>>> password2 = b"LiverKiteWorkerAgainst"
>>>
>>> # This is not really HMAC, it is for illustration ONLY:
```

```
>>> hashlib.sha256(password1 + b"hello world").hexdigest()
'ca7d4abd13bceb305eef2738e3592da77ed826aa1665ba684b80f36bd7522b32'
>>>
>>> hashlib.sha256(password2 + b"hello world").hexdigest()
'b22786bc894c8bb27d1e7e698a9bddfd6b95f35dcd063e37d764fa296216408a'
```

In this example, we used human-readable passwords as the keys. We hashed the input "hello world" two more times, but inserted a different password each time as a *prefix*. Basically we used the key to change what we were hashing. Each password results in a completely different output, meaning that the only way for someone to recreate the output MAC for the message "hello world" is to also *know the password* (or break it through brute force). As with any other cryptographic algorithm, the key/password must be both sufficiently large and sufficiently random.

Speaking of size, it is worth noting that the size of the password is not a factor in how effectively it changes the hash output. Do you recall the avalanche principle? Changing a single *bit* of input to a hash function completely changes the output hash value. You could have a terabyte document, change only a single character of it, and produce a new hash that has no relationship to the unaltered document's hash. Similarly, your password could be a single character, and it would effectively "scramble" the output for any given input, no matter how large. All you need to worry about is that your password length (and randomness) is sufficiently strong to prevent brute-force attacks.

EXERCISE 5.3. BRUTE FORCE AGAIN

You should already have done some brute-force attacks in previous chapters, but it's important to repeat the exercise until you develop intuition for the concept. Using our preceding fake HMAC, have the computer generate a random password of specific sizes and use brute-force methods to find out what it is. To be more specific, assume that you already know what the message is (e.g., "hello world," "happy birthday," or a message of your choosing). Write a program to create a random password of characters, prepend the password to the message, and then print out the MAC (hash). Take the output and iterate through all possible passwords until you find the right one. Start with a simple test of a single-letter character, then try two characters, and so forth. Mix things up by using different sets of characters such as all lowercase, lowercase and uppercase, either case plus numbers, and so forth.

EXERCISE 5.4. BRUTE FORCE FOUR-WORD PASSWORDS

Repeat the previous exercise. But instead of using letters drawn from a source of letters, use words drawn from a source of words. Find or create a text file with a list of common words. It should be at least 2000 words. Using this dictionary, create passwords by picking n random words. Attempt to brute force this password by trying every possible combination from the dictionary. Start with $n = 1$ (one-word password) and go up from there.

Even the preceding approach isn't quite good enough, so let's talk about the real HMAC. We have repeatedly said that merely prepending the password is not sufficiently secure. "HMAC" is the official name given to an algorithm defined in a standard document called "RFC 2104." If you haven't ever looked at an RFC before, these are documents from the Internet Engineering Task Force (IETF) that represent standards, best practices, experiments, and discussions for Internet protocols and algorithms. They are all freely available and can be found online. RFC 2104 can be found at `https://tools.ietf.org/html/rfc2104`.

The abstract for the document states:

> This document describes HMAC, a mechanism for message authentication using cryptographic hash functions. HMAC can be used with any iterative cryptographic hash function, e.g., MD5, SHA-1, in combination with a secret shared key.

That part should already make sense. The experiments we already did used SHA-256 and a secret shared key, but we obviously could have used SHA-1 or MD5. As a reminder, though, those hash algorithms are considered "broken" and should not be used except as necessary with legacy applications.

Returning to page 3 of the RFC, we see that once a hashing function H is picked, the HMAC over an input text is computed, thus

H(K XOR opad, H(K XOR ipad, text))

Let's take a look at each of these terms. We already know H; that's the underlying hash function. The term "text" refers to the input, but does not have to be composed of readable text characters any more than any "plaintext" message needs to be: it can be arbitrary binary data. Oh, and we need to address the commas. Because H is a function, you might be tempted to think that this definition is showing a hashing function that takes two parameters. But in this definition in the RFC, the comma can be thought of as concatenation. As in all of our other examples, a hash function only takes a single input.

The term K refers to the key, but it can't be just anything. The RFC has a number of requirements for the key that will often require some pre-processing. Most of these requirements are related to the block size of H. Recall from Chapter 3 that we used the term "block size" with block ciphers to describe the size of data that the block cipher operates on at one time. AES, for example, has a block size of 16 bytes (128 bits). Hashing algorithms can hash any size of input, so what is the block size of a hash algorithm?

In actuality, hashing functions typically operate on one block at a time, but feed the hash output from one chunk into the hashing computations of the next. SHA-1, for example, has a 64-byte (512-bit) block size, while SHA-256 has a 128-byte (1024-bit) block size. The RFC refers to the block size of H as B (bytes).

The first requirement for our key is that if it is *shorter* than the block size B, it has to be padded with zeros until it is B bytes long.

The second requirement is that if the key is *longer* than B, it is first reduced by hashing the key with H. Don't let this surprise you. We will use H multiple times in a single HMAC operation.

In summary, if K is too short, it is padded with zeros, and if K is too long, $H(K)$ is used instead.

The eagle-eyed reader will notice that the length of a hash may be *also* be shorter than the block size. SHA-1's hash is 20 bytes long and its block size is 64 bytes. SHA-256's hash is 32 bytes long but its block size is 128 bytes. After reducing the key that is *too long* with the hashing function, it will generally be *too short* and will then require padding.

In the end, we should have a key that is exactly B bytes long.

Next, we need to compute $K \oplus$ ipad (XOR). The term "ipad" stands for "inner padding" because this is the inner hashing operation in the HMAC. The RFC defines ipad as "the byte 0x36 repeated B times" and "opad" as "the byte 0x5c repeated B times." The values chosen for ipad and opad were picked arbitrarily. What is most important is that they are different.

The reasons for the pads go beyond the scope of this book, but they give HMAC some extra security in case the underlying hash function is broken. So, for example, these paddings made HMAC-MD5 relatively strong even after MD5 was shown to be broken. That's helpful, but not a good reason to use HMAC-MD5 for new applications. Please don't. HMAC's padding means that HMAC-SHA256 will be a reasonably strong MAC even if someone finds a vulnerability in the SHA-256 hashing function, which can help keep existing uses (that might not be easily upgraded to a better hash function immediately) relatively secure.

The computation of $K \oplus$ ipad is pretty easy because they are the same size. The subsequent value is prepended to the input "text," and the combined data is hashed by H. We have now computed $H(K \oplus (\text{ipad, text}))$. Again, this is the inner hash computation.

Now, for the outer hash, we compute $K \oplus$ opad. The subsequent value is prepended to the output of the inner hash, and the aggregated bytes are hashed again. The hash of the outer function is the HMAC of the input text keyed on K.

Fortunately for you, cryptographic libraries almost always have HMAC as a primitive.

```
>>> from cryptography.hazmat.backends import default_backend
>>> from cryptography.hazmat.primitives import hashes, hmac
>>>
>>> key = b"CorrectHorseBatteryStaple"
>>> h = hmac.HMAC(key, hashes.SHA256(), backend=default_backend())
>>> h.update(b"hello world")
>>> h.finalize().hex()
'd14110a202b607dc9243f83f5e0b1f4a1e59fba572fc5ea5f41d263dd4e78608'
```

Why go to all the trouble of learning how HMAC works on the inside, rather than just learning how to use a supplied library? There are a few reasons. First, it's good to have at least a little bit of an idea of how things work. It helps with intuition and reasoning about when to use it and why.

Second, and perhaps most important, it is to remind you that YANAC (You Are Not A Cryptographer... yet!). You must remember this principle! Use cryptographic libraries as much as possible and do not try to come up with your own "clever" algorithm. Take a look at HMAC again. It's built on some of the same concepts as simply prefixing an input with a key, but has much higher complexity. That complexity comes from deeper and subtler goals, including forward security in the event of a broken hash function. That complexity is not arbitrary; the HMAC operation was based on a research paper by cryptographers that *mathematically proved* certain security properties. Unless you are a cryptographer who publishes your work (often with formal proofs) for public peer scrutiny, test, and debate, then you really should not be creating your own algorithms except for the purposes of education or demonstration.

EXERCISE 5.5. TEST PYTHON'S HMAC

Although you should not roll your own crypto, it doesn't mean you shouldn't verify implementations! Create your own implementation of HMAC following the instructions from RFC 2104 and test some inputs and keys with both your implementation and Python's `cryptography` library's implementation. Ensure that they produce the same outputs!

CBC-MAC

HMAC is a very popular MAC and is used, for example, in TLS, but there are other ways to create MACs. For example, we can take what you learned in Chapter 3 about cipher block chaining (CBC) mode as another way to derive a secure MAC.

Let's quickly introduce some new terminology. A MAC is also sometimes called a "tag." When we create a MAC of a message, we can call it the "tag" of the message; it's like a tag on a gift or a piece of clothing: it's a little bit of information that is attached to the main article. In mathematical notation, a tag is often denoted t. Thus, a MAC over message m_1 produces a tag t_1, and the pair (m_1, t_1) is transmitted to the receiver for verification.

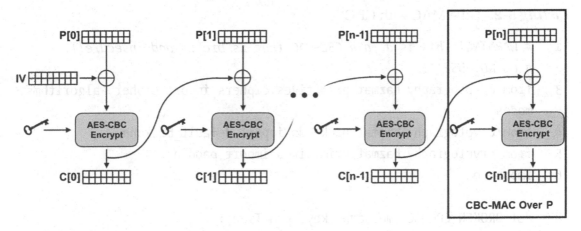

Figure 5-1. *Because all of the message impacts the value of the last encrypted block of data, C[n] is a MAC over all of P... with a few flaws.*

Recall that when encrypting with AES, we were limited to encrypting 128 bits at a time. If we encrypted each 128-bit block independently, there was still information that could "leak" through about the overall data. For example, large image features might still be recognizable. One of the solutions to the problem was to "chain" the encryption so that the input from one block carried over and influenced the encryption of the next. In other words, a change in a bit at the beginning would have a cascading effect all the way down to the very last block.

Put another way, the very last block of ciphertext is determined by the value of *every other block* in the chain: any changes anywhere in the input will be reflected in the last block! That makes the last block of a CBC encryption mode a MAC over the entire data as shown in Figure 5-1.

Hopefully as you have learned by this point in the book, all cryptography comes with limitations and critical parameters. As with HMAC, we will do some naive examples first to see both the basic concepts behind the CBC-MAC algorithm and how naive approaches are exploitable.

Let's start by taking a message and running it through AES-CBC encryption. For security reasons that we will explain shortly, we will fix the initialization vector to zero. In order to have our messages be a multiple of a block size, we will also use the same PKCS7 padding used for encryption. We will need some full block messages MAC'd without padding to simplify the next exercise, so we include a flag for turning padding off.

Listing 5-2. Fake MAC with CBC

```
1   # WARNING! This is a fake CBC-MAC that is broken and insecure!!!
2   # DO NOT USE!!!
3   from cryptography.hazmat.primitives.ciphers import Cipher, algorithms,
    modes
4   from cryptography.hazmat.backends import default_backend
5   from cryptography.hazmat.primitives import padding
6   import os
7
8   def BROKEN_CBCMAC1(message, key, pad=True):
9       aesCipher = Cipher(algorithms.AES (key),
10                          modes.CBC(bytes(16)), # 16 zero bytes
11                          backend=default_backend())
12      aesEncryptor = aesCipher.encryptor()
13
14      if pad:
15          padder = padding.PKCS7(128).padder()
16          padded_message = padder.update(message)+padder.finalize()
17      elif len(message) % 16 == 0:
18          padded_message = message
19      else:
20          raise Exception("Unpadded input not a multiple of 16!")
21      ciphertext = aesEncryptor.update(padded_message)
22      return ciphertext[-16:] # the last 16 bytes are the last block
23
24  key = os.urandom(32)
25  mac1 = BROKEN_CBCMAC1(b"hello world, hello world, hello world, hello
    world", key)
26  mac2 = BROKEN_CBCMAC1(b"Hello world, hello world, hello world, hello
    world", key)
```

The code in Listing 5-2, although not secure, does show the basic concept behind the MAC. A piece of data is first padded and then encrypted. No matter how long it is, however, the last block (16 bytes) is determined by all of the preceding input. Change the first letter from an "h" to an "H," and the MACs are completely different.

Nevertheless, it can be exploited. Recall that a MAC must be *unique* for a given message and key pair. If an attacker can generate the same MAC for a different message with the same key, the MAC algorithm is broken.

It turns out that for this naive version of CBC-MAC, you can do exactly that. Let's do it in code first and see if you can guess what's going on. Note that Listing 5-3 is intended to be combined with Listing 5-2.

Listing 5-3. MAC Prepend Attack

```
1    # Partial Listing: Some Assembly Required
2
3    # Dependencies: BROKENCBCMAC1
4    def prependAttack(original, prependMessage, key):
5        # assumes prependMessage is multiple of 16
6        # assumes original is at least 16
7        prependMac = BROKEN_CBCMAC1(prependMessage, key, pad = False)
8        newFirstBlock = bytearray(original [:16])
9        for i in range (16):
10           newFirstBlock[i] ^= prependMac[i]
11       newFirstBlock = bytes(newFirstBlock)
12       return prependMessage + newFirstBlock + original [16:]
13
14   key = os.urandom(32)
15   originalMessage = b"attack the enemy forces at dawn!"
16   prependMessage = b"do not attack. (End of message, padding follows)"
17   newMessage = prependAttack(originalMessage, prependMessage, key)
18   mac1 = BROKEN_CBCMAC1(originalMessage, key)
19   mac2 = BROKEN_CBCMAC1(newMessage, key)
20   print("Original Message and mac:", originalMessage, mac1.hex())
21   print("New message and mac    :", newMessage, mac2.hex())
22   if mac1 == mac2:
23       print("\tTwo messages with the same MAC! Attack succeeded!!")
```

The two MACs produced by Listing 5-3 are *identical*. Our attack prepends another message of our choosing to the original and *also* corrupts the first block. The only restriction on the prepended message is that it must also have the CBC-MAC value for the prepended message under the same key. We turned off padding for this prepended message to make the attack a little easier, but this is only for our convenience and not a prerequisite for the attack to succeed.

Sadly for the attacker, the original message requires modification to the first block; otherwise, the attack could have been even worse. The attacker could then create messages that say "do not attack the enemy forces at dawn!" The attacker also cannot scrub any of the data beyond the first block. In running the code, you probably noticed that "forces at dawn!" was still readable in the new message. Even so, this is still pretty bad: we added an entirely different message without changing the value of the MAC!

For this simple example, where we assume that a human is reading the output, we hope that our message that says the rest of the data is padding will be enough to convince the sender not to read further. In real attacks, transmitted data lengths and other similar mechanisms can often be used to achieve the same effect. If we are successful, we can basically send arbitrary message with the original MAC.

What went wrong? Before we give you an explanation, see if you can figure it out yourself. You might need to revisit how CBC mode works. If you need an additional hint, remember that $A \oplus B \oplus B = A$.

Let's work through it together anyway. Suppose that we have a message M composed of arbitrary blocks of data m_1 through m_n. In the formulas that follow, let E represent the AES encryption operation and let t be the CBC-MAC tag computed over the data:

$$t = E(m_n \oplus E(m_{n-1} \oplus ... E(m_2 \oplus E(m_1, k), k) ... , k), k)$$

Notice that m_1, the first block of the message, is encrypted by AES under key k and the output is XORed with m_2 before being encrypted.

Suppose that we prepended a message P that was exactly one block in length. How would that change things? The CBC-MAC would obviously produce something different because we're changing the first computation:

$$t_P = E(m_n \oplus E(m_{n-1} \oplus ... E(m_2 \oplus E(m_1 \oplus E(P, k), k), k) ... , k), k)$$

The outcome is as it should be. Changing the message (i.e., prepending a new block) changed the tag. But what if we already knew the output of the AES encryption of the prepended block $E(P, k)$? Let's call it C. If $E(P, k) = C$, then we can prepend P to the chain without changing the final tag *if* we also corrupt the original first block m_1 to be $m_1 \oplus C$.

$$t = E(m_n \oplus ... E(m_2 \oplus E(m_1 \oplus C \oplus E(P, k), k), k) ... , k), k)$$

When CBC operates on this corrupted chain, it attempts to XOR the encrypted output of the prepended block (C) into the plaintext of the corrupted first block ($m_1 \oplus C$). But the corrupted first block already has the XOR of C mixed in, the C values cancel! This just reduces to

$$t = E(m_n \oplus E(m_{n-1} \oplus \ldots E(m_2 \oplus E(m_1 \oplus C \oplus C, k), k) \ldots, k), k)$$

Effectively, we have canceled out the input of the prepended block on the final tag! We're back to the original MAC of the message!

$$t = E(m_n \oplus E(m_{n-1} \oplus \ldots E(m_2 \oplus E(m_1, k), k) \ldots, k), k)$$

This example was just for a single block. But it turns out that no matter how long the prepended message is, we only care about the part that will be XORed with m_1 before it is encrypted. In a CBC chain of arbitrary length, the only part that carries over into the next block is the *last encrypted block of the chain*. In other words, the MAC output of the CBC-MAC operation, t, is the only part of a prepended message that would impact what follows it!

Suppose, then, that you have two messages M_1 and M_2 and two corresponding tags t_1 and t_2, both of which were generated under the same key using our broken CBC-MAC algorithm. To create a falsified message, first XOR t_1 with the first block of M_2 to produce M_2'. Now create $M_3 = M_1 + M_2'$ (plus means concatenation). The CBC-MAC of M_3 will also be t_2 because (using $C(\cdot)$ to mean "MAC"):

$$t_2 = E(M_{2,n} \oplus E(M_{2,n-1} \oplus \ldots E(M_{2,1} \oplus t_1 \oplus C(M_1, k), k) \ldots, k), k)$$

As the MAC of M_1 is t_1, it cancels out with the other t_1 and the MAC of what is left is just the MAC of M_2.

A visualization of this attack, and the math we just worked through, is depicted in Figure 5-2.

Importantly, *you do not need the key to do this attack*. In our code example, we had the key ourselves and generated an arbitrary message. This is still an attack, because even the possessor of the shared key should not be able to send two messages with the same MAC.

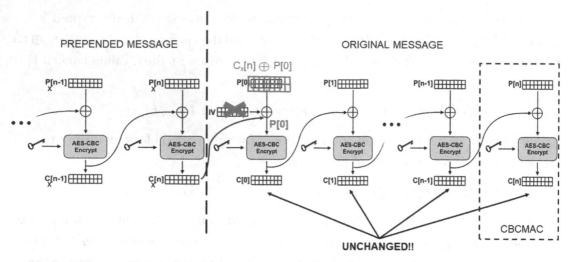

Figure 5-2. *An attacker can prepend a message without changing the (simple) CBC-MAC by corrupting just the first block*

But with this attack, an attacker *without* the key can generate a new message and a falsified tag from two existing messages (e.g., generated by the victim) and corresponding tags.

There are various solutions to this problem, but the only one we'll mention here is to enforce that each message is prepended with the length of the message, as in Listing 5-4.

Listing 5-4. Prepend Message Length

```
1    # Reasonably secure concept. Still, NEVER use it for production code.
2    # Use a crypto library instead!
3    from cryptography.hazmat.primitives.ciphers import Cipher, algorithms,
     modes
4    from cryptography.hazmat.backends import default_backend
5    from cryptography.hazmat.primitives import padding
6    import os
7
8    def CBCMAC(message, key):
9        aesCipher = Cipher(algorithms.AES(key),
10                           modes.CBC(bytes(16)), # 16 zero bytes
11                           backend=default_backend())
12       aesEncryptor = aesCipher.encryptor()
13       padder = padding.PKCS7(128).padder()
```

```
14
15        padded_message = padder.update(message)
16        padded_message_with_length = len(message).to_bytes(4, "big") +
          padded_message
17        ciphertext = aesEncryptor.update(padded_message_with_length)
18        return ciphertext[-16:]
```

To use CBC-MAC securely, there are a few additional caveats:

1. If you are also encrypting the data with AES-CBC, you must not
   use the same key for both encryption and MAC.

2. The IV should be fixed to zero.

A full explanation of each of these is beyond the scope of this book. Assuming
that you follow them, however, the included CBC-MAC code is reasonably secure.
We still don't recommend using it because it is *always* dangerous to create your own
cryptographic algorithms or even your own implementations of known cryptographic
algorithms. Instead, always use algorithms in trusted cryptographic libraries.

The Cryptography library that we are using for our example code includes
CMAC. This algorithm is an updated and improved CBC-MAC defined in RFC 4493.
Either CMAC or HMAC are good choices for a MAC algorithm; HMAC might be faster on
most systems without specialized AES encryption hardware.

Using CMAC from the library is straightforward. The following is taken directly from
the online documentation:

```
>>> from cryptography.hazmat.backends import default_backend
>>> from cryptography.hazmat.primitives import cmac
>>> from cryptography.hazmat.primitives.ciphers import algorithms
>>> c = cmac.CMAC(algorithms.AES(key), backend=default_backend())
>>> c.update(b"message to authenticate")
```

Encrypting and MACing

In many circumstances a message needs to be encrypted and protected from
modification. In the first code example in this chapter, Alice and Bob used an unkeyed
hash to protect an encrypted message. Obviously, that doesn't work because without a
key, anyone can generate the corresponding hash. Now that our intrepid (or dastardly)
duo know how to use HMAC and CMAC, they can update their code.

EXERCISE 5.6. ENCRYPT THEN MAC

Update the code from the beginning of the chapter to do a proper MAC by replacing the
SHA-256 operation with HMAC or CMAC. Use *two* keys.

Pay attention to when you use MAC and what you use it on in the previous exercise. You will notice that it is the *ciphertext* that the MAC is applied to, not the plaintext. As the name of the exercise implied, this is called *Encrypt-Then-MAC*. There are two other ways of sending an encrypted and authenticated message that have been done in the past.

One is MAC-Then-Encrypt. In this version, the MAC is applied to the *plaintext,* and then both the plaintext and the MAC are encrypted together. This approach was taken by early versions of TLS (which is used for HTTPS connections).

Another approach is called Encrypt-And-MAC. To take this approach, the MAC is again computed over the plaintext, but the MAC itself is not encrypted. It is sent (unencrypted) along with the ciphertext. If you've ever used Secure Shell (SSH or PuTTY), it uses Encrypt-And-MAC.

It is strongly recommended by most cryptographers, with a few dissenters, as there are always some of those, to use Encrypt-Then-MAC[3] over these other two approaches. In fact, certain practical vulnerabilities have been found against certain combinations of MAC-Then-Encrypt. You have already demonstrated one! The padding oracle attack against CBC in the previous chapter only works against MAC-Then-Encrypt scenarios.

There's an even better approach called AEAD (authenticated encryption with additional data) that we will learn about in Chapter 7 that combines encryption and message integrity into a single operation. If, for whatever reason, you need to combine encryption and MAC, make sure you choose Encrypt-Then-MAC (i.e., encrypt the plaintext and then compute a MAC over the ciphertext).

We won't go into the various arguments for why Encrypt-Then-MAC is generally considered better but one point is worth mentioning. As we have talked about in other circumstances, we generally don't want bad guys messing around with our ciphertext. It can be unintuitive because we tend to think about the end goal: protecting the *plaintext*. But bad things happen when the bad guys can change the ciphertext without us being

---

[3]Are you confused, yet? "Encrypt-*And*-MAC" means to apply them both to the plaintext, while "Encrypt-*Then*-MAC" means to apply the MAC to the ciphertext: *after* encryption.

able to detect it. When you do Encrypt-Then-MAC, the ciphertext should be protected against modification.

EXERCISE 5.7. KNOW THY WEAKNESS

Encrypt-Then-MAC is the recommended approach to combining encryption and MACs. However, it is good to understand all three approaches. If nothing else, if you ever have to maintain code you did not write, or have to be compatible with legacy systems, you may encounter this in the future. Modify your (highly recommended) Encrypt-Then-MAC system to create a MAC-Then-Encrypt variant. Finally, create a MAC-And-Encrypt version as well.

Digital Signatures: Authentication and Integrity

Alice and Bob love sending encrypted messages with HMACs (using Encrypt-Then-MAC). On their current assignment in West Antarctica, they each have four keys. One pair allows them to send encrypted and MAC-protected messages to each other (remember, one key for encryption, one key for MAC generation), and the second pair allows them to send and receive encrypted and MAC-protected messages to and from HQ back in East Antarctica.

Unfortunately, one day Alice is captured as she attempts to infiltrate the West Antarctic Snowball Testing Edifice. Instantly, everything is thrown into disarray as Eve now has access to all of her keys.

This is a terrible compromise. Eve is now able to send messages as though they are from Alice or HQ! Trying to mitigate this loss of confidentiality and authentication is a nightmare. Bob's situation is bad. He needs two new keys to communicate with HQ and perhaps two new keys for communicating with a new partner in the field. This can only be done by returning to HQ, which means pulling him out of the field, potentially wasting time and resources he has spent infiltrating his targets and gathering data. Worse, he can't even be reliably told about what is going on! If he doesn't have first-hand knowledge of Alice's capture, any messages sent by HQ informing him of the event or instructing him to come home can be intercepted and changed.

As bad as things are for Bob, HQ is in far worse shape. They were using the same shared keys for encrypting and tagging all of their messages. Every single agent in the field has the compromised keys lost by Alice. Eve can impersonate HQ to any of them.

And Eve can send messages to HQ as any of the agents, because they did not have their own individual keys for communicating with HQ.

The loss of the shared keys sets EATSA back at least 12 months.

As bad as it is that Eve can read the traffic between HQ and their agents using the encryption keys, it might be worse that she can send messages pretending to be any of these parties by using the MAC keys. To repeat one of our earlier comments, when people first start to learn about cryptography, they typically think about "encryption" as its main purpose or characteristic. As our fictional example illustrates, authentication—knowing who sent a message—is at least as important, and arguably more so.

Even once EATSA manages to get all of their agents' home and is no longer using the old keys (the old keys are thus "revoked"), they have the problem of coming up with a key management system to avoid the same problem in the future. One option they consider is for each agent to have their own individual key. If either HQ or an agent wants to send a message, they use their individual key to tag it.

The problem is MACs require *shared* keys. The receiver of the message must have the same key as the sender. How will they obtain it? Will every agent have every other agent's key? If so, an agent's capture is just as bad as if there was only one key. Worse, nothing keeps an agent from using another agent's key (impersonating them) either by accident or because they go rogue.

Eventually, one of the scientists remembers asymmetric encryption from Chapter 4, specifically that it can be used for something called a *digital signature*. Like message authentication codes, digital signatures are designed to provide authenticity (you can tell who sent the message) and message integrity (the message cannot be changed undetectably). Furthermore, because they use asymmetric encryption, there are *no shared keys*. At the time the EA started playing around with asymmetric encryption, they became very, very focused on encryption of messages (confidentiality) and digital signatures fell off to the side.

It is time to remedy that.

What exactly is a digital signature? First, let's review how asymmetric encryption works for the RSA algorithm we studied in Chapter 4. Unlike symmetric encryption where there is a single shared key between parties, RSA's asymmetric encryption involves a *pair* of keys: the public key and the private key. These keys work as opposites of one other: what one encrypts, the other decrypts. Moreover, the RSA public key can be derived from the private key but not the other way around.

As the name implies, a party should keep the RSA private key private and disclose it to nobody, ever. On the other hand, the RSA public key can and typically should be widely disseminated. This setup enables two very interesting operations.

First, because the RSA public key is held by anyone (and potentially by everyone!), it is easy for anyone in the world to send an encrypted message to the owner of the corresponding RSA private key. Anyone can use the public key to encrypt the message, but *only* the party with the private key can decrypt it.

This is important! The person that sends the encrypted message knows that *only* the party possessing the private key can decrypt the message. This is a different kind of reverse authenticity. The recipient of the message has no idea who sent it, but the sender can be certain (if the keys are secure) that only the intended party can *read* the message. Our introduction to RSA asymmetric encryption in Chapter 4 focused on this use case.

But, the direction of the encryption can be *reversed*: RSA private keys can also be used to *encrypt* messages. The party that has the private key can thus use it to encrypt something that can only be decrypted by the public key. What good would that do? Anybody (everybody!) could have the public key. This encryption certainly won't keep data confidential!

This is true! But, a message sent encrypted under the RSA private key can only have been encrypted by someone *who has that private key*. Even if everyone can *decrypt* it, the fact that it can be decrypted by a particular public key is a *proof that the sender holds the private key*. In other words, if you get a message that you can decrypt using my public key, *you know that it came from me*; nobody else could have encrypted it. That sounds useful!

Let's suppose that the EA wants to publish a manifesto of West Antarctica's crimes to the whole world. First they could disseminate their RSA public key everywhere and then encrypt the document under the associated private key. Now, when they distribute the document, anyone in the world can decrypt it, and that fact proves to them that it came from the EA.

This system is great, but it has a couple of important flaws. First of all, how does the world know that the RSA public key really belongs to the EA (and is not a fake from the WA, for example)? This is a critically important question and we'll get to it a bit later. For now, we will assume that recipients have a legitimate, trusted RSA public key for the intended party.

Another problem is efficiency. RSA encryption is *slow*. Decrypting long documents to verify the sender is not a remotely efficient way of doing things. Worse, some asymmetric algorithms do not have any built-in message integrity. Oh, and while we're talking about RSA's limitations, it can't encrypt something as long as a document anyway.

These latter two problems of efficiency and integrity are fortunately easily addressed. Recall that we are not encrypting for *confidentiality*, but for *proof of origin or authenticity*. Instead of encrypting the message itself, how about encrypting a *hash* of the message?

That is the basic idea of an RSA digital signature over arbitrary data. It consists of two steps. First, hash the data. Second, encrypt the hash with the private key. The encrypted hash is the sender's signature applied to the data. The signature can now be transmitted along with the original (potentially unencrypted) data. When the recipient receives data and a signature, the recipient generates the hash, decrypts the signature with the public key, and verifies that the two hashes (generated and decrypted) are identical.

Here is how cryptographers might represent this. First, for a message M, we generate a hash using a hash function: $h = H(M)$.

Once we have the hash h, we encrypt it under the RSA private key. To depict this operation, we are going to use some notation that is often used in cryptographic protocols. Specifically, we will use $\{\cdot\}$ to indicate RSA-encrypted data. Everything within the braces is plaintext, but the braces indicate that the plaintext is within some cryptographic envelope. The braces will also have a subscript indicating the key. So, for example, the ciphertext C is the plaintext P encrypted under some key K, and this is depicted as $C = \{P\}_K$.

From this point forward in the book, a *shared* key between two parties will be depicted with a subscript indicating both parties. So, for example, a key between Alice and Bob can be depicted as $K_{A,B}$. This would be an example of a symmetric key.

Public keys, such as RSA public keys, will be denoted by a key with just one identifying party. For example, Alice's public key could be denoted K_A and Bob's would similarly be K_B. Because the public key is what is distributed, it is what is named. The private key is denoted instead as the inverse of a public key: K^{-1}_A and K^{-1}_B).

In this chapter, we will also typically use the letter t to represent RSA signatures because a signature is also sometimes called a tag, just like a MAC is. Thus, we represent an R:

$$t_M = \{H(M)\}_{K^{-1}}$$

When another party with possession of the RSA public key K receives $M, \{H'(M)\}_{K^{-1}}$, the signature is decrypted by the public key to recover $H'(M)$. The receiving party generates their own $H(M)$, and the signature is considered authentic if $H'(M) = H(M)$.

At the risk of being repetitive, remember that RSA public key encryption is used for different things than private key encryption. Encryption with the RSA public key keeps the message *confidential*: only the private key owner can *read* it. Encrypting with the RSA private key proves *authenticity*: only the owner could have *authored* it.

In the EA spy agency, this seems miraculous! The agency generates an RSA key pair for itself and also has all of the agents generate an RSA key pair. The agency keeps a copy of all the public keys of all the agents, and every agent takes a copy of the agency's public key.

When the agency sends an encrypted message to Alice, they encrypt it under her public key and only Alice will be able to decrypt it. They *also* sign the message with their private key, and Alice can use the agency public key to verify that the message is authentic and uncorrupted. So long as Alice and Bob have a copy of each other's public keys, they can likewise send encrypted and authenticated messages to each other.

This is a big step forward, and it seems pretty great.

It really is, but as has so often been true with the EA's cryptographic experiences, there are complications, caveats, and subtleties. Before we get into that, however, let's help Alice and Bob learn how to send each other some signed communications. For simplicity, we are not going to encrypt them.

Again, the cryptography library comes to our rescue with its signing and verification functions: we do not need, nor should we attempt, to implement digital signatures ourselves. Rather, using our library, we will generate some RSA signatures.

Listing 5-5. Sign Unencrypted Data

```
1   from cryptography.hazmat.backends import default_backend
2   from cryptography.hazmat.primitives.asymmetric import rsa
3   from cryptography.hazmat.primitives import hashes
4   from cryptography.hazmat.primitives.asymmetric import padding
5
6   private_key = rsa.generate_private_key(
7       public_exponent=65537,
8       key_size=2048,
9       backend=default_backend()
10  )
11  public_key = private_key.public_key()
12
13  message = b"Alice, this is Bob. Meet me at Dawn"
14  signature = private_key. sign(
```

```
15      message,
16      padding.PSS(
17          mgf=padding.MGF1(hashes.SHA256()),
18          salt_length=padding.PSS.MAX_LENGTH
19      ),
20      hashes.SHA256()
21  )
22
23  public_key.verify(
24      signature,
25      message,
26      padding.PSS(
27          mgf=padding.MGF1(hashes.SHA256()),
28          salt_length=padding.PSS.MAX_LENGTH
29      ),
30      hashes.SHA256()
31  )
32  print("Verify passed! (On failure, throw exception)")
```

There's probably a bit more in Listing 5-5 than expected, particularly in the padding configuration. Let's walk through it all.

First, we generate a key pair. For RSA, the public key is derivable from the private key, so generating the private key generates the key pair. The API includes a call to obtain the public key from the private key. In this example, both keys are used. In a real example, the signing and verification code would live in completely different programs, and the verification program would only have access to the public key, not the private key.

In Chapter 4 we also learned how to serialize and de-serialize these kinds of RSA keys from disk.

In the next part of the code, we sign the message. You will notice that we are using padding here just as we did for RSA encryption, but it is a different scheme. The recommended paddings for RSA are OAEP for encryption and PSS for signatures. Perhaps that surprises you given that RSA signatures are generated by encrypting a hash. If it's all encryption anyway, why do we need different padding schemes?

The answer is that, because signatures are operating on a hash, there are certain characteristics that must be true about the data. The nature of arbitrary data encryption vs. hash encryption drives the two different padding schemes.

Like the OAEP padding used in Chapter 4, PSS padding function also requires the use of a "mask generation function." At the time of this writing, there is only one such function, MGF1.

Finally, the signature algorithm requires a hashing function. In this example, we are using SHA-256.

The parameters to the verification algorithm should be self-explanatory. Note that the validation function does not return a true or false, rather it raises an exception if the data does not match the signature.

Important Please pay careful attention to this next paragraph. It is very important and somewhat counter-intuitive.

If you wanted to encrypt and sign, should you sign first and then encrypt, or should you encrypt first and then sign? After the discussion in the previous section on Encrypt-Then-MAC, you might be thinking Encrypt-Then-Sign.

But signatures are *not MACs*, and you should generally *not* use Encrypt-Then-Sign. There are two very important reasons.

First, remember that the goal of the signature is not just message *integrity* but also sender *authentication*. Suppose that Alice is sending an encrypted message to Bob, and she encrypts the message *before* signing it. Anyone can intercept the message, strip off the signature, and send the message re-signed under their own key. Oops.

It isn't clear how practical this attack is because the data was encrypted under the *receiver's* public key that everyone already has. The attacker could just send their own encrypted message to Bob (encrypted by Bob's public key) anyway. The attacker can't even decrypt Alice's message to see if he/she wants to take credit for it. But the point is, there is no association between the plaintext and the signature, and there really needs to be: Bob is interested in knowing that the *message he can read* comes from Alice and not someone else. If the encrypted data is signed instead of the plaintext, when Bob receives the ciphertext and the signature, he cannot reliably determine who authored the original message.

In short, if you sign an encrypted message, it is too easy for it to be intercepted and signed by someone else instead, which compromises its authenticity. The signature should be applied to the plaintext.

Second, and far more important, signatures cannot prevent the bad guys from altering the ciphertext. Remember, the number one reason for using Encrypt-Then-MAC was to prevent undetectable alteration of the encrypted data. With Encrypt-Then-Sign, Eve, for example, could intercept a message from Alice to Bob, strip off Alice's signature, *alter the ciphertext*, and then sign the altered data with her own key. What good is this, you might ask? After all, Bob will see that the message is now signed by Eve and not Alice. Why would he trust it?

There are any number of reasons Bob will accept the signature. For example, Eve may have compromised another agent's key. The whole reason for using RSA encryption was to prevent the compromise of one agent's key from compromising the communications of another. But if Eve gets a legitimate signing key, she can strip off Alice's signature, modify the ciphertext, and re-sign with something Bob will accept.

Once this happens, Eve can observe Bob's behavior to learn things about Alice's message. As we used in earlier examples, even Bob throwing away a message is information that Eve can use to her advantage (e.g., she knows that the message she sent to him was unreadable).

Does this sound far-fetched? Well, exactly this kind of vulnerability in Apple's iMessage was discovered by Matt Green. You can read about it on his blog [6]. We won't discuss his attack in detail here other than to say that this kind of attack is actually very practical.

So please, do *not* Encrypt-Then-Sign.

Why is this so different from MACs? Why does Encrypt-Then-MAC work? The fundamental difference comes back to the keys. With a MAC, there is a shared key, typically shared between just the two parties. Nobody should be able to replace a MAC created by a key shared between Alice and Bob because nobody else should have the key. The private key used to create a digital signature, however, is not shared and does not bind any parties together.

What *should* you do? In the first place, there don't seem to be many crypto systems this applies to. If you are using symmetric encryption, it is usually no problem to include a symmetric MAC. If Apple had done this, the iMessage attack we mentioned wouldn't have been possible. Asymmetric encryption is not generally used for bulk encryption. When encrypting a lot of data is necessary, the usual approach is to exchange or create a symmetric key using the asymmetric cryptography and then switch to symmetric algorithms. We will talk about this in the next chapter.

If you absolutely must sign and encrypt without the benefit of a symmetric MAC (e.g., RSA encryption plus some signatures), the plaintext message should be signed and both the plaintext and signature should be encrypted (Sign-Then-Encrypt). Although this means that an attacker can try to mess around with the ciphertext, a good RSA padding scheme like OAEP should make this very difficult.

While there are no known attacks against Sign-Then-Encrypt, some of the most paranoid still Sign-Then-Encrypt-Then-Sign-Again. The inner signature is over the plaintext, proving authorship, and the outer signature is over the ciphertext, ensuring the integrity of the message. One other alternative is something called "signcryption." Because signcryption isn't supported by the Python `cryptography` library, we won't spend any time on it here, but the curious can read this paper about it: `www.cs.bham.ac.uk/~mdr/teaching/modules04/security/students/SS3/ IntroductiontoSigncryption.pdf`.

For now we will stick with the slightly less paranoid Sign-Then-Encrypt strategy. Remember, however, that RSA encryption can only encrypt a very limited number of bytes. When OAEP padding is used with SHA-256, the maximum plaintext that can be encrypted is only 190 bytes! If you start encrypting signatures, there may be very little room left for anything else. If your message is too long, you will have to break it up and encrypt it in 190-byte chunks. This is all the more reason to use the combined asymmetric and symmetric operations we will see in the next chapter.

EXERCISE 5.8. RSA RETURNS!

Create an encryption and authentication system for Alice, Bob, and EATSA. This system needs to be able to generate key pairs and save them to disk under different operator names. To send a message, it needs to load a private key of the operator and a public key of the recipient. The message to be sent is then signed by the operator's private key. Then the concatenation of the sender's name, the message, and the signature is encrypted.

To receive a message, the system loads the private key of the operator and decrypts the data extracting the sender's name, the message, and the signature. The sender's public key is loaded to verify the signature over the message.

EXERCISE 5.9. MD5 RETURNS!

In Chapter 2, we discussed some of the ways that MD5 is broken. In particular, we emphasized that MD5 is still not broken (in practice) for finding the preimage (i.e., working backward). But it *is* broken in terms of finding collisions. This is very important where signatures are concerned because signatures are typically computed over the hash of data and not the data itself.

For this exercise, modify your signature program to use MD5 instead of SHA-256. Find two pieces of data with the same MD5 sum. You can find some examples at or with a quick search of the Internet. Once you have the data, verify that the hashes are the same for the two files. Now, create a signature for both files and verify that they are the same.

One last thing should be mentioned. In some cases, you may not have all of the data to be signed all at once. The sign function does not have an update method like hashing functions do. It does have an API to submit pre-hashed data, however. This allows you to hash the data that needs to be signed separately. Here is an example drawn from the cryptography module documentation:

```
>>> from cryptography.hazmat.primitives.asymmetric import utils
>>> chosen_hash = hashes.SHA256()
>>> hasher = hashes.Hash(chosen_hash, default_backend())
>>> hasher.update(b"data & ")
>>> hasher.update(b"more data")
>>> digest = hasher.finalize()
>>> sig = private_key.sign(
...     digest,
...     padding.PSS(
...         mgf=padding.MGF1(hashes.SHA256()),
...         salt_length=padding.PSS.MAX_LENGTH
...     ),
...     utils.Prehashed(chosen_hash)
... )
```

Elliptic Curves: An Alternative to RSA

It's time we told you the truth about asymmetric cryptography. Everything we've told you so far has been RSA-specific and quite a bit of what RSA does is actually unique.

When we talk about asymmetric, or public key, cryptography, we are referring to any cryptographic operations that involve a public and private key pair. In Chapter 4 we looked almost exclusively at RSA encryption, and in this chapter, we explored RSA signatures. Conveniently, RSA signatures are also based on RSA encryption (i.e., encrypting a hash of the data to be signed). But most other asymmetric algorithms do not even support encryption as a mode of operation at all and do not use encryption for generating a signature. Other asymmetric algorithms, for example, generate a signature or tag that does not involve any encryption and verify the signature without any kind of reversible operation such as decryption.

This is one reason why we have tried to qualify our conversations about asymmetric cryptography through the book by referring specifically to "RSA public keys," "RSA encryption," and "RSA asymmetric operations." You should not assume that other asymmetric algorithms provide the same operations or do them in the same way.

Why focus so much on RSA encryption? We do this here because RSA has been one of the most popular algorithms for asymmetric operations for decades. It is still found absolutely everywhere, and you will be hard-pressed not to run into it somewhere. DSA (digital signing algorithm) is another asymmetric algorithm, but it is only usable for signatures, not for encryption. For educational and practical purposes, then, RSA is a great place to start.

With that said, RSA is slowly getting phased out. It has been found to have a lot of weaknesses, some of which we have explored already. Cryptography based on "elliptic curves"[4] has been used both to sign data and to exchange keys. In this chapter we will look at ECDSA's signing capabilities. In Chapter 6 we will look at something called Elliptic-Curve Diffie-Hellman (ECDH) that is used to create and agree on session keys. ECDH's key agreement provides an alternative (arguably a better alternative) to the key transport functionality enabled by RSA encryption.

To sign data with elliptic curves, you make use of the ECDSA algorithm. Just as you must choose parameters for RSA (such as e, the public exponent), you must also choose parameters in EC-based operations. The most obvious of these is the underlying curve.

---

[4]The math upon which elliptic-curve cryptography is based is beyond the scope of the book. The goal of this section is simply to make you aware of the algorithms and show you how to use them.

Again, the actual mathematics are not discussed in this book, so we will satisfy ourselves by saying that different elliptic curves can be used in these algorithms.

For ECDSA, the `cryptography` library provides a number of NIST-approved curves. It should be noted that some cryptographers are wary of these curves because it is possible that the US government recommends curves that it knows can be broken. With that said, these are the only curves currently provided by the library. If you use these in production, you should keep an eye out for additional information about security vulnerabilities and potential replacements.

For this test, we will use NIST's P-384 curve, which is referred to as SECP384r1 in the library. From the `cryptography` documentation

```
>>> from cryptography.hazmat.backends import default_backend
>>> from cryptography.hazmat.primitives import hashes
>>> from cryptography.hazmat.primitives.asymmetric import ec
>>> private_key = ec.generate_private_key(
...     ec.SECP384R1(), default_backend()
... )
>>> data = b"this is some data I'd like to sign"
>>> signature = private_key.sign(
...     data,
...     ec.ECDSA(hashes.SHA256())
... )
>>> public_key = private_key.public_key()
>>> public_key.verify(signature, data, ec.ECDSA(hashes.SHA256()))
```

As with RSA signing, you do have to pick a hash function. Again, we have chosen SHA-256. You will notice that, although it might seem daunting to pick a curve function, once that's done, the rest of the operation is very straightforward.

ECDSA also has the same pre-hashed API as RSA for processing large amounts of data.

Certificates: Proving Ownership of Public Keys

In our example with Alice and Bob and public keys, we assumed that every interested party had the public key of every other interested party. In our scenario, this *might* be possible. The HQ could gather all the spies together and have everyone exchange public keys.[5]

This might not be feasible over time, however.

What if Noel, a new spy, enters the field after everyone else? Assume agent Charlie has been captured and Noel has been sent to take his place. Alice and Bob already had Charlie's key, but they don't yet have Noel's key.

Of course, Noel can't just show up and hand out a public key. Otherwise, Eve could send in fake agents handing out public keys claiming to be real EA agents. She can create certificates just as easily as HQ. How can Alice and Bob recognize that Noel is a true EATSA agent and is not working for Eve?

One possibility is to have HQ send Alice and Bob a message with the name and public key of the new agent. Alice and Bob already trust HQ and already have HQ's public key. HQ can act as a *trusted third party* between them and Noel. In the early days of PKI, this was exactly what was proposed to establish trust. This model was called a "registry." A registry would be a central repository of identity-to-public-key mappings. The registry's own public key would be disseminated everywhere: newspapers, magazines, textbooks, physical mailings, and so forth. So long as everyone had a true copy of the registry's key, they could look up the public key of anyone registered within it.

The problem at the time, although it is less of a problem now, was scale. Although contemporary computing envisions the Googles, Amazons, and Microsofts of the world handling billions of connections from all over the world all the time, such was not the case in the 1990s. It was believed that an online registry was simply not scalable.

In the case of our spies, they have to assume they may be cut off from HQ. They may have to go into deep cover, or they may be on the run from Eve, or maybe the EA wants to disavow any of their activities for a time. For any or all of these reasons, they may not be able to get a timely message from HQ. If they're on the run from Eve, it would be great if they could tell whether the spy who meets them at the safe house is on their side.

This brings us to certificates. A public key certificate is just data; it generally includes a public key, the metadata related to ownership of the key, and a signature over all of the

---

[5]An analog of this happens in the real world: PGP signing parties. You might want to look for more information about this using your favorite web search engine.

contents by a known "issuer." The metadata includes information such as the identity of the owner, the identity of the issuer, an expiration date, a serial number, and so forth. The concept is to bind the metadata, especially for identity, to the public key. The identity can be a name, an email address, a URL, or any other agreed-upon identifier.

Instead of simply handing out public keys to their agents, HQ can now hand out *certificates*.[6] First, the agent generates their own key pair (nobody, not even HQ, should ever have the agent's private key). Next, HQ takes the agent's public key and starts creating a certificate by including the identifying information about the agent, such as their code name.[7] To complete the certificate, HQ *signs* it with the HQ private key and becomes the issuer.

To repeat, the public key in the certificate belongs to the agent. The agent keeps their own private key private.[8] As illustrated in Figure 5-3, the signature *on* the certificate was generated by the issuer's private key (in this case, HQ's private key).

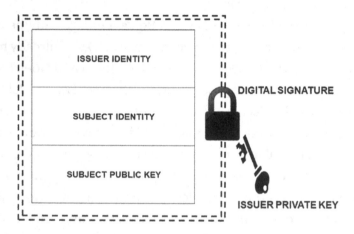

Figure 5-3. *The primary purpose of a certificate is to bind an identity and a public key together. An issuer can sign the certificate data preventing modification and providing trust.*

---

[6]Remember, these *contain* public keys, but are also signed, etc.

[7]Although, remember that certificates are *public*! Don't put information in a certificate that you don't want other people to see. Maybe that's not the right place for a code name?

[8]Apparently, some web servers ask for a "certificate" to be installed but require both a certificate and a private key. This is an unfortunate misuse of words that have clear meanings. Certificates are public and only contain public keys. Private keys are private and are not part of a certificate.

Let's go back to our scenario where Alice is on the run in West Antarctica with Eve's agents hot on her trail. She gets to a safe house and sees an agent she's never met before: Charlie. To prove that he is who he says he is, Charlie presents his certificate. Alice checks that the identity data matches his claim (e.g., that the identity in the certificate is "charlie"). Next, Alice checks that the issuer of the certificate is HQ and then verifies the signature included in the certificate. Remember, the signature in the certificate is signed by the *issuer* (HQ). Using HQ's public key issued to her before she left on the mission, Alice's signature check is successful. Thus, Alice knows that the certificate must have been issued by HQ because nobody else could have generated a valid signature. The certificate is authentic, and Alice now has (and trusts) Charlie's public key for future communications.

Of course, there is one more wrinkle. Charlie's certificate is *public*! There's nothing to stop Eve from having a copy and present it to Alice herself. How does Alice know that the person at the door that claims to be Charlie, with certificate in hand, really is Charlie?

Charlie must now prove his identity by signing some data for Alice. Alice gives him some kind of test message, and Charlie signs it with his private key. Alice verifies the signature on this data using the public key from his certificate. The signature check passes, so Alice knows that Charlie must be the owner of the certificate. Only the owner has (or should have!) the private key associated with the public key necessary to sign data. Of course, if Charlie were captured and his private key compromised, all bets would be off!

In summary, Charlie signs with his private key to prove it is his certificate, but Alice checks the signature in the certificate to ensure that the certificate itself was issued by someone she trusts. Alice's point of view for this process is shown in Figure 5-4.

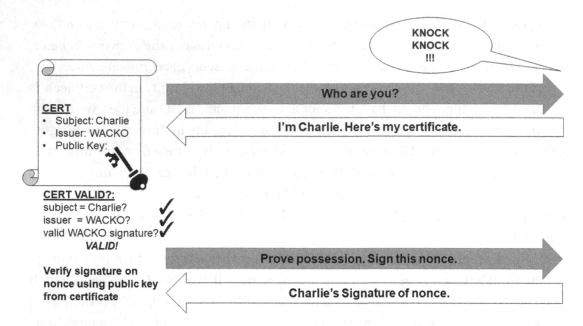

Figure 5-4. *Who's knocking at the door? Alice would like to know before she lets in whoever it is!*

Let's go through some examples to see how this works. For the first exercise, we are not going to use real certificates, at least not yet. For now, we're going to use a simple dictionary as our certificate data structure, and we're going to use the Python json module to convert it to bytes.

Warning: Not for Production Use

My, we do say that "not for production use" thing a lot, don't we? We kind of have to. Cryptography is uniquely and simultaneously subtle and alluring: the concepts are relatively simple to describe, but tiny details can make the difference between good security and no security. Those details are sometimes hard to discover, and proving that they are correct is *hard*.

Don't use *any* of the non-library implementations from this book in production and do not assume that even our use of libraries is an appropriate solution. Don't assume that an example has taught you enough to roll your own crypto, and don't assume that you have mastered the correct use of the libraries. Don't even assume that our list of things that go wrong is complete!

Remember, YANAC (You Are Not A Cryptographer... yet!). We'll be saying this again. It's what we do.

___

The example we're going to work has three parties: the party claiming an identity (Charlie), also known as the *subject*, the party verifying the claim (Alice), and the trusted third party that issued the certificate (HQ). Two of these parties, Charlie and HQ, will need RSA key pairs. You can generate RSA key pairs and save them to disk using the rsa_simple.py script from Chapter 4. For the rest of this exercise, we will assume that HQ's keys are saved in hq_public.key and hq_private.key and Charlie's keys are saved in charlie_public.key and charlie_private.key.

Also, for clarity, we have created three separate scripts for each one of these parties. The first script is used *by the issuer* (HQ) to generate a certificate from an existing public key.

Listing 5-6. Fake Certificate Issuer

```
1   from cryptography.hazmat.backends import default_backend
2   from cryptography.hazmat.primitives.asymmetric import rsa
3   from cryptography.hazmat.primitives.asymmetric import padding
4   from cryptography.hazmat.primitives import hashes
5   from cryptography.hazmat.primitives import serialization
6
7   import sys, json
8
9   ISSUER_NAME = "fake_cert_authority1"
10
11  SUBJECT_KEY = "subject"
12  ISSUER_KEY = "issuer"
13  PUBLICKEY_KEY = "public_key"
14
15  def create_fake_certificate(pem_public_key, subject, issuer_private_key):
16      certificate_data = {}
17      certificate_data[SUBJECT_KEY] = subject
```

```
18        certificate_data[ISSUER_KEY] = ISSUER_NAME
19        certificate_data[PUBLICKEY_KEY] = pem_public_key.decode('utf-8')
20        raw_bytes = json.dumps(certificate_data).encode('utf-8')
21        signature = issuer_private_key.sign(
22            raw_bytes,
23            padding.PSS(
24                mgf=padding.MGF1(hashes.SHA256()),
25                salt_length=padding.PSS.MAX_LENGTH
26            ),
27            hashes.SHA256()
28        )
29        return raw_bytes + signature
30
31    if __name__=="__main__":
32        issuer_private_key_file = sys.argv[1]
33        certificate_subject = sys.argv[2]
34        certificate_subject_public_key_file = sys.argv[3]
35        certificate_output_file = sys.argv[4]
36
37        with open(issuer_private_key_file, "rb") as private_key_file_object:
38            issuer_private_key = serialization.load_pem_private_key(
39                        private_key_file_object.read(),
40                        backend=default_backend(),
41                        password=None)
42
43        with open(certificate_subject_public_key_file, "rb") as public_
    key_file_object:
44            certificate_subject_public_key_bytes = public_key_file_object.
        read()
45
46        certificate_bytes = create_fake_certificate(certificate_subject_
    public_key_bytes,
47                                                    certificate_subject,
48                                                    issuer_private_key)
49
```

```
50        with open(certificate_output_file, "wb") as certificate_file_object:
51            certificate_file_object.write(certificate_bytes)
```

Let's walk through Listing 5-6. There is only one function: `create_fake_certificate`. We are using the name "fake" not to indicate fraud, but rather that this is not a real certificate. Again, please don't ever use this in production.[9]

The function creates a dictionary and loads three fields: a subject name (identity), an issuer name, and a public key. Note that there are (parts of) two key pairs being used in this file. There is an issuer private key and the subject public key. It is the subject's private key that is being stored in the certificate. This public key in many ways *represents* the subject as it will be used to prove his or her identity. That is why it is so important that the certificate be signed.[10] Otherwise, anyone could create a certificate to claim any identity they like.

Once the dictionary is loaded, we use `json` to serialize the dictionary to a string. JSON is a common and standard format, but in Python 3.x, it cannot encode bytes directly and it outputs a text string. For compatibility with the Python `cryptography` library, we load the PEM-encoded keys as binary bytes rather than as text. The public key to be stored in this JSON certificate has to be converted to a string first, but because it is PEM-encoded (i.e., it is already plaintext), we can convert it to UTF-8 safely. Similarly, the entire output of the `json.dumps()` operation is converted to bytes with a safe UTF-8 conversion.

The bytes are then signed using the *issuer's* private key. Only the issuer should have access to this private key because it is the issuer's way of proving to the world that it (the issuer) has created the certificate. Our final certificate is the raw bytes from json concatenated with the bytes from the signature.

In our hypothetical example, Charlie wants to claim the identity "charlie." Charlie starts out by generating a key pair. The public key (*not the private key*) is sent to the HQ certificate-issuing department and a request to make a certificate. The human beings within the issuing department should verify that Charlie has the right to claim the identity "charlie." For example, the officer in charge might ask to see Charlie's agency ID, review paperwork from a superior officer, check fingerprints, and so forth to ensure that the real Charlie will be given the certificate.

---

[9]Told you.
[10]By a trusted authority.

The issuer script takes four parameters: the issuer private key file, the claimed identity that will be put into the certificate, the public key associated with the identity, and an output filename for the certificate. Using the keys you generated for this exercise, run the script as shown in the following:

```
python fake_certs_issuer.py \
  hq_private.key \
  charlie \
  charlie_public.key \
  charlie.cert
```

This will generate a (fake) certificate for Charlie with the claimed identity and associated public key, all signed by HQ.

Now Charlie can prove that he has the identity "charlie" to Alice. He starts by giving her the claimed identity ("charlie") and providing the certificate.

The second script here is for Alice to verify Charlie's claimed identity.

Listing 5-7. Verify Identity in a Fake Certificate

```
1    from cryptography.hazmat.backends import default_backend
2    from cryptography.hazmat.primitives.asymmetric import rsa
3    from cryptography.hazmat.primitives.asymmetric import padding
4    from cryptography.hazmat.primitives import hashes
5    from cryptography.hazmat.primitives import serialization
6
7    import sys, json, os
8
9    ISSUER_NAME = "fake_cert_authority1"
10
11   SUBJECT_KEY = "subject"
12   ISSUER_KEY = "issuer"
13   PUBLICKEY_KEY = "public_key"
14
15   def validate_certificate(certificate_bytes, issuer_public_key):
16       raw_cert_bytes, signature = certificate_bytes[:-256], certificate_
         bytes [-256:]
17
```

```
18        issuer_public_key.verify(
19            signature,
20            raw_cert_bytes,
21            padding.PSS(
22                mgf=padding.MGF1(hashes.SHA256()),
23                salt_length=padding.PSS.MAX_LENGTH
24            ),
25            hashes.SHA256())
26        cert_data = json.loads(raw_cert_bytes.decode('utf-8'))
27        cert_data[PUBLICKEY_KEY] = cert_data[PUBLICKEY_KEY].encode('utf-8')
28        return cert_data
29
30    def verify_identity(identity, certificate_data, challenge, response):
31        if certificate_data[ISSUER_KEY] != ISSUER_NAME:
32            raise Exception("Invalid (untrusted) Issuer!")
33
34        if certificate_data[SUBJECT_KEY] != identity:
35            raise Exception("Claimed identity does not match")
36
37        certificate_public_key = serialization.load_pem_public_key(
38            certificate_data[PUBLICKEY_KEY],
39            backend=default_backend())
40
41        certificate_public_key.verify(
42            response,
43            challenge,
44            padding.PSS(
45                mgf=padding.MGF1(hashes.SHA256()),
46                salt_length=padding.PSS.MAX_LENGTH
47            ),
48            hashes.SHA256())
49
50    if __name__ == "__main__":
51        claimed_identity = sys.argv[1]
52        cert_file = sys.argv[2]
```

```
53          issuer_public_key_file = sys.argv[3]
54
55      with open(issuer_public_key_file, "rb") as public_key_file_object:
56          issuer_public_key = serialization.load_pem_public_key(
57                          public_key_file_object.read(),
58                          backend=default_backend())
59
60      with open(cert_file, "rb") as cert_file_object:
61          certificate_bytes = cert_file_object.read()
62
63      cert_data = validate_certificate(certificate_bytes, issuer_public_key)
64
65      print("Certificate has a valid signature from {}".format(ISSUER_NAME))
66
67      challenge_file = input("Enter a name for a challenge file: ")
68      print("Generating challenge to file {}".format(challenge_file))
69
70      challenge_bytes = os.urandom(32)
71      with open(challenge_file, "wb+") as challenge_file_object:
72          challenge_file_object.write(challenge_bytes)
73
74      response_file = input("Enter the name of the response file: ")
75
76      with open (response_file, "rb") as response_object:
77          response_bytes = response_object.read()
78
79      verify_identity(
80          claimed_identity,
81          cert_data,
82          challenge_bytes,
83          response_bytes)
84      print("Identity validated")
```

Listing 5-7 requires three arguments: the claimed identity of the party, the certificate presented, and the issuer's public key.

The verification of the claimed identity has to run in two parts. First, it loads the certificate to see if it is signed by HQ's public key. This is performed by the `verify_certificate` function. Remember that the signature verification function raises an exception if the signature check fails. You will notice that to get the signature, the script just takes the last 256 bytes of the certificate. Because the signature is concatenated at the end, and because we always use an RSA signature from a 2048-bit key, the signature is always 256 bytes.

If the signature verifies, we take the other bytes and load them into a dictionary using the `json` module (again converting bytes to string for the JSON operation and then from string to bytes for the public key data).

Alice runs the script:

```
python fake_certs_verify_identity.py \
  charlie \
  charlie.cert \
  hq_public.key
```

At this point Alice's script has given her some information, but it is waiting for more input. What does Alice know right now, at this phase of the process? She knows that she has been presented with a true certificate that was actually signed by HQ. What happens next? She doesn't yet know if the party presenting the certificate is really Charlie. To do that, she needs to test him or her to see if they have the private key.

She generates a random message and saves it to the file `charlie.challenge`, which she will ask the person claiming to be Charlie to sign with his private key. The script is waiting for that random message, so Alice provides the name of the file she just created, `charlie.challenge`.

Although Alice isn't finished, we now need to switch over to Charlie's operations. Leave Alice's script running until we get back. Charlie will use another script, and his private key, to answer Alice's challenge.

Listing 5-8. Prove Identity on a Fake Certificate

```
1   from cryptography.hazmat.backends import default_backend
2   from cryptography.hazmat.primitives.asymmetric import rsa
3   from cryptography.hazmat.primitives.asymmetric import padding
4   from cryptography.hazmat.primitives import hashes
5   from cryptography.hazmat.primitives import serialization
```

```
6
7   import sys
8
9   def prove_identity(private_key, challenge):
10      signature = private_key.sign(
11          challenge,
12          padding.PSS(
13              mgf = padding.MGF1(hashes.SHA256()),
14              salt_length = padding.PSS.MAX_LENGTH
15          ),
16          hashes.SHA256()
17      )
18      return signature
19
20  if __name__ == "__main__":
21      private_key_file = sys.argv[1]
22      challenge_file = sys.argv[2]
23      response_file = sys.argv[3]
24
25      with open(private_key_file, "rb") as private_key_file_object:
26          private_key = serialization.load_pem_private_key(
27                          private_key_file_object.read(),
28                          backend=default_backend(),
29                          password=None)
30
31      with open(challenge_file, "rb") as challenge_file_object:
32          challenge_bytes = challenge_file_object.read()
33
34      signed_challenge_bytes = prove_identity(
35          private_key,
36          challenge_bytes)
37
38      with open(response_file, "wb") as response_object:
39          response_object.write(signed_challenge_bytes)
```

Charlie's script in Listing 5-8 is straightforward. It takes in three arguments: the certificate subject's private key, the challenge filename, and the response filename that will be used to store the response. The response is generated simply by taking the challenge bytes and signing them with the private key. Run this script (in a separate terminal from Alice's) as shown:

```
python fake_certs_prove_identity.py \
  charlie_private.key \
  charlie.challenge \
  charlie.response
```

Charlie has thus answered Alice's challenge and put the response into the file `charlie.response`. Now we can finally finish Alice's script, which is waiting for the response filename. Enter the filename generated by Charlie (`charlie.response`) to proceed.

Alice's script loads the response and verifies it. To do this, Alice's script now moves to the `verify_identity` function. It starts by checking that the name in the certificate matches the identity claimed (e.g., "charlie") and that the issuer is HQ. Next, it loads the public key from the certificate and verifies that the signature on the challenge bytes is valid.

This proves to Alice that not only is the certificate Charlie presented valid, but Charlie is the subject (owner). The person claiming to be Charlie must have the associated private key or he would not have been able to answer her challenge.

EXERCISE 5.10. DETECT FAKE CHARLIES

Experiment with the preceding scripts to check out the various errors from trying to deceive Alice. Create a false issuer and sign the certificate with this private key. Have someone with the wrong private key present Charlie's certificate. Make sure to understand all the different checks being performed in the code.

Although our certificates are "fake," they are designed to teach the basic principles behind the certificate concept. Real certificates typically use a format called X.509. We will discuss X.509 in detail in Chapter 8.

Certificates and Trust

One question you might have asked yourself is, why did we name the issuer? After all, if Alice, Bob, and all the other agents are always going to trust HQ, why require the issuer to be named in the certificate?

In our hypothetical world in which Antarctica is locked in its civil cold war, there may be many issuers of certificates. For example, other agencies besides the espionage unit may want to issue certificates. What if the EA military starts to issue certificates? What if the EA Department of Education starts to issue certificates? Should Alice and Bob trust those as well? Maybe they will want to trust military certificates but not education certificates?

In certificate parlance, we also call an issuer a "certificate authority" (CA), and certificate validators have to decide which certificate authorities they will trust. In fact, CAs also have their own certificates with their identity name and their public key. Thus, the *Issuer* field of a certificate should be the same identity as the *Subject* in the CA's certificate.

If the CA has a certificate, who signs *that*? There is a concept called an "intermediate" CA. An intermediate CA has its certificate signed by a "higher" CA. In the EA government, perhaps, there might be a top-level CA that signs all other CAs for defense, education, espionage, and so forth. This creates a hierarchical chain of certificates with the highest certificate called a "root" certificate.

Who signs this ultimate root CA?

The answer is: itself. This CA's certificate is known as a *self-signed* certificate. Note that anyone can generate a self-signed certificate, so great care must be taken in deciding which self-signed, root certificates to trust. Basically, they become axiomatically trusted *along with all of the certificates that they sign*!

While this can be a little complicated to visualize, it does make things a little bit easier to manage. The entire EA government could have a single top-level CA. All employees, agents, or even citizens need only have the very top-most, root CA certificate. All other identities can be verified in a chain. For example, Charlie might keep three certificates: his personal certificate, the intermediate certificate for the espionage CA that signed his certificate, and the root EA certificate itself. Charlie can present these three certs to any other EA employee and have him or her verify the chain back to the root.

Things become slightly more complicated (and introduce potential security risks) when there are multiple roots. For example, perhaps the EA government doesn't have a single, top-level root. After all, do you really want your espionage orders to be signed by a CA that can be traced back to the government? Suppose then that the EA government keeps two roots: one for departments and organizations that operate "visibly" and one for groups and individuals that operate covertly.

Should Charlie and the other agents trust both roots?

EXERCISE 5.11. THE CHAINS WE FORGED IN LIFE

Modify the identity validation programs to support a chain of trust. First, create some self-signed certificates for the EA government (at least two as described previously). The existing issuer script can already do this. Just make the issuer private key for the self-signed certificate to be the organization's own private key. Thus, the organization is signing its own cert, and the private key used to sign the certificate matches the public key *in* the certificate.

Next, create certificates for intermediate CAs such as "Department of Education," "Department of Defense," "Espionage Agency," and so forth. These certificates should be signed by the self-signed certificates in the previous step.

Finally, sign certificates for Alice, Bob, and Charlie by the espionage CA. Perhaps create some certificates for employees of the defense department and the education department. These certificates should be signed by the appropriate intermediate CA.

Now modify the verification program to take a chain of certificates instead of just a single certificate. Get rid of the command-line parameter for the issuer's public key and instead hard-code which of the root certificate filenames are trusted. To specify the chain of certificates, have the program take the claimed identity as the first input (as it already does) and then an arbitrary number of certificates to follow. Each certificate's issuer field should indicate the next certificate in the chain. For example, to validate Charlie, there may be three certificates: `charlie.cert`, `espionage.cert`, `covert_root.cert`. The issuer of `charlie.cert` should have the same subject name as `espionage.cert` and so forth. The verify program should only accept an identity if the last certificate in the chain is already trusted.

Certificates are very important to modern cryptography and computer security. In Chapter 8, we will introduce real X.509 certificates and discuss how real CAs operate and additional issues and solutions as part of learning about TLS.

Revocation and Private Key Protection

Certificates and the public keys they contain are very powerful. At the same time, they come with a very dangerous Achilles heel. How do you disable them if the associated private key is compromised?

What we are talking about here is a concept called "revocation." To revoke a certificate is to reverse the endorsement of the issuer. HQ might have issued a certificate to Charlie, but if Charlie is captured and his private key lost, HQ needs to figure out a way to tell all of the other agents not to trust that certificate anymore.

Unfortunately, this is not easily done. If you recall, one of the reasons why CAs came into existence instead of online registries was the desire for offline verification. How can an offline verification process provide real-time revocation data?

The simple answer is, "It can't." There are only two options. Either the verification process must have a real-time component or the revocation cannot be updated in real time. Both options are available for certificates today in the form of the Online Certificate Status Protocol (OCSP), which checks a certificate's status on the fly, and Certificate Revocation Lists (CRLs), which are lists published from time to time with revoked certs. We will review both of these in more detail in Chapter 8.

Because of the difficulty of revoking a certificate, private keys **must** be protected with the utmost care. When real-time signing is not needed, private keys should be kept offline and in a secure environment. If they must be used in real time, and must be stored on a server, certificates should be stored with the minimum permissions necessary and readable on a strictly need-to-know basis. For end-user keys, such as those used for email and other applications, private keys stored on disk should be adequately protected by symmetric encryption with a strong password. Ideally, avoid storing private keys on desktops and servers altogether (especially in the modern era of continuous backups) and, instead, store private keys in a hardware security module.

It might not be a bad idea to keep certificates with a relatively short expiration date and rotate them as necessary.

Replay Attacks

There is one last security issue to address before moving on from message integrity. It applies equally to both MACs and signatures. The issue is *replay attacks*.

A replay attack occurs when a legitimate message from a previous communication is used by an attacker at a later time when it should no longer be valid.

Let's consider the following message: "We attack at dawn!"

We can secure this message from modification and authenticate the sender with either MACs or signatures. But what would prevent Eve from intercepting that message and sending it on *a different day*? Perhaps she would choose to send it on a day when the EA is *not* planning an attack? Eve may not be able to change the message contents; perhaps she cannot even read them, but that does not stop her from resending (replaying) the message whenever she wants.

For this reason, almost all cryptographically secured messages typically need some kind of unique component that distinguishes them from all other messages. This piece of data is often referred to as a *nonce*. In many circumstances a nonce can be a random number. If you take a quick peek back at Chapter 3, you will see that the IV value passed to AES counter mode was called a nonce. Nonces, especially random number nonces, are also used to keep messages from being the same when doing so would introduce security vulnerabilities.

However, to prevent replay attacks, simply using a random number won't do. In order to detect a replay, the receiver must *keep track* of the nonces that have been used and reject them when seen a second time.

This can be terribly problematic. How big of a list of nonces should be kept? A hundred? A thousand? Do you remove a nonce from the list after a certain period of time? If you do and the attacker knows it, the attacker can now use it in a replay. For example, if the attacker knows you only keep track of nonces received in the last 5 minutes, the attacker can replay something from 6 minutes ago with a reasonable amount of success.

Some systems use timestamps instead of random nonces. Using a timestamp, a receiver can reject data that is too old. The problem with this approach is that all of the computers have to have synchronized clocks for it to work reliably. Plus, data with an "old" timestamp must be accepted within some window. After all, the message won't arrive instantaneously. How large a window do you permit? However big it is, the bad guy will figure out a way to use it against you.

It's possible to combine both approaches together. You can send data with a timestamp *and* a random number. The timestamp is used to get rid of data that is *really* old and the nonce is used to prevent replays within the time window permitted. This means that the clocks only need to be relatively close (perhaps even within 24 hours) and that the list of nonces to be stored is bounded.

You have now seen *two* pieces of metadata that you need to consider sending in a message: the nonce and/or timestamp to prevent replays and the sender/receiver names. In general, you should put all relevant context into the message so that it cannot be used outside of that context.

EXERCISE 5.12. REPLAY IT AGAIN SAM!

Use either MAC or signatures to send a message from Alice to Bob or vice versa. Include a nonce in the message to prevent replays using all three mechanisms described in this section. Send some replays from Eve and try to get around Alice and Bob's defenses.

Summarize-Then-MAC

Another chapter, another firehose of information! In this chapter we covered message authentication codes, which are keyed codes computed over a series of data. Without the key, it is impossible to change the data undetectably. Moreover, when two parties share a MAC key, they can be sure that (unless the shared key has been compromised) if one of them received a correctly MACed message, it came from the other party.

Using asymmetric operations, one can use a private key to create a signature over a piece of data (typically over the hash of the data). Unlike MAC operations, which can only ensure correctness and authenticity to those individuals sharing the key, a widely distributed public key can be used theoretically by anyone (that trusts it) to validate the signature over the data.

And we also provided a quick overview of basic certificate operations.

And now that our summary is complete, here is the HMAC-SHA256 (in hex) over the preceding three paragraphs (i.e., from "Another chapter..." through "... certificate operations.") using our twice-cited XKCD password:

c4d60c7336911cd0a23132f11ae1ca8ba392a05ae357c81bc995876693886b9e

Now you have a way of telling if any corrections or changes were made to this summary by our editors after we submitted it to them!

CHAPTER 6

Combining Asymmetric and Symmetric Algorithms

In this chapter, we'll spend time getting familiar with how asymmetric encryption is typically used, where it is a critical *part* of communication privacy, but not responsible for *all* of it. Typically, asymmetric encryption, also known as "public key cryptography", is used to establish a trusted *session* between two parties, and the communication while within that session is protected with much faster symmetric methods.

Let's dive in with a short example and some code!

Exchange AES Keys with RSA

Armed with their newer cryptography technologies, Alice and Bob have become more brazen in their covert operations. Alice has managed to infiltrate the Snow Den Records Center in West Antarctica and is attempting to steal a document related to genetic experiments to turn penguins completely white, thus creating a perfectly camouflaged Antarctic soldier. WA soldiers are quickly moving on her position, and she decides to risk transmitting the document over a short-wave radio to Bob who is monitoring from outside the building. Eve is certainly listening and Alice does not want her to know which document has been stolen.

The document is nearly ten megabytes. RSA encryption of the entire document will take *forever*. Fortunately, she and Bob agreed beforehand to use RSA encryption to send AES session keys and then transmit the document using AES-CTR with HMAC. Let's create the code they will use to make this alphabet soup work.

© Seth James Nielson, Christopher K. Monson 2019
S. J. Nielson and C. K. Monson, *Practical Cryptography in Python*,
https://doi.org/10.1007/978-1-4842-4900-0_6

First, let's assume that Alice and Bob already have each other's certificates and public keys. Bob cannot risk giving away his position by transmitting; he will be limited to monitoring the channel, and Alice will just have to hope that the message is received. The agreed-upon transmission protocol is to transmit a single stream of bytes with all data concatenated together. The transmission stream includes

- An AES encryption key, IV, and a MAC key encrypted under Bob's public key

- Alice's signature over the hash of the AES key, IV, and MAC key

- The stolen document bytes, encrypted under the encryption key

- An HMAC over the entire transmission under the MAC key

As we have done before, let's create a class to manage this transmission process. The code snippet in Listing 6-1 shows key pieces of the operations.

Listing 6-1. RSA Key Exchange

```
1    import os
2    from cryptography.hazmat.primitives.ciphers import Cipher, algorithms,
     modes
3    from cryptography.hazmat.primitives import hashes, hmac
4    from cryptography.hazmat.backends import default_backend
5    from cryptography.hazmat.primitives.asymmetric import padding, rsa
6
7    # WARNING: This code is NOT secure. DO NOT USE!
8    class TransmissionManager:
9        def __init__(self, send_private_key, recv_public_key):
10           self.send_private_key = send_private_key
11           self.recv_public_key = recv_public_key
12           self.ekey = os.urandom(32)
13           self.mkey = os.urandom(32)
14           self.iv = os.urandom(16)
15
16           self.encryptor = Cipher(
17                   algorithms.AES(self.ekey),
18                   modes.CTR(self.iv),
```

```
19                backend=default_backend()).encryptor()
20          self.mac = hmac.HMAC(
21              self.mkey,
22              hashes.SHA256(),
23              backend=default_backend())
24
25      def initialize(self):
26          data = self.ekey + self.iv + self.mkey
27          h = hashes.Hash(hashes.SHA256(), backend=default_backend())
28          h.update(data)
29          data_digest = h.finalize()
30          signature = self.send_private_key.sign(
31              data_digest,
32              padding.PSS(
33                  mgf=padding.MGF1(hashes.SHA256()),
34                  salt_length=padding.PSS.MAX_LENGTH),
35              hashes.SHA256())
36          ciphertext = self.recv_public_key.encrypt(
37              data,
38              padding.OAEP(
39                  mgf=padding.MGF1(algorithm=hashes.SHA256()),
40                  algorithm=hashes.SHA256(),
41                  label=None)) # rarely used.Just leave it 'None'
42          ciphertext = data+signature
43          self.mac.update(ciphertext)
44          return ciphertext
45
46      def update(self, plaintext):
47          ciphertext = self.encryptor.update(plaintext)
48          self.mac.update(ciphertext)
49          return ciphertext
50
51      def finalize(self):
52          return self.mac.finalize()
```

Hopefully, all of the pieces here are familiar, and if you follow the code paths, it should also be pretty easy to see how things come together. Perhaps you've noticed that we are drawing on concepts from Chapter 3, Chapter 4, and Chapter 5! All of these pieces are coming together to shape a more advanced whole.

A few points are worth noting. First, we chose to use AES-CTR, so there is no need for padding. Earlier in the book, we used the term "nonce" to describe the initialization value to the algorithm, as this is what the `cryptography` library calls it. In other literature it is still called an IV, however, so we use that term here. Either way, the IV (or nonce) is the starting value for the counter.

Note that we are not using Sign-Then-Encrypt as we discussed in Chapter 5. As always, this is an example program not meant to be used for real security. You might want to review the issues we discussed in relation to Sign-Then-Encrypt to see how Eve could strip out the signature, change the keys, and re-sign.

Nevertheless, that's not the major vulnerability we will discuss. After all, in our scenario, Bob is probably only going to accept data from Alice. The issues of swapping out a signature are more applicable when more than one signature can be accepted.

Like most of the APIs you've seen so far, we use `update` and `finalize`, but we added a new method called `initialize`. For transmission, Alice would call `initialize` first to get the signed and encrypted header with the session keys. Next, she would call `update` as many times as needed to feed the entire document through. When everything is finished, she would call `finalize` to get the HMAC trailer over all of the transmitted contents.

EXERCISE 6.1. BOB'S RECEIVER

Implement the reverse of this transmitter by creating a `ReceiverManager`. The exact API might vary a little, but you will probably need at least an `update` and `finalize` method. You will need to unpack the keys and IV using Bob's private key and verify the signature using Alice's public key. Then, you will decrypt data until it's exhausted, finally verifying the HMAC over all received data.

Remember, the last bytes of the transmission are the HMAC trailer and are not data to be decrypted by AES. But when `update` is called, you may not yet know whether these are the last bytes or not! Think through it carefully!

Asymmetric and Symmetric: Like Chocolate and Peanut Butter

Hopefully, Alice's transmission to Bob in the exercise at the beginning of this chapter gave you a small taste for how asymmetric and symmetric cryptography work together. The protocol we outlined in code works, but lacks some important subtlety, as is often the case with our first attempts. As you might expect by now, the preceding code is *not secure* and we will demonstrate at least one problem with it shortly. It does illustrate the ideas behind putting the two systems together, though.

Let's see what we can learn from what we have. We'll start with session keys.

We first introduced the term *session key* in Chapter 4 but did not discuss it much. A session key is by nature a temporary thing; it is used for a single communication session and then discarded permanently, never to be reused. In the preceding code, notice that the AES and MAC keys are generated at the beginning of a session by the communications manager. Every time a new communications manager is created, a new set of keys is created. The keys are not stored or recorded anywhere. Once all the data is encrypted, they are thrown away.[1]

On the receiving end, the session keys are decrypted using the recipient's private key. Once these keys are decrypted, they are then used to decrypt the rest of the data and process the MAC. Again, after the transmitted data is processed, the keys can—and should—be destroyed.

Symmetric keys make good session keys for multiple reasons. First of all, symmetric keys are easy to create; in our example, we simply generated random bytes. We could also *derive* symmetric keys from a base secret by using key derivation functions. This is a common approach, and we will see later that you almost always need to derive *multiple* keys for typical secure communication. Regardless of how they are created, symmetric keys (and IVs) are plain old ordinary bytes, unlike most asymmetric keys that require some additional structure (e.g., public exponents, chosen elliptic curves, etc.).

Second, symmetric keys are good session keys because symmetric algorithms are *fast*. We have already mentioned this a time or two, but it is worth repeating. AES is typically on the order of hundreds of times faster than RSA, so the more data that can be

---

[1]Well, they *should* be thrown away. In real applications, this might mean securely overwriting memory with zeros and ensuring that all copies are accounted for. It's not paranoia when they are actually out to get you.

encrypted by AES, the better. This is another reason that symmetric keys are sometimes called "bulk data transfer" keys.

Finally, let's also recognize that symmetric keys are good session keys because they are *not* always good long-term keys! Remember, symmetric keys cannot be *private* keys because they must always be shared between at least two parties. The longer a shared key is in use, the higher the risk that trust breaks down between the parties and the key should no longer be shared. In the case of Alice's break-in to the Snow Den archive, she risks capture and the compromise of any keys she has with her. The loss of her asymmetric private key is serious, as we discussed when we talked about certificate revocation, but if Alice and Bob were using the same shared symmetric key for all of their communications, the loss of that key would be even worse as any intercepted communications between them that were encrypted using that key could now be decrypted.

On the other hand, asymmetric keys are very useful for long-term identification. Using certificates, asymmetric keys can establish a sort of proof of identity; once this is done, the shorter-term keys do the work of actually transmitting data between the authenticated parties. That said, sometimes *ephemeral* (quickly discarded) asymmetric keys are incredibly valuable. We will see this both with key exchanges that have the "forward secrecy" attribute and with how ransomware attackers lock up their victims' files.

Measuring RSA's Relative Performance

Even though we've hammered home just how much slower RSA is than AES, let's have some fun and run a few experiments. We're going to write a tester that will generate random test vectors for encryption and decryption. Then we can compare the performance of RSA and AES for ourselves.

For this walk-through, we are going to create a more complex file from smaller bits. Listing 6-2 shows the imports for the overall script. You can start with this as a skeleton and build/copy the other pieces in.

Listing 6-2. Imports for Encryption Speed Test

```
1   # Partial Listing: Some Assembly Required
2
3   # Encrypt ion Speed Test Component
4   from cryptography.hazmat.backends import default_backend
5   from cryptography.hazmat.primitives.asymmetric import rsa
```

```
6    from cryptography.hazmat.primitives import serialization
7    from cryptography.hazmat.primitives import hashes
8    from cryptography.hazmat.primitives.asymmetric import padding
9    from cryptography.hazmat.primitives.ciphers import Cipher, algorithms,
     modes
10   import time, os
```

Let's start by creating some algorithms to test. We will define one class for each algorithm, and the instances of the class will build encryption and decryption objects. Builders will be self-contained, providing all keys and necessary configuration. Each will have a name attribute with a human-readable label and a get_cipher_pair() method to create a new encryptor and decryptor. This method must generate new encryption and decryption objects each time it is called.

AES is very straightforward because the cryptography library already provides most of the machinery, as shown in Listing 6-3.

Listing 6-3. AES Library Use

```
1    # Partial Listing: Some Assembly Required
2
3    # Encryption Speed Test Component
4    class AESCTRAlgorithm:
5        def __init__(self):
6            self.name = "AES-CTR"
7
8        def get_cipher_pair(self):
9            key = os.urandom(32)
10           nonce = os.urandom(16)
11           aes_context = Cipher(
12               algorithms.AES(key),
13               modes.CTR(nonce),
14               backend=default_backend())
15           return aes_context.encryptor(), aes_context.decryptor()
```

The get_cipher_pair() operation creates new keys and nonces each time it is invoked. We could put this in the constructor because we don't really care if we reuse keys for these speed tests, but the re-generation of a few bytes for a key and a nonce is probably not really a limiting factor for speed.

RSA encryption is a little more complicated. It really wasn't meant to encrypt arbitrary amounts of data. Unlike AES, which has counter and CBC modes to tie blocks together, RSA must encrypt its data all at once, and the size of data it can manipulate is limited by various factors. An RSA key with a 2048-bit modulus cannot encrypt more than 256 bytes at a time. In fact, once you add in the OAEP (with SHA-256 hash) padding, it's significantly less: only 190 bytes![2]

If we were actually concerned about the security of the encryption, we could thus not use RSA for more than 190 bytes of data. However, what we are really testing here is a *hypothetical* RSA encryptor that does not exist in the real world. What we want to explore is this: *if* RSA could encrypt arbitrary amounts of data, how long would it take? For this test, we will encrypt each chunk of 190 bytes one at a time and concatenate the results together. Note that when we encrypt with the OAEP padding, the 190 bytes of plaintext becomes 256 bytes of ciphertext. When we are decrypting, we need to decrypt 256-byte chunks.

Although a truly secure RSA encryption algorithm would have to bind the bytes of the different individual encryption operations together, this version is the *fastest* it could ever be, so it gives us an upper bound on speed, making for an interesting comparison.

With this in mind, we can construct our RSA encryption and decryption algorithm like Listing 6-4.

Listing 6-4. RSA Implementation

```
1    # Partial Listing: Some Assembly Required
2
3    # Encryption Speed Test Component
4    class RSAEncryptor:
5        def __init__(self, public_key, max_encrypt_size):
6            self._public_key = public_key
7            self._max_encrypt_size = max_encrypt_size
8
9        def update(self, plaintext):
```

---

[2]Don't confuse bytes and bits here! Even an AES-256 key is 256 *bits*, or just 32 bytes. So RSA can safely hold even a "large" AES key.

```
10          ciphertext = b""
11          for offset in range(0, len(plaintext), self._max_encrypt_size):
12              ciphertext += self._public_key.encrypt(
13                  plaintext[offset:offset+self._max_encrypt_size],
14                  padding.OAEP(
15                      mgf=padding.MGF1(algorithm=hashes.SHA256()),
16                      algorithm=hashes.SHA256(),
17                      label=None))
18          return ciphertext
19
20      def finalize(self):
21          return b""
22
23  class RSADecryptor:
24      def __init__(self, private_key, max_decrypt_size):
25          self._private_key = private_key
26          self._max_decrypt_size = max_decrypt_size
27
28      def update(self, ciphertext):
29          plaintext = b""
30          for offset in range(0, len(ciphertext), self._max_decrypt_size):
31              plaintext += self._private_key.decrypt(
32                  ciphertext[offset:offset+self._max_decrypt_size],
33                  padding.OAEP(
34                      mgf=padding.MGF1(algorithm=hashes.SHA256()),
35                      algorithm=hashes.SHA256(),
36                      label=None))
37          return plaintext
38
39      def finalize(self):
40          return b""
41
42  class RSAAlgorithm:
43      def __init__(self):
44          self.name = "RSA Encryption"
```

```
45
46    def get_cipher_pair(self):
47        rsa_private_key = rsa.generate_private_key(
48          public_exponent=65537,
49          key_size=2048,
50          backend=default_backend())
51        max_plaintext_size = 190 # largest for 2048 key and OAEP
52        max_ciphertext_size = 256
53        rsa_public_key = rsa_private_key.public_key()
54        return (RSAEncryptor(rsa_public_key, max_plaintext_size),
55                RSADecryptor(rsa_private_key, max_ciphertext_size))
```

Note that we created our encryptor and decryptor to have the same API as the AES encryptor and decryptor. Namely, we provide update and finalize methods. The finalize methods don't do anything as RSA encryption (with padding) processes each chunk exactly the same way. The chunk-by-chunk encryption takes each 190-byte piece of the input, encrypts it to the 256-byte ciphertext, and returns the concatenation of all of these pieces. The decryptor reverses the processes, taking each 256-byte chunk in for decryption. Our RSAAlgorithm class constructs the appropriate encryptor and decryptor using these classes.

Now that we have a couple of algorithms to test, we need to create a mechanism for generating plaintext and keeping track of the encryption and decryption times. To this end, we created a class in Listing 6-5 that generates plaintexts randomly and receives notification of each individual ciphertext chunk produced. When the test calls for ciphertexts for the subsequent decryption test stage, it replays those ciphertext chunks exactly how it received them. Based on the notification of encrypted ciphertexts and decrypted plaintexts, it can also keep track of how long the overall operation takes.

Listing 6-5. Random Text Generation

```
1    # Partial Listing: Some Assembly Required
2
3    # Encryption Speed Test Component
4    class random_data_generator:
5        def __init__(self, max_size, chunk_size):
6            self._max_size = max_size
7            self._chunk_size = chunk_size
```

```
8
9              # plaintexts will be generated,
10             # ciphertexts recorded
11             self._ciphertexts = []
12
13             self._encryption_times = [0, 0]
14             self._decryption_times = [0,0]
15
16         def plaintexts(self):
17             self._encryption_times[0] = time.time()
18             for i in range(0, self._max_size, self._chunk_size):
19                 yield os.urandom(self._chunk_size)
20
21         def ciphertexts(self):
22             self._decryption_times[0] = time.time()
23             for ciphertext in self._ciphertexts:
24                 yield ciphertext
25
26         def record_ciphertext(self, c):
27             self._ciphertexts.append(c)
28             self._encryption_times [1] = time.time()
29
30         def record_recovertext(self, r):
31             # don't store, just record time
32             self._decryption_times[1] = time.time()
33
34         def encryption_time(self):
35             return self._encryption_times [1] - self._encryption_times [0]
36
37         def decryption_time(self):
38             return self._decryption_times [1] - self._decryption_times [0]
```

Notice that a new random_data_generator contains timing and data specific to each individual test run. So a new object needs to be created for each test.

Now, armed with an algorithm and a data generator, we can, as in Listing 6-6, write a fairly generic test function.

Listing 6-6. Encryption Tester

```
1    # Partial Listing: Some Assembly Required
2
3    # Encryption Speed Test Component
4    def test_encryption(algorithm, test_data):
5        encryptor, decryptor = algorithm.get_cipher_pair()
6
7        # run encryption tests
8        # might be slower than decryption because generates data
9        for plaintext in test_data.plaintexts():
10           ciphertext = encryptor.update(plaintext)
11           test_data.record_ciphertext(ciphertext)
12       last_ciphertext = encryptor.finalize()
13       test_data.record_ciphertext(last_ciphertext)
14
15       # run decryption tests
16       # decrypt the data already encrypted
17       for ciphertext in test_data.ciphertexts():
18           recovertext = decryptor.update(ciphertext)
19           test_data.record_recovertext(recovertext)
20       last_recovertext = decryptor.finalize()
21       test_data.record_recovertext(last_recovertext)
```

Using these building blocks, we can test these encryption algorithms over various chunk sizes to see if speed increases or decreases based on the amount of data they're handling. For example, Listing 6-7 is a test of AES-CTR and RSA on 100MB of data with chunk sizes ranging from 1 KiB to 1 MiB.

Listing 6-7. Algorithm Tester

```
1    # Encryption Speed Test Component
2    test_algorithms = [RSAAlgorithm(), AESCTRAlgorithm()]
3
4    data_size = 100 * 1024 * 1024 # 100 MiB
5    chunk_sizes = [1*1024, 4*1024, 16*1024, 1024*1024]
6    stats = { algorithm.name : {} for algorithm in test_algorithms }
```

```
7    for chunk_size in chunk_sizes:
8        for algorithm in test_algorithms:
9            test_data = random_data_generator(data_size, chunk_size)
10           test_encryption(algorithm, test_data)
11           stats[algorithm.name][chunk_size] = (
12               test_data.encryption_time(),
13               test_data.decryption_time())
```

The stats dictionary is used for holding encryption and decryption times for the various algorithms in the various tests. These can be used to generate some fun graphs. For example, Figure 6-1 and Figure 6-2 are the encryption and decryption graphs for the tests we ran.

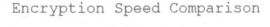

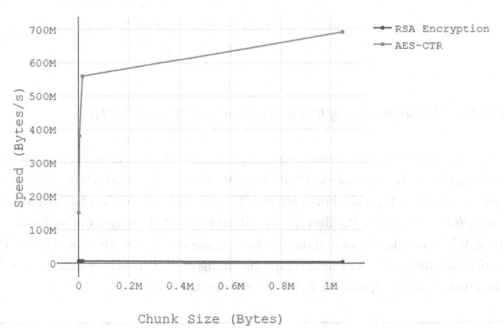

Figure 6-1. *A Comparison of RSA encryption speeds vs. AES-CTR*

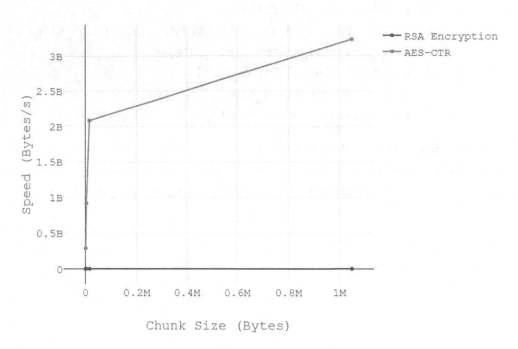

Figure 6-2. *A Comparison of RSA decryption speeds vs. AES-CTR*

As you can see, RSA operations are so much slower, it's not even really a comparison. By the way, if you run the tests we did, RSA encryption over 100 MiB can be slow (about 20 seconds on our computer), but decryption is so bad, it's just off the charts (about *400 seconds* for our tests!). RSA decryption is slower than RSA encryption, so this isn't a surprise. When you have tests that run this long, make sure to save the statistics in raw, numerical format and then generate graphs from this data. That way you can regenerate graphs quickly and easily without running the entire test again.

EXERCISE 6.2. RSA RACING!

Use your preceding tester to compare the performance of RSA with a 1024-bit modulus, a 2048-bit modulus, and a 4096-bit modulus. Please note, you will need to change your chunk size to 62 bytes for 1024-bit RSA keys with OAEP (and SHA-256 hashing) and 446 bytes for 4096-bit RSA keys with OAEP (and SHA-256 hashing).

EXERCISE 6.3. COUNTERS VS. CHAINS!

Use your tester to compare the performance of AES-CTR against AES-CBC.

EXERCISE 6.4. MACS VS. SIGNATURES

Modify your algorithms to sign or apply a MAC to the data in the `finalize` methods. Try disabling encryption (just have the update methods return the unmodified plaintext) so that you can compare only the speed of the MAC and signature. Is the difference as extreme? Can you think why this is so?

EXERCISE 6.5. ECDSA VS. RSA SIGNING

In addition to testing the speed of MAC vs. RSA signing, also compare the speed of RSA signing with ECDSA signing. It's hard to get a fair comparison because it isn't always obvious what your key size is with ECDSA, but look at the list of supported curves in the `cryptography` library documentation and try them out to see which ones are faster in general, as well as how they compare to RSA signing using different modulus sizes.

Hopefully, these timed tests have helped to reinforce why, security reasons aside, symmetric ciphers are preferred over asymmetric ciphers for bulk data transfer.

Diffie-Hellman and Key Agreement

For the last couple of sections in this chapter, we will look at another type of asymmetric cryptography known as Diffie-Hellman (or DH) and a more recent variant called Elliptic-Curve Diffie-Hellman (or ECDH).

DH is a little different than RSA. Where RSA can be used to encrypt and decrypt messages, DH is only used for exchanging keys. In fact, it is technically called the Diffie-Hellman key exchange. As we have already explored in this chapter, outside of signatures, RSA encryption is largely used only for transmitting keys, also called "key transport." This means that if Alice has Bob's RSA public key, Alice can send Bob an encrypted key that only Bob can decrypt.

Figure 6-3 shows key transport in a TLS 1.2 handshake. We will discuss the TLS 1.2 handshake in more detail in Chapter 8, where this figure will also make an appearance.

But notice that the client in this figure can generate a random session key, encrypt it under the server's public key, and "transport" it back. This process also proves the server is in possession of the certificate because only the server could decrypt the session key and use it to communicate. No signatures are required for the server.[3]

On the other hand, DH and ECDH actually create a key seemingly out of thin air. No secrets are transmitted between the parties, encrypted or otherwise. Instead, they exchange public parameters that allow them to simultaneously compute the same key on both sides. This process is called *key agreement*.

To get started, Diffie-Hellman creates a pair of mathematical numbers, one private, one public, for each participant. The DH and ECDH key agreement protocol requires that *both* Alice and Bob have key pairs. In over-simplistic terms, Alice and Bob share their public keys with each other. The foreign public key and the local private key—when combined—create a shared secret on both sides.

A non-mathematical explanation in A. J. Han Vinck's course "Introduction to Public Key Cryptography" [14] is depicted in Figure 6-4.

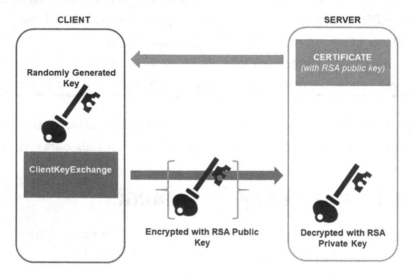

Figure 6-3. *An illustration of key transport using TLS*

Please note that, unlike RSA, DH and ECDH do not allow for the transmission of arbitrary data. Alice can send Bob any message she chooses, encrypted under Bob's RSA public key. Using DH or ECDH, however, all that the two can do is agree upon some

---

[3]TLS does not typically authenticate the client. But if client authentication is requested, it will have to independently prove it is the owner of a certificate by signing a challenge nonce from the server.

random data; they don't get to choose the message contents. The random data can be, and typically is, used as a symmetric key or for deriving symmetric keys.

In addition to not being able to exchange arbitrary contents, key exchange is also limited in that it requires *bidirectional* information exchange. In our scenario at the beginning of this chapter, Bob could not transmit for fear of discovery. Were that actually the case, DH and ECDH key exchanges would be impossible and RSA encryption would be the only option. This really isn't an issue in almost all real-world scenarios. In real Internet applications, we typically assume that both sides are free to communicate with each other.

Coding a DH key exchange in Python is straightforward. The example in Listing 6-8 is taken, with a few simplifications, directly from the cryptography module's online documentation.

Listing 6-8. Diffie-Hellman Key Exchange

```
1   from cryptography.hazmat.backends import default_backend
2   from cryptography.hazmat.primitives import hashes
3   from cryptography.hazmat.primitives.asymmetric import dh
4   from cryptography.hazmat.primitives.kdf.hkdf import HKDF
5   from cryptography.hazmat.backends import default_backend
6
7   # Generate some parameters. These can be reused.
8   parameters = dh.generate_parameters(generator=2, key_size=1024,
9                                       backend=default_backend())
10
11  # Generate a private key for use in the exchange.
12  private_key = parameters.generate_private_key()
13
14  # In a real handshake the peer_public_key will be received from the
15  # other party. For this example we'll generate another private key and
16  # get a public key from that. Note that in a DH handshake both peers
17  # must agree on a common set of parameters.
18  peer_public_key = parameters.generate_private_key().public_key()
19  shared_key = private_key.exchange(peer_public_key)
20
21  # Perform key derivation.
22  derived_key = HKDF(
```

```
23        algorithm=hashes.SHA256(),
24        length=32,
25        salt=None,
26        info=b'handshake data',
27        backend=default_backend()
28   ).derive(shared_key)
```

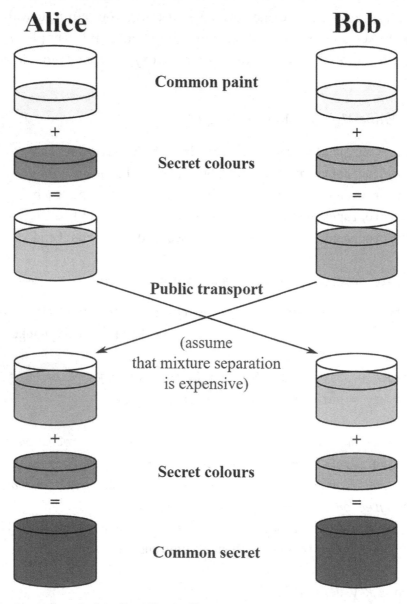

Figure 6-4. *Intuition behind Diffie-Hellman*

Unlike RSA there are a lot fewer pitfalls and gotchas.

There are only two parameters to the exchange: the generator and the key size. There are only two legal values for the generator, 2 and 5. Strangely enough, for a cryptographic protocol, the choice of generator doesn't matter for security reasons but must be the same for both sides of the exchange.

The key size, however, is important and should be at least 2048 bits. Key lengths between 512 and 1024 bits are vulnerable to known attack methods.

Warning: Slow Parameter Generation

Diffie-Hellman is touted as being pretty fast for generating keys on the fly. However, generating the parameters that can generate keys can be pretty slow. We warned you against using key sizes smaller than 2048 and then used 1024 in our own code example. We wanted to give you code that wouldn't take forever to run to illustrate the basic operations.

So if parameter generation is so slow, why do we say DH is fast? The same parameters can generate many keys so the cost is amortized. So make sure not to regenerate the parameters with every key generation, or DH will run unacceptably slow. Alternatively, use ECDH which is much faster.

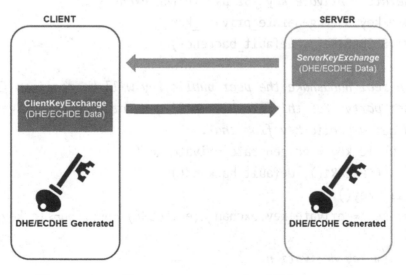

Figure 6-5. *An illustration of key agreement using TLS*

The other recommended setting is to derive another key from the shared key rather than using the shared key directly. The key derivation function is similar to the ones we looked at in Chapter 3.

The TLS 1.2 handshake can either do the key transport using RSA encryption or key agreement using DH/ECDH. Again, this will be discussed in Chapter 8 in detail, but Figure 6-5 shows that both sides exchange the public data, derive a key, and can communicate using the agreed-upon keys. Unlike key transport, however, there is no authentication. Either or both sides will have to sign the public data to prove that possession of a public key.

Elliptic-Curve Diffie-Hellman (or ECDH) is a variant of DH that is becoming popular in modern use. It works in the same way but uses elliptic curves for some of the internal mathematical computations. The code for using ECDH is almost identical to DH in the cryptography module as shown in Listing 6-9.

Listing 6-9. Elliptic-Curve DH

```
1    from cryptography.hazmat.backends import default_backend
2    from cryptography.hazmat.primitives import hashes
3    from cryptography.hazmat.primitives.asymmetric import ec
4    from cryptography.hazmat.primitives.kdf.hkdf import HKDF
5
6    # Generate a private key for use in the exchange.
7    private_key = ec.generate_private_key(
8        ec.SECP384R1(), default_backend()
9    )
10   # In a real handshake the peer_public_key will be received from the
11   # other party. For this example we'll generate another private key
12   # and get a public key from that.
13   peer_public_key = ec.generate_private_key(
14       ec.SECP384R1(), default_backend()
15   ).public_key()
16   shared_key = private_key.exchange(ec.ECDH(), peer_public_key)
17
18   # Perform key derivation.
19   derived_key = HKDF(
20       algorithm=hashes.SHA256(),
```

```
21      length=32,
22      salt=None,
23      info=b'handshake data ',
24      backend=default_backend()
25  ).derive(shared_key)
```

In most circumstances, creating keys with DH or ECDH key agreement is preferred over RSA key exchange. There are a number of reasons but perhaps the biggest one is *forward secrecy*.

Diffie-Hellman and Forward Secrecy

Using RSA encryption, we can generate a symmetric key, encrypt it under someone's public key, and send it to them. This allows both parties to share a session key securely, provided that the exchange protocol follows certain rules. There are even ways to have both sides contribute to a key. Each party could send the other some random data, and the concatenation of both could be fed to a hash function to produce the session key.

Unfortunately, RSA key transport does *not* provide a really fantastic property called *forward secrecy*. Forward secrecy means that even if a key is eventually compromised, it *does not reveal anything about **previous** communications*.

Let's go back to Alice, Bob, and Eve. Alice and Bob already assume that Eve is recording everything that is transmitted. That's why they are encrypting the transmission in the first place. So, after the transmission is complete, Eve has a recording of the ciphertext that she cannot yet decrypt. But, rather than toss it aside, Eve files it away in storage.

But also recall that, in our scenario, Alice actually believed she was on the verge of being captured. If the guards capture her and her keys are compromised, what is lost? Fortunately, nothing. Remember that Alice encrypted the session keys under *Bob's* public key. Capturing Alice won't make it any easier to decrypt that data (do you see the advantage of this over shared keys?).

But suppose that Eve finds Bob, perhaps even a long time in the future. Even if it's years later, if Eve manages to get Bob's private key, she can go back to her recording of Alice's previous transmission and decrypt it! Bob's private key will still decrypt the session keys, and Eve will then be able to decrypt the entire transmission.

Forward secrecy is much stronger than this. If a protocol has forward secrecy, Eve can *never* recover data from a terminated session no matter what long-term keys she manages to obtain. Forward secrecy is not possible when session keys are sent directly via RSA encryption (in the way we've just described) because once the RSA private key is compromised, any recorded data from previous sessions is now vulnerable.

With Diffie-Hellman (DH) and Elliptic-Curve Diffie-Hellman (ECDH), forward secrecy is achieved by the use of *ephemeral keys*. RSA produces an ephemeral *symmetric* session key, but DH and ECDH actually produce ephemeral *asymmetric* keys as well! A new ephemeral key pair is (or should be!) generated with every single key agreement operation and then *thrown away*. The symmetric key is also ephemeral and thrown away after each session. Because DH and ECDH are typically used in this fashion, an "E" is often tacked onto the end of the acronym (DHE or ECDHE).[4]

Now that a new key pair is used for every exchange, compromising a single asymmetric key only reveals a single symmetric key and, accordingly, a single communications session. And when the ephemeral DH and ECDH private keys are properly disposed of, there is no key left for Eve to compromise and no way that she could ever decrypt these sessions. In some ways, it is akin to the old spy trope of swallowing the key so the spy's nemesis can't unlock the movie's McGuffin.

Observe that, in theory, Alice and Bob could also do an *ephemeral* RSA key exchange. They *could* generate new RSA key pairs for *every single key transport*, sending each other their new public keys before transmitting the session key, then destroying the key pair after transmission.

The problem is that generating RSA keys is slow in computer terms. You might not have thought it took very long to generate your RSA keys for the examples in this book, but for computers involved in rapid communications (such as setting up a secure connection from your browser to a web site), RSA is mind-numbingly slow. DH and ECDH are much, much faster. Because of the key generation speed, DH and ECDH are the common choices for forward-secrecy-style communications.

This ephemeral mode of operation is the preferred mode for DH and ECDH under almost all circumstances, which is why DH and ECDH often mean DHE and ECDHE.

---

[4]The TLS protocol, which we'll talk about at the end of this book, is very strict. When TLS says "DH," it does *not* mean DHE and vice versa. This distinction is not always so clear in other contexts.

EXERCISE 6.6. OFF TO THE RACES!

Write a python program to generate a thousand or so 2048-bit RSA private keys and a program to generate a thousand or so DH and ECDH keys. How does the performance compare?

There's only one other limitation to Diffie-Hellman methods: they have no *authentication*. Because the keys are completely ephemeral, there is no way to tie them to an identity; you don't know with whom you are speaking. Remember that beyond communicating confidentially, we need to know with whom we're communicating confidentially. By itself, DH and ECDH do not provide any such assurances.

For this reason, many DH and ECDH key exchanges also require a long-term public key, such as RSA or ECDSA, and that key is typically protected within a signed certificate. These long-term keys, however, are never used for encryption or key transport and are not used in the actual exchange of key data in any way. Their sole purpose is to establish the identity of the other party, usually by signing some of the ephemeral DH/ECDH data being exchanged, and to ensure freshness via some kind of challenge or nonce.

Remember, to ensure forward secrecy, the Diffie-Hellman parameters must be regenerated for *every key exchange*. If you take a look through the cryptography library documentation, you'll notice that they include sample code that, as written, does *not* provide forward secrecy. This code sample saves what should be a single-use key for later. Make sure that your keys are destroyed after use (never logged).

Now that we've walked through the very high-level concepts, let's help Alice and Bob with authenticated ECDH key exchange code. First we will create some code for the key exchange (Listing 6-10), and then we'll modify it to be authenticated.

Listing 6-10. Unauthenticated ECDH

```
1    from cryptography.hazmat.backends import default_backend
2    from cryptography.hazmat.primitives import hashes, serialization
3    from cryptography.hazmat.primitives.asymmetric import ec
4    from cryptography.hazmat.primitives.kdf.hkdf import HKDF
5
6    class ECDHExchange:
7        def __init__(self, curve):
8            self._curve = curve
9
```

```
10          # Generate an ephemeral private key for use in the exchange.
11          self._private_key = ec.generate_private_key(
12              curve, default_backend())
13
14      self.enc_key = None
15      self.mac_key = None
16
17  def get_public_bytes(self):
18      public_key = self._private_key.public_key()
19      raw_bytes = public_key.public_bytes(
20          encoding=serialization.Encoding.PEM,
21          format=serialization.PublicFormat.SubjectPublicKeyInfo)
22      return raw_bytes
23
24  def generate_session_key(self, peer_bytes):
25      peer_public_key = serialization.load_pem_public_key(
26          peer_bytes,
27          backend=default_backend())
28      shared_key = self._private_key.exchange(
29          ec. ECDH(),
30          peer_public_key)
31
32      # derive 64 bytes of key material for 2 32-byte keys
33      key_material = HKDF(
34          algorithm=hashes.SHA256(),
35          length=64,
36          salt=None,
37          info=None,
38          backend=default_backend()).derive(shared_key)
39
40      # get the encryption key
41      self.enc_key = key_material[:32]
42
43      # derive an MAC key
44      self.mac_key = key_material[32:64]
```

To use the ECDHExchange, both parties instantiate the class and call the `get_public_bytes` method to get the data that needs to be sent to the other party. When those bytes are received, they are passed to `generate_session_key` where they are de-serialized into a public key and used to create a shared key.

So, what's with HKDF? This is a key derivation function that is useful for real-time network communications, but should not be used for data storage. It takes the shared key as input and derives a key (or key material) from it. Notice that in our example, we derive both an encryption key and a MAC key. This is done by using HKDF to derive 64 bytes of key material and then splitting it into two 32-byte keys. In reality, we need to derive a lot more data, and we'll discuss this in the next section. But for now, it demonstrates the basics of the ECDH exchange.

To repeat one last time, notice that ECDH is *generating* its private key on the fly. This key must be destroyed after every key exchange, along with any session keys created.

EXERCISE 6.7. RUDIMENTARY ECDH EXCHANGE

Use the ECDHExchange class to create shared keys between two parties. You will need to have two instances of the program running. Each program should write their public key bytes to disk for the other program to load. When they're finished, have them print out the bytes of the shared key so that you can verify that they both come up with the same key.

EXERCISE 6.8. NETWORK ECDH EXCHANGE

In the upcoming chapters, we will start using the network to exchange data between two peers. If you already know how to do some client-server programming, modify the previous ECDH exchange program to send the public data over the network instead of saving it to disk.

Our ECDH code so far just does the ECDH ephemeral key exchange. Both sides have a key, but since we aren't yet doing any authentication, neither side can be certain about whom they're talking to! Remember, the ephemeral nature of the ECDH keys means that they cannot be used to establish identity.

To remedy this, we are going to modify our ECDHExchange program to *also* be authenticated. In addition to an ephemeral asymmetric key, it will also use a long-term asymmetric key to sign the data.

Let's modify our ECDHExchange class and rename it AuthenticatedECDHExchange, which we do in Listing 6-11. First, we need to modify the constructor to take a long-term (*persistent*) private key as a parameter. This will be used for signing.

Listing 6-11. Authenticated ECHD

```
1    # Partial Listing: Some Assembly Required
2
3    from cryptography.hazmat.backends import default_backend
4    from cryptography.hazmat.primitives import hashes, serialization
5    from cryptography.hazmat.primitives.asymmetric import ec
6    from cryptography.hazmat.primitives.kdf.hkdf import HKDF
7    import struct # needed for get_signed_public_pytes
8
9    class AuthenticatedECDHExchange:
10       def __init__(self, curve, auth_private_key):
11           self._curve = curve
12           self._private_key = ec.generate_private_key(
13                   self._curve,
14                   default_backend())
15           self.enc_key = None
16           self.mac_key = None
17
18           self._auth_private_key = auth_private_key
```

Please note the difference between _private_key, which is generated and is ephemeral, and _auth_private_key. The latter is passed in as a parameter. This persistent key will be used to establish identity. We could use an RSA key here and it would work just fine, but in keeping with the elliptic-curve theme, we will assume this is an ECDSA key.

Instead of just generating public bytes to send to the other side, we will use Listing 6-12 to generate *signed* public bytes.

Listing 6-12. Authenticated ECDH Signed Public Bytes

```
1    # Partial Listing: Some Assembly Required
2
3    # Part of AuthenticatedECDHExchange class
4    def get_signed_public_bytes(self):
5        public_key = self._private_key.public_key()
6
7        # Here are the raw bytes.
8        raw_bytes = public_key.public_bytes(
9            encoding=serialization.Encoding.PEM,
10           format=serialization.PublicFormat.SubjectPublicKeyInfo)
11
12       # This is a signature to prove who we are.
13       signature = self._auth_private_key.sign(
14           raw_bytes,
15           ec.ECDSA(hashes.SHA256()))
16
17       # Signature size is not fixed.Include a length field first.
18       return struct.pack("I", len(signature)) + raw_bytes + signature
```

When the other side receives our data, they will need to unpack the first four bytes to get the length of the signature before they do anything else. The signature can be verified using the other party's long-term public key (just like we did with RSA). If the signature works out, we have some confidence that the ECDH parameters we received came from the expected party.

EXERCISE 6.9. ECDH LEFT TO THE READER

We did not show code for verifying the public parameters received in the AuthenticatedECDHExchange class. Luckily for you, we've left it as an exercise to the reader! Update the generate_session_key method to be generate_authenticated_session_key. This method should implement the algorithm previously described for getting the signature length, verifying the signature using a public key, and then deriving the session keys.

The principles in this section are important. You might consider working through this section a couple of times until you are comfortable with both sending a key encrypted under RSA and generating an ephemeral key on the fly using DH or ECDH. Make sure you also understand why the DH/ECDH approach has forward secrecy and the RSA version does not.

EXERCISE 6.10. BECAUSE YOU LOVE TORTURE

To emphasize that RSA technically could be used as an ephemeral exchange mechanism, modify your preceding ECDH program to generate an ephemeral set of RSA keys. Exchange the associate public keys and use each public key to send 32 bytes of random data to the other party. Combine both 32-byte transmissions with XOR to create a "shared key" and run it through HKDF just as the ECDH example does. Once you've proved to yourself that this works, review your results from Exercise 6.2 to see why this is too slow to be practical.

Also, creating a shared key with RSA encryption requires a round trip to create the key (transmission of certificate and reception of encrypted key), whereas DH and ECDH only require one transmission from each party to the other. When we learn about TLS 1.3, for example, you'll see how this can greatly impact performance.

Challenge-Response Protocols

We have briefly introduced challenge-response protocols in Chapter 5. In particular, Alice used challenge-response to validate that the man claiming to be Charlie was the owner of the certificate with the identity "charlie." At its core, a challenge-response protocol is about one party proving to another that they *currently* control either a shared secret or a private key. Let's look at both examples.

First, suppose that Alice and Bob share some key $K_{A,B}$. If Alice is communicating over a network with Bob, a simple authentication protocol is to send Bob a nonce N (potentially unencrypted) and ask him to encrypt it. For security reasons, it's a good idea for the response to include the identity of the communicating parties. Accordingly, Bob should reply with $\{A, B, N\}_{K_{A,B}}$. If only Alice and Bob share the key $K_{A,B}$, then only Bob could have responded to Alice's challenge correctly. Even if Eve overhears the challenge and knows N, she should not be able to encrypt it without the key.

For the asymmetric example, it is more or less the same, but uses signatures generated by private keys. This time, Bob is communicating with Alice over the network and wishes to be sure that he is talking to the real Alice. So he sends a nonce N and asks her to sign it with her public key. As with Bob's challenge, Alice should also send her name and Bob's. Her transmission should therefore look like $\{H(B, A, N)\}_{K^{-1}_A}$ (for RSA signatures anyway). Bob verifies with the Alice's public key that the signature is correct. Only the possessor of the private key could have signed that challenge.

Challenge-response algorithms are relatively simple, but they can go wrong in many ways. For one thing, the nonce must be sufficiently large and sufficiently random to be unguessable, even with knowledge of previous transmissions. In the early days of remote keys for cars, for example, the transmitter used a 16-bit nonce. Thieves only had to record a transmission once and then interrogate the system over and over until it cycled through all the possible nonces and returned to the one they recorded. At that point, they could replay the nonce and gain access to the car.

Another way this can go wrong is via a "(hu)man-in-the-middle" (MITM) attack. Suppose that Eve wants to convince Alice that she is Bob. Eve waits until Bob wants to talk to Alice and then intercepts all of their communications. Then, she initiates communication with Alice pretending to be Bob. Alice responds with a challenge N to prove that the person she is talking to (Eve) is Bob. Eve immediately turns around and sends the challenge to Bob who, wanting to talk to Alice, was already expecting it. Bob happily signs the challenge and sends it back to Eve who forwards it directly on to Alice. (For a fascinating, but probably fictional example, Ross Anderson describes a "MIG-in-the-middle" scenario of this attack [1, Chap. 3].)

One way to defeat this MITM problem is to transmit information that only the true party can use. For example, even if Eve forwards along Bob's response to the challenge it won't help her if Alice's response is to send Bob a session key encrypted under his public key. Eve won't be able to decrypt it. If all subsequent communication takes place using that session key, Eve is still locked out. Alternatively, Alice and Bob could use ECDH plus signatures to generate a session key. Even if Eve can intercept every transmission between the two of them, Alice and Bob can create a session key that only they can use. The most Eve can do is block the communications.

The point here is to illustrate all the different kinds of considerations that need to go into authenticating the party you're talking to.

Once the identity of a party has been established, all subsequent communications of the session *must be tied to that authentication.* For example, Alice and Bob might authenticate one another using challenge-response, but unless they establish a session MAC key and use it to digest all of their subsequent communications, they cannot be sure who is sending the message.

Sometimes, initialization data must be sent in the clear before encrypted communications can be established. All of this data must also be tied together at some point. After session keys have been established, one option is to send a hash of all the unauthenticated data sent so far using the newly established secure channel. If the hash doesn't match what is expected, then the communicating parties can assume that an attacker, like Eve, has modified some of the initialization data.

In summary, when combining asymmetric and symmetric cryptography, don't just think about the confidentiality part (encryption). Remember that knowing to whom you are speaking is just as important as, if not more important than, knowing that the communications between the two of you are unreadable to anyone else. You might not want the whole world to read your love poetry, but you definitely don't want your amorous expressions to be received by the wrong person! Keep in mind that after establishing the other party's identity, you must ensure that there is a chain of authenticity for all the remaining communications for the rest of the session. If the initial identity is proved with signatures and the remaining data is authenticated by MACs, ensure that there is no break in the chain as you switch from one to the other.

Common Problems

After seeing a bit about how asymmetric and symmetric keys work together, you might be tempted to create your own protocol. Definitely resist that urge. The goal of these exercises is to teach you the *principles* and to illuminate your *understanding*, but that alone is not sufficient to prepare you to develop cryptographic protocols. The history of cryptography is littered with protocols that were later found to be exploitable even though they were written by cryptographers with more experience than you or I have.

Let's take the example we used with Alice sending the encrypted document to Bob. Did you notice that we broke one of our recommendations from previous chapters? Our data has no nonce! This means that Bob has no idea if the message from Alice is "fresh." What if that data was recorded by Eve from a year ago and is just being replayed now?

Here's another example. In our derivation of encryption keys, we only generated a single encryption key between both parties. This is only secure for *one-way communication!* If you want full-duplex communication (the ability to send data in both directions), you will need an encryption key for each direction!

But wait. Why can't we use the same key to send data from Alice to Bob as we use to send data from Bob to Alice?

Do you remember what you learned about in Chapter 3? You do not reuse the same key and IV to encrypt two different messages! In full-duplex communication, that is exactly what you would be doing. Suppose that AEC-CTR mode is being used for the bulk data transport. If Alice uses a key to encrypt messages she sends to Bob, and Bob uses the same key to encrypt messages to Alice, both data streams could be XORed together to get the XOR of the plaintext messages! As we have seen, that is catastrophic. In fact, if Eve can trick Alice or Bob into encrypting data on her behalf (e.g., by planting "honeypot" data that will certainly be picked up and transmitted), she can XOR that data out leaving the other data as plaintext.

A naive key exchange using RSA encryption could be exploited using this very same principle. Suppose that Alice sends Bob an initial secret K encrypted under Bob's public key. Alice and Bob correctly derive session keys and IVs for full-duplex communication from K. As an example, Bob has a key $K_{B,A}$ that he uses to send encrypted messages to Alice, and Alice has a key $K_{A,B}$ that she uses to send encrypted messages to Bob. (Bob uses $K_{A,B}$ to decrypt Alice's messages and Alice uses $K_{B,A}$ to encrypt Bob's messages.)

But suppose that Eve records all of these transmissions. Then, at a much later date, she replays the initial transmission of K to Bob. Bob doesn't know that it's a replay and he uses K to derive $K_{B,A}$. Now he starts sending data to Eve encrypted under this key.

While it's true that Eve does not have $K_{B,A}$ and cannot decrypt Bob's messages directly, she does have the messages Bob sent to Alice under the same key from the earlier transmissions. Again, assuming that Alice and Bob use AES-CTR, the two transmission streams can be XORed together to potentially extract sensitive information. There are ways to solve this (e.g., by reintroducing challenge-response) but there are many ways it can go wrong even still.

It is very difficult to get all the parts of a cryptographic protocol right, even for the experts. In general, do not design your own protocols. Use existing protocols as much as possible and existing implementations whenever feasible. Above all, we want to remind you one more time, YANAC (You Are Not A Cryptographer... yet!).

EXERCISE 6.11. EXPLOITING FULL-DUPLEX KEY REUSE

In previous exercises, you XORed some data together to see if you could still find patterns, but you didn't actually XOR the two cipher streams together. Imagine if Alice and Bob used your ECDH exchange and derived the same key for full-duplex communication. Use the same key to encrypt some documents together for Alice to send to Bob and for Bob to send to Alice. XOR the cipher streams together and validate that the result is the XOR of the plaintext. See if you can figure out any patterns from the XORed data.

EXERCISE 6.12. DERIVING ALL THE PIECES

Modify the ECDH exchange program to derive six pieces of information: a write encryption key, a write IV, a write MAC key, a read decryption key, a read IV, and a read MAC key. The hard part will be getting both sides to derive the same keys. Remember, the keys will be derived in the same order. So how does Alice determine that the first key derived is her write key and not Bob's write key? One way to do this is to take the first *n* bytes of each side's public key bytes as an integer and whoever has the lowest number goes "first."

An Unfortunate Example of Asymmetric and Symmetric Harmony

Most of our examples of cryptography are beneficial in some way, or are at least not *inherently* evil. Unfortunately, bad guys can use cryptography just as well as the good guys. And given that they can make a lot of money from evil, they can be highly motivated to produce creative, efficient uses of the technology.

One area where bad guys are incredibly good at using cryptography is *ransomware*. If you've been living in a cave in West Antarctica for the past decade and haven't heard about ransomware, it's basically software that encrypts your files and refuses to unlock them until you pay the extortionists behind it.

The cryptography behind early ransomware was simplistic and naive. The ransomware encrypted every file with a different AES key, but all of the AES keys were stored *on the system* in a file. The ransomware's decryptor could easily find the keys and decrypt the file, but so could security researchers. If you don't want somebody to unlock a file, it's bad idea to leave the keys just lying around (under the doormat, so to speak).

Ransomware authors logically turned to asymmetric encryption as a solution. The immediately obvious advantage of asymmetric cryptography is that a public key could be on the victim's system and a private key could be somewhere else. For all of the reasons you've seen in this chapter, the files themselves cannot be encrypted with RSA directly. RSA doesn't even have the capacity to encrypt data larger than between 190 and 256 bytes, and if it did, it would be too slow. The user might notice their system getting locked down long before the encryption was complete.

Instead, the ransomware could encrypt all of the AES keys individually. After all, an AES key is just 16 bytes for AES-128 and 32 bytes for AES-256. Each key can be easily RSA encrypted before being stored on the victim's system. RSA encrypts with the public key, so as long as the private key isn't available to the victim, they won't be able to decrypt the AES keys.

There are two naive variants of this approach, both of which are problematic. The first approach is to generate the key pair ahead of time and hard-code the public key into the malware itself. After the malware encrypts all the AES keys with the public key, a victim has to pay the ransom to have the private key sent to them for decryption. The obvious flaw in this design is that the *same* private key would unlock all of the systems attacked by the ransomware, as each copy of the malicious attack file had the same public key baked into it.

The second approach is for the ransomware to generate the RSA key pair on the victim's system and transmit the private key to the command and control server. Now there is a unique public key encrypting the AES keys, and when the attacker releases the private key for decryption, it only unlocks the specific victim's files. The problem here is that the system has to be *online* to get rid of the private key, and many network monitoring systems will detect transmissions to risky IPs where command and control servers often operate. Transmitting the private key might give away the ransomware before it has even started encrypting files on the system. It is stealthier to do everything locally until the system is fully locked.

Modern ransomware solves all of these problems with a pretty clever approach. First, the attacker generates a long-term asymmetric key pair. For our purposes, let's just assume it is an RSA key pair, and we will call these keys the "permanent" asymmetric keys.

Next the attacker creates some malware and hard-codes the permanent public key into the malware. When the malware activates on a victim's machine, the first thing that it does is generate a *new* asymmetric key pair. Again, for simplicity, let's assume that it is an RSA key pair. We will call it the "local" key pair. It immediately encrypts the newly generated local private key by the attacker's permanent public key embedded in the malware. The unencrypted local private key is *deleted*.

Now the malware begins to encrypt the files on the disk using AES-CTR or AES-CBC. Each file is encrypted under a different key, and then each key is encrypted by the *local* public key. The unencrypted version of the key is destroyed as soon as the file is finished being encrypted.

When the whole process is done, the victim's files are encrypted by AES keys that are themselves encrypted by the local RSA public key. These AES keys could be decrypted by the local RSA private key, but that key is encrypted under the attacker's permanent public key, and the private key is not on the computer.

Now the attacker contacts the victim and demands the ransom. If the victim agrees and pays the ransom (usually by way of Bitcoin), the attacker provides some kind of authentication code to the malware. The malware transmits the encrypted local private key to the attacker. Using his or her permanent private key, he or she decrypts the local private key and sends it back to the victim. Now all of the AES keys can be decrypted and the files subsequently decrypted.

What's clever about this algorithm is that the attacker does not disclose his or her permanent private key. It remains private. A secondary private key is decrypted by the attacker for the victim to use in unlocking the rest of the system.

Warning: Risky Exercise

The upcoming exercise is somewhat risky. You should not do this exercise unless you have a virtual machine that can be restored to a snapshot or a jail (e.g., a chroot jail) with files that can be permanently lost.

Furthermore, this exercise has you create a simplified version of ransomware. We do not condone nor encourage any actual use of ransomware in any form. Don't be stupid, don't be evil.

EXERCISE 6.13. PLAYING THE VILLAIN

Help Alice and Bob create some ransomware to infect WA servers. Start by creating a function that will encrypt a file on disk using an algorithm of your choice (e.g., AES-CTR or AES-CBC). The encrypted data should be saved to a new file with some kind of random name. Before moving on, test encrypting and decrypting the file.

Next, create the fake malware. This malware should be configured with a target directory and the permanent public key. The public key can be hard-coded directly into the code if you wish. Once up and running, it needs to generate a new RSA key pair, encrypt the local private key with the permanent public key, and then delete any unencrypted copies of the local private key. If the private key is too big (e.g., more than 190 bytes), encrypt it in chunks.

Once the local key pair is generated, begin encrypting the files in the target directory. As an extra precaution, you can ask for manual approval before encrypting each file to make sure you don't accidentally encrypt the wrong thing. For each file, encrypt it under a new random name and store a plaintext metadata file with the original name of the file, the encrypted key, and IV. Delete the original file if you feel that you can do so safely (we will **not** be held responsible for any mistakes on your part! Use a VM, only operate in a target directory on copies of unimportant files, and manually confirm each deletion!).

The rest should be straightforward. Your "malware" utility needs to save the encrypted private key to disk. This should be decrypted by a separate command and control utility that has access to the permanent private key. Once decrypted, it should be loaded by the malware and used to decrypt/release the files.

While you are hopefully not a malware/ransomware author, this section should also be helpful to you in thinking about how to encrypt "data at rest." Much of what we talk about in this book is to protect "data in motion," which is data traveling across a network or in some other way between two parties. The ransomware example illustrates protecting data that stays largely in place, typically to be encrypted and decrypted by the same party.

Utilities that encrypt files on disk have to deal with the wretched key management problem just like they do with data in motion. In general, there will have to be one key per file just like there has to be one key per network communications session; this prevents key reuse. The keys (and IVs) must be stored, or it must be possible to regenerate them. If they are stored, they must be encrypted by some kind of master key and stored along with additional metadata about the algorithm used and so forth. This information can be prepended to the beginning of the encrypted file, or it can be stored somewhere in a manifest.

If the keys are regenerated later, this is typically done by deriving the keys from a password, as we have already discussed in Chapter 2. As there needs to be a different key for each file, a random per-file salt is used in the derivation process to ensure that key's uniqueness. The salt must be stored with the file, and the loss of the salt would result in a lost file that could never be decrypted.

This is the basic cryptographic concept behind securing data at rest, but production systems are usually far more complicated. NIST, for example, requires that compliant systems have a defined cryptographic key *life cycle*. This includes a pre-operational, operational, post-operational, and deletion stages as well as an operational "crypto" period for each key. This period is further broken down into an "originator usage period" (OUP) for when sensitive data can be generated and encrypted and a "recipient usage period" (RUP) for when this data can be decrypted and read. Key management systems are expected to handle key rollover (migrating encrypted data from one key to another), key revocation, and many other such functions.

We won't bother you with another reference to YANAC… but by this point in the book, we hope your own subconscious is starting to do it for us!

That's a Wrap

The main thrust of this chapter is that you can wrap up a temporary symmetric communication session within an initial asymmetric session establishment protocol. A lot of the world's asymmetric infrastructure is focused on long-term identification of parties and that infrastructure is useful for establishing identities in some way and based on some model of trust. But once that trust is established, it's more secure and more efficient to create a temporary symmetric key (well, actually several of them) to handle encrypting and MACing the data going forward.

We reviewed, for example, that you can transport a key from one party to another using RSA encryption. This approach was the primary approach used for a long time. Although still present in many systems, it is being retired for many reasons. More favored these days is using an ephemeral key agreement protocol, such as DH and ECDH (actually, DHE and ECDHE to be precise) to create a session key with perfect forward secrecy.

Either way, whether by key transport or key agreement, the parties can then derive the suite of keys necessary for communications. Or, a single party can derive the keys necessary for encrypting data on a hard drive. In both cases, the asymmetric operations are primarily used to establish identity and get an initial key, while the symmetric operations are used for the actual encryption of data.

If you can understand these principles, you can be conversant about most cryptography systems you'll find.

CHAPTER 7

More Symmetric Crypto: Authenticated Encryption and Kerberos

In this chapter we'll be covering some advanced symmetric cryptography, and we'll get deeper into authenticated encryption.

Let's dive right into an example and some code using AES-GCM.

AES-GCM

Alice and Bob have had a few close calls with Eve over the past month. During that time, they have been exchanging USB drives with encrypted files. This has worked out for them so far, but they seem to have trouble remembering a handful of key things: that they should Encrypt-Then-MAC, that the MAC needs to cover unencrypted data, and that they need to have two separate keys. After some exasperation and close calls due to their understandably imperfect memory under pressure, they let HQ know that they would like something less error-prone.

As it happens, there *is* something new that they can use. New symmetric modes of operation are available called "authenticated encryption" (AE) and "authenticated encryption with additional data" (AEAD). These new modes of operation provide *both* confidentiality and authenticity for the data. AEAD can also provide authenticity over "additional data" that is *not* encrypted. This is far more important than it might sound, so we're actually going to leave AE behind and focus exclusively on AEAD.

In this exercise, we're going to use a mode of AES called "Galois/Counter Mode" (GCM). The API for this mode is just a little different than what we have seen before,

© Seth James Nielson, Christopher K. Monson 2019
S. J. Nielson and C. K. Monson, *Practical Cryptography in Python*,
https://doi.org/10.1007/978-1-4842-4900-0_7

so let's give Alice and Bob a crash course in using it. In Listing 7-1, we use AES-GCM to encrypt a document *and* authenticate the IV and salt used in the encryption process.

Listing 7-1. AES-GCM

```
1   from cryptography.hazmat.backends import default_backend
2   from cryptography.hazmat.primitives.kdf.scrypt import Scrypt
3   from cryptography.hazmat.primitives.ciphers import Cipher, algorithms,
    modes
4   import os, sys, struct
5
6   READ_SIZE = 4096
7
8   def encrypt_file(plainpath, cipherpath, password):
9       # Derive key with a random 16-byte salt
10      salt = os.urandom(16)
11      kdf = Scrypt(salt=salt, length=32,
12                   n=2**14, r=8, p=1,
13                   backend=default_backend())
14      key = kdf.derive(password)
15
16      # Generate a random 96-bit IV.
17      iv = os.urandom(12)
18
19      # Construct an AES-GCM Cipher object with the given key and IV.
20      encryptor = Cipher(
21          algorithms.AES(key),
22          modes.GCM(iv),
23          backend=default_backend()).encryptor()
24
25      associated_data = iv + salt
26
27      # associated_data will be authenticated but not encrypted,
28      # it must also be passed in on decryption.
29      encryptor.authenticate_additional_data(associated_data)
30
```

```
31        with open(cipherpath, "wb+") as fcipher:
32            # Make space for the header (12 + 16 + 16), overwritten last
33            fcipher.write(b"\x00"*(12+16+16))
34
35            # Encrypt and write the main body
36            with open(plainpath, "rb") as fplain:
37                for plaintext in iter(lambda: fplain.read(READ_SIZE), b''):
38                    ciphertext = encryptor.update(plaintext)
39                    fcipher.write(ciphertext)
40                ciphertext = encryptor.finalize() # Always b''.
41                fcipher.write(ciphertext) # For clarity
42
43                header = associated_data + encryptor.tag
44                fcipher.seek(0,0)
45                fcipher.write(header)
```

Most of this function should look familiar. Because we're storing this data on disk, we are using Scrypt instead of HKDF, and we use this to generate a key from a password. As described in the previous chapter, because a user might use the same password across multiple files, each file needs its own salt in order to generate a per-file key. Remember, we do not want to use the same key and IV on different files or even on the same file (e.g., if we encrypt, then modify the file and encrypt again). To be extra cautious, we won't even use the same key.

Similar to what we've done before, we also create a Cipher object. But instead of using CTR or CBC modes, we use GCM mode. That mode takes an IV, and we'll talk momentarily about why it is 12 bytes instead of the 16 bytes we've seen in the past. The only new method on the encryptor is authenticate_additional_data. As you can probably guess, this method takes in the data that will *not* be encrypted, but that still needs to be authenticated.

The unencrypted data that we're authenticating in this case is the salt and the IV. This data *must* be in plaintext because we can't decrypt without it. By authenticating it, we can be certain—once the decryption is done—that nobody has tinkered with these unencrypted values.

The other unique part of this GCM operation is the encryptor.tag. This value is computed after the finalize method and is more or less the MAC over the encrypted and additional data. In our implementation, we choose to put the associated data (the salt and the IV) and the tag at the *beginning* of the file. Because that data (at least the tag data) won't be available until the end of the encryption process, we preallocate several bytes (initially zeros) that we'll overwrite when we finally have the tag at the end of the process. In some operating systems, there is no way to prepend data, so the preallocated prefix bytes ensure that we have room for the header when finished.

The function in Listing 7-2 doesn't delete or overwrite the original file, so it's pretty safe to play with. Use it to create an encrypted copy of a file on your system. Examine the bytes using a utility like *hexdump* to ensure that the data is, in fact, encrypted.

Warning: Beware the Files of Unusual Size

Do not encrypt a file greater than 64 GiB, as there are limits to GCM that we will discuss shortly.

Now, let's write a decrypt_file function, shown in Listing 7-2.

Listing 7-2. AES-GCM Decryption

```
1   from cryptography.hazmat.backends import default_backend
2   from cryptography.hazmat.primitives.kdf.scrypt import Scrypt
3   from cryptography.hazmat.primitives.ciphers import Cipher, algorithms,
    modes
4   import os, sys, struct
5
6   READ_SIZE = 4096
7   def decrypt_file(cipherpath, plainpath, password):
8       with open(cipherpath, "rb") as fcipher:
9           # read the IV (12 bytes) and the salt (16 bytes)
10          associated_data = fcipher.read(12+16)
11
12          iv = associated_data[0:12]
13          salt = associated_data[12:28]
14
15          # derive the same key from the password + salt
16          kdf = Scrypt(salt=salt, length=32,
17                  n=2**14, r=8, p=1,
```

```
18                  backend=default_backend())
19          key = kdf.derive(password)
20
21          # get the tag. GCM tags are always 16 bytes
22          tag = fcipher.read(16)
23
24          # Construct an AES-GCM Cipher object with the given key and IV
25          # For decryption, the tag is passed in as a parameter
26          decryptor = Cipher(
27              algorithms.AES(key),
28              modes.GCM(iv, tag),
29              backend=default_backend()).decryptor()
30          decryptor.authenticate_additional_data(associated_data)
31
32          with open(plainpath, "wb+") as fplain:
33              for ciphertext in iter(lambda: fcipher.read(READ_SIZE),b''):
34                  plaintext = decryptor.update(ciphertext)
35                  fplain.write(plaintext)
```

This decryption operation starts by first reading out the unencrypted salt, IV, and tag. The salt is used in conjunction with the password to derive the key. The key, the IV, and the tag are parameters to the GCM decryption process. The associated data (the salt and the IV) are also passed into the decryptor using the `authenticate_additional_data` function.

When the decryptor's `finalize` method is called and any data has been changed, either in the ciphertext or the additional data, the method throws an invalid tag exception.

This function does not attempt to recreate the original filename. You can thus safely restore the encrypted file to a new filename and then compare the newly recovered file with the original.

EXERCISE 7.1. TAG! YOU'RE IT!

Artificially "damage" different parts of an encrypted file including both the actual ciphertext and the salt, IV, or tag. Demonstrate that decrypting the file throws an exception.

AES-GCM Details and Nuances

In our introductory exercise, Alice and Bob were introduced to the GCM mode of operation for AES. AES-GCM is an AEAD (authenticated encryption and associated data) mode. A summary of key details includes

- The mode both encrypts and authenticates data *with a single key*.

- The encryption and authentication is integrated; there is no need to worry about when to do what (i.e., Encrypt-Then-MAC vs. MAC-Then-Encrypt).

- AEAD includes authentication over data that is *not* encrypted.

You may have noticed that these features address Alice and Bob's concerns. It significantly reduces misuse and misconfiguration, making it easier for Alice and Bob (and you) to do it right.

One element of this that deserves particular emphasis is the authentication of additional data. There have been many issues in the history of cryptography where an attacker takes data out of one context to misuse it in another. Replay attacks, for example, are classic examples of this kind of problem. In many cases, these attacks would fail if the context of the sensitive data were enforced.

In our file encryption example, we authenticated the IV and salt values, but we could have easily thrown in the filename and a timestamp. One problem with encrypted files is recognizing a replay of an older, but correctly encrypted, version of the file. If a timestamp is authenticated with a file, or alternatively a version number or other nonce is included, the encrypted file is more tightly bound to a recognizable context.

When you are encrypting data, think carefully over what data needs to be *authentic*, not just *private*. The better you can identify and secure the surrounding context of encryption, the more secure your system will be.

In terms of securing data against modification, it is important to note that the AEAD algorithm decrypts data *before* it knows if the data is unmodified. In your experimentation with the preceding file decryption, you may have noticed that even if the encrypted file is damaged, the decryptor will still create a decrypted file. The exception thrown by GCM is thrown after everything is decrypted and (in our implementation) written to the recovered file.

In summary, remember that the decrypted data *cannot be trusted* until the tag is verified!

AEAD is great, but the combined operation introduces an interesting problem. How long do you have to wait for a tag? Suppose that, instead of file decryption, Alice and Bob are using AES-GCM to send data over a network. Suppose it's a lot of data. Suppose it will take many hours to completely transmit the data. If we encrypt this data like we encrypted the file, the tag will not be sent until the entire transmission is complete.

Do you really want to wait until the very end of those hours to finally receive the tag?

Worse, how do you calculate the "end" of a secure channel? If you have an encrypted channel open for days sending arbitrary amounts of data, at what point do you decide to stop, calculate, and send the tag?

In network protocols like TLS, which we will explore more fully in Chapter 8, each individual TLS record (a TLS packet more or less) is individually GCM-encrypted with its own individual tag. That way, malicious or accidental modifications are detected almost in real time, rather than at the end of transmission. In general, a more bite-sized approach to GCM encryption is recommended for streams.

The `cryptography` library has a simpler user interface for this bite-sized AES-GCM encryption operation. It has an added bonus in that the decryption operation will not return the decrypted data unless the tag is correct, preventing you from accidentally using bad data. Here is some sample code from the `cryptography` library documentation demonstrating its use:

```
>>> import os
>>> from cryptography.hazmat.primitives.ciphers.aead import AESGCM
>>> data = b"a secret message"
>>> aad = b"authenticated but unencrypted data"
>>> key = AESGCM.generate_key(bit_length=128)
>>> aesgcm = AESGCM(key)
>>> nonce = os.urandom(12)
>>> ct = aesgcm.encrypt(nonce, data, aad)
>>> aesgcm.decrypt(nonce, ct, aad)
b'a secret message'
```

This API is easy to use and the concept is not too difficult, but it comes with one critical security consideration: the nonce. Recall that the "C" in GCM stands for "Counter." GCM is more or less like CTR with a tag operation integrated into it. This is important because many of the problems with counter mode that we've discussed previously still apply. In particular, while you should never reuse a key and IV pair in *any* mode of AES encryption, it is *especially* bad for counter mode (and GCM). Doing so makes it possible to trivially expose the XOR of the two plaintexts. The IV/nonce to GCM must **never be reused**.

To illustrate the issue, let's briefly revisit how counter mode works. Remember that unlike CBC mode, AES counter mode does not actually encrypt the plaintext with AES block encryption. Rather, a monotonically increasing counter is encrypted with AES, and this *stream* is XORed with the plaintext. It's worth repeating that the AES block cipher is first applied to the counter, and then to the counter +1, and then to the counter +2, and so on to generate the full stream. Reusing the *nonce* results in reusing the *stream*.

That's important. If you are not even more careful, though, you might run into a slightly similar problem that is equally disastrous. For example, suppose that you decide to start with a nonce of 0 (16 bytes of 0) instead of picking a random IV for counter mode. You use that nonce (0) to encrypt a bunch of data (maybe a file) under a key and then you increase your nonce by 1 to initialize a new AES counter context to encrypt a new set of data (such as another file) under the same key. Your nonce is thus nothing more than an ever-incrementing counter.

The problem with this is that—even though you think you're not reusing a nonce (it's different every time)—counter mode works by increasing the nonce by one for each block. The first operation encrypted 0, then 1, then 2, and so forth; the second operation encrypted 1, then 2, then 3, and so forth. In other words, the second file encrypted with the second nonce repeats the same key stream after the first 128-bit block. There is a *very large amount of overlap* between subsequent streams.

For relatively small amounts of data like we are using in examples, using a completely random 16-byte IV is probably enough for standard counter mode. In production code, you would have to do a security analysis to determine exactly how long you have on average before you create cipher streams that overlap. This calculation is dependent on how much data you plan to encrypt under the same key. If you want to explicitly control your IVs to ensure that it is not possible to overlap a key/counter pair, there are some rules that you can follow that help.

GCM, for example, mandates a 12-byte IV to explicitly solve this problem (it does permit longer IVs, but this introduces new problems and is beyond the scope of the book). The selected 12-byte nonce is then padded with 4 zero bytes to produce a 16-byte counter. Even if a nonce is chosen that is just one more than the previous nonce, the counters will not overlap, provided you do not overflow the 4-byte block counter.

A 4-byte counter on 128-bit blocks means no more than 2^{36} bytes (or 64 GiB) of data can be encrypted before overflowing the counter, which is why 64 GiB of data is designated as an upper bound for GCM encryption.

Using 12-byte IVs and no more than 64 GiB of plaintext per key/IV pair means that there will never be any overlap. For reasons that are beyond the scope of this book, the only other requirement on GCM IVs is that they not be zero.

Let's return to the problem of using AES-GCM to encrypt a bunch of smaller messages in a stream. How do we keep from reusing a key/IV pair? We could try to come up with a deterministic way of rotating the key on each side of the transmission, but that's too complicated and error-prone. What we can do instead is use different IV/ nonce values for each individual encryption. In a worst-case scenario, the nonce can be sent with each packet. Unlike the key, the nonce does not have to be *secret*, merely *authentic*.

Additionally, we can use certain nonce construction algorithms to help prevent reuse. It is not OK to limit the randomness of a key because the key must be secret, and any bits chosen deterministically reduce the brute-force difficulty of discovering that secret. It *is* acceptable to reduce the randomness of some bits in an IV so long as the IV is never reused with the same key.

For example, some number of bytes of the IV could be device-specific. This ensures that two different devices can never generate the same nonce. Alternatively—or additionally—some bytes of the IV could be *inferred*, reducing the amount of IV data that has to be stored or transmitted. Perhaps part of the IV for a file encryption could depend on where the file is stored on disk.

For now, we will continue to generate random IVs and transmit them as needed, but it's good to understand some of the different ways that IVs can be generated and used.

EXERCISE 7.2. CHUNKY GCM

Modify the document encryption code from earlier in the chapter to encrypt in chunks no larger than 4096 bytes. Each encryption will use the same key, but a different nonce. This change means that rather than storing one IV and one tag at the top of the file, you will need to store an IV and a tag with each encrypted chunk.

Other AEAD Algorithms

In addition to AES-GCM mode, there are two other popular AEAD algorithms supported by the `cryptography` library. The first one is AES-CCM. The second is known as ChaCha.

AES-CCM is very similar to AES-GCM. Like GCM, it uses counter mode for the encryption; however, the tag is generated by a method similar to, but also superior to, CBC-MAC.

One critical difference between AES-CCM and AES-GCM is that the IV/nonce can be of variable length: between 7 and 13 bytes. The smaller the IV/nonce, the larger the data size that can be encrypted by the key/IV pair. Like GCM, this nonce is just a part of the full 16-byte counter value. Thus, the fewer of the 16 bytes used by the nonce, the more bytes that can be used by the counter before overflowing.

For reasons beyond the scope of this book, the nonce is constrained to be 15-L bytes long, where L is the size of the length field: if your data requires 2 bytes to store the length, the nonce can be up to 13 bytes. On the other hand, if the size of the data would require 8 bytes to store the length, the nonce is limited to 7 bytes. These two values represent the minimum and maximum values supported by the CCM mode.

Assuming that you want to use CCM for large amounts of data, just select a nonce of 7 bytes and move on. The security of the algorithm doesn't change based on nonce size, *so long as you do not reuse a nonce with a key*.

Besides this painful nonce issue, CCM has no other API differences over GCM. In terms of performance, however, GCM is more easily parallelized. That may not make much of a difference in your python programming, but it does make a difference if you want to use your graphics card as a cryptographic accelerator.

When using the `cryptography` library, CCM is not supported as a mode of operation to the AES cipher context. Only the self-contained `AESCCM` object is available.

```
>>> import os
>>> from cryptography.hazmat.primitives.ciphers.aead import AESCCM
>>> data = b"a secret message"
>>> aad = b"authenticated but unencrypted data"
>>> key = AESCCM.generate_key(bit_length=128)
>>> aesccm = AESCCM(key)
>>> nonce = os.urandom(7)
```

```
>>> ct = aesccm.encrypt(nonce, data, aad)
>>> aesccm.decrypt(nonce, ct, aad)
b'a secret message'
```

The last AEAD mode that we'll introduce to you is known as ChaCha20-Poly1305. This cipher is unique among the AEAD approaches discussed in this book, as it is the only AEAD algorithm not based on AES. Designed by Daniel J. Bernstein, it combines a stream cipher he designed named ChaCha20 with a MAC algorithm also designed by Bernstein named Poly1305. Bernstein is quite the cryptographer and is currently working on a number of projects related to elliptic curves, hashing, encryption, and asymmetric algorithms resistant to quantum-enabled attacks. He is also a programmer and has written a number of security-related programs.

Some in the security community worry that the popularity of AES means that if a severe vulnerability were ever found in AES, the cryptographic wheels of the Internet might grind to a halt. Establishing ChaCha as an effective alternative means that, should such a vulnerability be found, there would be a well-tested, well-established alternative already available. The fact that ChaCha20-Poly1305 is available as *authenticated* encryption is even better.

ChaCha20 has some other advantages. For purely software-powered implementations, ChaCha is typically faster than its peers. Moreover, it is a stream cipher by design. Whereas AES is a block cipher that can be used as a stream cipher, ChaCha is only a stream cipher. In the earlier days of the Internet, RC4 was a stream cipher that was used in a lot of security contexts including TLS and Wi-Fi. Unfortunately, it was found to have major vulnerabilities and weaknesses that have all but eliminated its use. ChaCha is seen by some as its spiritual successor.

Like AES-GCM, ChaCha20-Poly1305 expects a 12-byte nonce. Its API within the cryptography library is pretty much identical:

```
>>> import os
>>> from cryptography.hazmat.primitives.ciphers.aead import
    ChaCha20Poly1305
>>> data = b"a secret message"
>>> aad = b"authenticated but unencrypted data"
>>> key = ChaCha20Poly1305.generate_key()
>>> chacha = ChaCha20Poly1305(key)
>>> nonce = os.urandom(12)
```

```
>>> ct = chacha.encrypt(nonce, data, aad)
>>> chacha.decrypt(nonce, ct, aad)
b'a secret message'
```

Any of these AEAD algorithms can be used with more or less the same security guarantees. All three of them are considered to be much better than creating authenticated encryption by doing a separate cipher along with an accompanying MAC. Whenever AEAD algorithms are available, you should take advantage of them.

You may have noticed the generate_key methods for these three different modes. This is a convenience function, not a requirement. You can still use, for example, a key derivation function to create keys just as you always have. But as you can see with ChaCha, you don't even have to specify a bit size. It just gives you an appropriately sized key, which can eliminate a common class of errors.

EXERCISE 7.3. SPEEDY CHACHA

Create some speed comparison tests for AES-GCM, AES-CCM, and ChaCha20-Poly1305. Run one set of tests where a large amount of data is fed into each encrypt function exactly once. Test the speed of the decryption algorithm as well. Note that this also tests the tag check.

Run a second set of tests where large data is broken up into smaller chunks (perhaps 4 KiB each), and each chunk is individually encrypted.

Working the Network

The spies of East Antarctica are finally getting out of the stone age and have begun hooking computers up to the Internet. It's time that Alice and Bob learned to write some network-capable code for sending their codes back and forth.

Because they're using Python 3, Alice and Bob are going to do some asynchronous network programming using the asyncio module. If you've programmed with sockets before, this is going to be a little bit different.

By way of explanation, sockets are typically a *blocking* or *synchronous* approach to network communications. Sockets can be configured to be non-blocking, and in that mode you can use them with something like the select function to keep the program from getting stuck while you wait for data. Alternatively, sockets can be put in a thread to keep data flowing into the main program loop.

The `asyncio` module takes an asynchronous approach and attempts to model the data structure after the conceptual model of network communications. In particular, network data is processed by a `Protocol` object that has methods for handling `connection_made`, `data_received`, and `connection_lost` events. The `Protocol` object is plugged into an asynchronous event loop, and the `Protocol`'s event handlers are called when events are triggered.

A `Protocol` class typically looks something like Listing 7-3.

Listing 7-3. Network Protocol Intro

```
1    import asyncio
2
3    class ConcreteProtocol(asyncio.Protocol):
4        def connection_made(self, transport):
5            self.transport = transport
6
7        def data_received(self, data):
8            pass
9            # process data
10           # send data using transport.write as needed
11
12       def connection_lost(self, exc):
13           pass
14           # do cleanup
```

The contract for a `Protocol` object is that, after construction, there will be one call to `connection_made` when the underlying network is ready. This event will be followed by zero or more calls to `data_received`, followed by a single `connection_lost` call when the underlying network connection is broken.

A protocol can send data to the peer by calling `self.transport.write` and can force the connection to close by calling `self.transport.close`.

It should be noted that there is exactly one protocol object created per connection: when a *client* makes an outbound connection, there is only ever one connection and there is only ever one protocol. But, when a *server* is listening for connections on a port, there are potentially many connections at one time. A server spawns connections for each incoming client, and `asyncio` spawns a protocol object for each new connection.

That was a really fast overview of `asyncio`'s network API. A more detailed explanation is beyond the scope of this book, but if you need more information, the `asyncio` documentation is very thorough. Also, much of this will probably become clear as you follow along with the examples. Speaking of which, let's use what we have learned and create a "secure" echo server.

The echo protocol is the "Hello World" of network communications. Basically, a server listens on a port for client connections. When a client connects, it sends to the server a string of data (usually human readable). The server responds by mirroring back the exact same message (hence, "echo") and closing the connection. You can find plenty of examples of this on the Web, including an example in the `asyncio` documentation.

We are going to add a twist. We're going to build a variant that encrypts on transmission and decrypts on reception.

Let's start by creating the server, shown in Listing 7-4.

Listing 7-4. Secure Echo Server

```
1    from cryptography.hazmat.primitives.ciphers.aead import
     ChaCha20Poly1305
2    from cryptography.hazmat.primitives import hashes
3    from cryptography.hazmat.primitives.kdf.hkdf import HKDF
4    from cryptography.hazmat.backends import default_backend
5    import asyncio, os
6
7    PW = b"password"
8
9    class EchoServerProtocol(asyncio.Protocol):
10       def __init__(self, password):
11           # 64 bytes gives us 2 32-byte keys.
12           key_material = HKDF(
13               algorithm=hashes.SHA256(),
14               length=64, salt=None, info=None,
15               backend=default_backend()
16           ).derive(password)
17           self._server_read_key = key_material[0:32]
18           self._server_write_key = key_material[32:64]
19
```

```
20      def connection_made(self, transport):
21          peername = transport.get_extra_info('peername')
22          print('Connection from {}'.format(peername))
23          self.transport = transport
24
25      def data_received(self, data):
26          # Split out the nonce and the ciphertext.
27          nonce, ciphertext = data[:12], data[12:]
28          plaintext = ChaCha20Poly1305(self._server_read_key).decrypt(
29              nonce, ciphertext, b"")
30          message = plaintext.decode()
31          print('Decrypted message from client: {!r}'.format(message))
32
33          print('Echo back message: {!r}'.format(message))
34          reply_nonce = os.urandom(12)
35          ciphertext = ChaCha20Poly1305(self._server_write_key).encrypt(
36              reply_nonce, plaintext, b"")
37          self.transport.write(reply_nonce + ciphertext)
38
39          print('Close the client socket')
40          self.transport.close()
41
42  loop = asyncio.get_event_loop()
43  # Each client connection will create a new protocol instance
44  coro = loop.create_server(lambda: EchoServerProtocol(PW),
    '127.0.0.1', 8888)
45  server = loop.run_until_complete(coro)
46
47  # Serve requests until Ctrl+C is pressed
48  print('Serving on {}'.format(server.sockets[0].getsockname()))
49  try:
50      loop.run_forever()
51  except KeyboardInterrupt:
52      pass
53
```

```
54   # Close the server
55   server.close()
56   loop.run_until_complete(server.wait_closed())
57   loop.close()
```

There is a single protocol class in this file: EchoServerProtocol. For illustrative purposes, the connection_made method reports the details of the connecting client. This will typically be the client's IP address and outbound TCP port. This is for flavor only and not essential to the operation of the server.

The real meat is in data_received method. This method receives data, decrypts it, re-encrypts it, and sends it back to the client.

Actually, we're getting a little ahead of ourselves: for this encryption, where does the key come from? The password is a parameter to the EchoServerProtocol constructor, but if you look down at the create_server line later in the code, you will see that we are passing in a hard-coded value. In honor of the fact that "password" is still a common password, we have chosen that string as the "secret"[1].

Using the password, the EchoServerProtocol derives two keys: a "read" key and a "write" key. Because we will be using randomized nonces, we could use the same key for both the client and the server, but having two separate keys is easy to do and is good practice. We use HKDF to generate 64 bytes of key material and split that into two keys: the server's read key and the server's write key.

Going back to the data_received method, remember that this method is called when we have received something from the client. Thus, the data variable is what the client sent us. We are assuming (without any error checking) that the client sent a 12-byte nonce followed by an arbitrary amount of ciphertext. Using that nonce and our server's read key, we can decrypt the ciphertext. Note that the third parameter is just an empty byte string because we are not authenticating any additional data for now.

Once the data is decrypted, the recovered plaintext is re-encrypted under the server's write key and a newly generated nonce. We could have reused the nonce because we have a different key, but using a separate nonce is good practice and keeps both sides of the transmission using the same message format. The new nonce and the re-encrypted message are then sent back to the client.

---

[1]If anyone reading this book is still using "password" for any passwords that actually matter, please stop reading and go change it. Really. We'll wait.

The rest of this sets up the server. You can ignore most of it, with the exception of the create_server method. This method sets up a listener on local port 8888 and associates it with an anonymous factory function. That lambda will get called each time there is a new incoming connection. In other words, for each incoming client connection, a new EchoServerProtocol object is produced.

With the server code finished, we create the client code in Listing 7-5 that sends the initial message and decrypts the response.

Listing 7-5. Secure Echo Client

```
1    from cryptography.hazmat.primitives.ciphers.aead import ChaCha20Poly1305
2    from cryptography.hazmat.primitives import hashes
3    from cryptography.hazmat.primitives.kdf.hkdf import HKDF
4    from cryptography.hazmat.backends import default_backend
5    import asyncio, os, sys
6
7    PW = b"password"
8
9    class EchoClientProtocol(asyncio.Protocol):
10       def __init__(self, message, password):
11           self.message = message
12
13           # 64 bytes gives us 2 32-byte keys
14           key_material = HKDF(
15               algorithm=hashes.SHA256(),
16               length=64, salt=None, info=None,
17               backend=default_backend()
18           ).derive(password)
19           self._client_write_key = key_material[0:32]
20           self._client_read_key = key_material[32:64]
21
22       def connection_made(self, transport):
23           plaintext = self.message.encode()
24           nonce = os.urandom(12)
25           ciphertext = ChaCha20Poly1305(self._client_write_key).encrypt(
26               nonce, plaintext, b"")
```

```
27            transport.write(nonce + ciphertext)
28            print('Encrypted data sent: {!r}'.format(self.message))
29
30        def data_received(self, data):
31            nonce, ciphertext = data[:12], data[12:]
32            plaintext = ChaCha20Poly1305(self._client_read_key).decrypt(
33                nonce, ciphertext, b"")
34            print('Decrypted response from server: {!r}'.format(plaintext.
              decode()))
35
36        def connection_lost(self, exc):
37            print('The server closed the connection')
38            asyncio.get_event_loop().stop()
39
40    loop = asyncio.get_event_loop()
41    message = sys.argv[1]
42    coro = loop.create_connection(lambda: EchoClientProtocol(message, PW),
43                                  '127.0.0.1', 8888)
44    loop.run_until_complete(coro)
45    loop.run_forever()
46    loop.close()
```

This code has some similarities to the server that should be readily apparent. First of all, we have the same hard-coded (really bad) password. Obviously we need the same password or the two sides wouldn't be able to communicate with each other. We also have the same key derivation routine in the constructor.

There are important differences, though. If you look at how the key material is divided up, this time the first 32 bytes is the client's *write* key and the second 32 bytes is the client's *read* key. In the server code, this is of course reversed.

This is not an accident. We are dealing with symmetric keys; what the client writes, the server reads and vice versa. In other words, the client's write key is the server's read key. When you derive keys, you have to make sure that the order in which key material is split up is correctly managed on both sides. There were a few earlier exercises that dealt with this without so much explanation. If those exercises didn't make as much sense at the time, now might be a good time to go revisit them.

Another way to solve this problem is to always call the derived keys the same thing on both sides. So, for example, instead of deriving a "read" key and a "write" key, you could instead choose to use the names "client write" key and a "server write" key for both the client and the server. That way, the first 32 bytes can always be the client's write key and the second 32 bytes is the server's write key.

Once these two keys are created, the other names are just aliases. That is, "client read" key is just an alias for "server write" key and "server read" key is just an alias for "client write" key.

EXERCISE 7.4. WHAT'S IN A NAME?

In many circumstances, "read" and "write" are the correct names to use because despite calling one computer a client and one computer a server, they behave as *equal* peers.

But, if you are dealing with a context where a client *only* makes requests and the server *only* responds to requests, you can rename your keys appropriately. The echo client/server we have created is an example of this pattern.

Starting with the code in Listings 7-4 and 7-5, change all references to "read" and "write" data or keys to be "request" and "response" instead. Name them appropriately! The client writes a request and reads a response, while the server reads a request and writes a response. What happens to the relationship between client and server code?

Another difference from the server code is that we transmit data in the client's `connection_made` method. This is because the server waits for the client to send something before it responds, while the client just transmits as soon as it can.

The transmission of the data itself should look familiar. A nonce is generated and the nonce and ciphertext are written using `transport.write`.

The server's response is handled in `data_received`. This should also look familiar. The nonce is split out and the ciphertext is decrypted using the read key and the received nonce.

In the `create_connection` method, you will notice that we still use an anonymous lambda function to build instances of the client protocol class. This might surprise you. In the server, using a factory function makes sense because there may be multiple connections requiring multiple protocol instances. In an outbound connection, though, there is just one protocol instance and one connection. Practically speaking, the factory is unnecessary. It is used so that the APIs for `create_server` and `create_connection` are as similar as possible.

This code is a good start for playing around with network protocols that use cryptography. For real network communications, though, additional machinery is often needed. One problem that might appear in production code is messages that get split across multiple `data_received` calls, or multiple messages that get condensed into a single `data_received` call. The `data_received` method treats incoming data as a *stream*, which means that there are no guarantees on how much data will be received in a single call. The `asyncio` library has no idea whether the data you send is meant to be split up or not. To solve this problem, you need to be able to recognize where one message ends and another begins. That typically requires some buffering in case not all data is received at once and a protocol that indicates where to split out the individual messages.

An Introduction to Kerberos

Although PKI is widely used today for establishing and authenticating identity, there are algorithms for establishing identity and trust between two parties using only symmetric encryption. As with PKI, these algorithms require a trusted third party.

One of the most well-known protocols for authenticated communications between two parties is *Kerberos*. Kerberos is a type of single sign-on (SSO) service that was developed into its current (version 5) form by the early 1990s. Although it has had updates since then, the protocol has remained largely the same. It allows someone to log in to the Kerberos system first and then have access to other network resources without logging in again. What's really cool about it is that, while extensions have been added to use PKI for certain components, the core algorithms all use symmetric cryptography.

Alice and Bob have heard that Kerberos is now being deployed on systems within certain WA networks. In order to explore various opportunities for infiltrating these systems and looking for weaknesses therein, Alice and Bob spend some time back at HQ learning how Kerberos works.

We are going to help Alice and Bob create some Kerberos-like code. As with most of the examples in this book, this is not real Kerberos and the full system is beyond the scope of this book. We can still explore the basic components and get a feel for how Kerberos performs its magic using relatively simple network protocols. We will attempt to identify the more advanced and complicated pieces that we are leaving out, but if you really want to understand production Kerberos in depth, you will need to research additional sources.

We are also going to introduce some new notation for describing messages sent in a cryptographic protocol. Building upon how we already denote ciphertext under a key ({plaintext}K), we now add in some notation to express one party (principal) sending a message to another. Suppose Alice wants to send a message to Bob that includes her name (in the clear) and some ciphertext encrypted under a shared key. Our notation for this intended exchange looks like this:

$$A \rightarrow B : A, \{\text{plaintext}\} K_{A,B}.$$

The arrow you see does not represent *receiving* the message. Bob may never get it because of data loss or because Eve intercepts it. The arrow represents *intent*, so $A \rightarrow B$ means that A (Alice) intends to send a message to B (Bob). For practical purposes, however, it is sometimes simpler to just think of it as sending and receiving, so we will make that simplifying assumption as well.

The A represents Alice's name, or identity string. Identity strings can be a lot of things. It could be Alice's legal name, a username, a URI, or just an opaque token. Because the A in the message is not within any braces, it is plaintext. The ciphertext under $K_{A,B}$ is the same notation we've used before to represent a key shared by A and B. However, when A is sending data to B encrypted under a secret that "belongs" to B (e.g., under a key derived from a password associated with B), we will label this key as K_B. Even though A knows this secret and, technically, it is a shared key, the idea is that the message is being encrypted exclusively for use by B.

Kerberos has multiple principals and the message exchange can be a little complicated. We will use this notation to help express who is sending data to whom.

Thus prepared, Alice and Bob sit down for a class on how Kerberos works. The first lesson is about how Kerberos uses a central repository of identities *and passwords*. Unlike a certificate authority that does not necessarily keep an online registry of all signed certificates—and certainly does not store any private keys—the Kerberos authentication server (AS) tracks every usable identity and maps it to a password. This data must be available at all times.

The Kerberos AS is a very sensitive part of the system obviously. Should the AS be compromised, the attacker gains knowledge of every password for every user. Thus, this system should be carefully guarded. Moreover, if the AS *goes down*, the rest of Kerberos falls apart. The AS must, therefore, be resistant to denial-of-service (DoS) attacks.

Let's pause and build a quick skeletal framework of our toy AS. Throughout this example and starting in Listing 7-6, we will refer to our system as SimpleKerberos to indicate that this is not the full protocol. We'll start by creating a protocol class for the AS and hard-coding a dumb dictionary-based password database. We don't know what the AS *does* yet, so we'll leave all the networking methods blank.

Listing 7-6. Kerberos Authentication Server

```
1    # Partial Listing: Some Assembly Required
2
3    # Skeleton for Kerberos AS Code, User Database, initial class decl
4    import asyncio, json, os, time
5    from cryptography.hazmat.backends import default_backend
6    from cryptography.hazmat.primitives import hashes
7    from cryptography.hazmat.primitives.ciphers import Cipher, algorithms,
     modes
8    from cryptography.hazmat.primitives import padding
9    from cryptography.hazmat.primitives.kdf.hkdf import HKDF
10
11   # we used the most common passwords
12   # from 2018 according to wikipedia
13   # https://en.wikipedia.org/wiki/List_of_the_most_common_passwords
14   USER_DATABASE = {
15       "johndoe": "123456",
16       "janedoe": "password",
17       "h_world": "123456789",
18   }
19
20   class SimpleKerberosAS(asyncio.Protocol):
21       def connection_made(self, transport):
22           self.transport = transport
23
24       def data_received(self, data):
25           pass
```

There's nothing complicated in Listing 7-6 so far: just a username-to-password dictionary and an empty protocol class. To fill in these methods, we need to know how the AS works.

At this point, some *really cool* cryptography appears! How should a user log in? We definitely don't want to send a password *in the clear* over the wire. The user obviously had to register with the AS in order for their password to be stored there, so should we have used that as an opportunity to create a shared encryption key?

It turns out that none of these things are necessary! A user can log in *just by sending their name*. Using our protocol notation, here is how Alice logs in to the AS:

$$A \rightarrow AS : A.$$

Really? How does that work? What keeps Eve from just sending Alice's name?

The magic is in the *response*. The AS is going to send back encrypted data that only the *real* Alice can decrypt. This assumes that Alice knows her password and nobody else does.

First, the AS is going to derive Alice's key K_A from her password. Then, the AS will send back a newly generated session key encrypted under Alice's K_A key!

$$AS \rightarrow A : \left\{ K_{session} \right\} K_A$$

If Alice knows the password, she will be able to derive K_A and decrypt the session key, the purpose of which we will explain in just a moment. For now, we'll just say that it's needed as part of the SSO operation.

Kerberos resists replay attacks by using both timestamps and nonces. While configurable, Kerberos will typically not accept messages that are more than 5 minutes old. The timestamp is also used as a nonce, meaning that the same timestamp cannot be used twice. The timestamp includes a microsecond field; it is difficult to imagine a client sending two requests within the same microsecond. The real Kerberos checks to see if, by some small chance, it is sending multiple packets with the same time (down to the microsecond). If that happens, it should artificially increase the value of the microsecond field in the timestamp by one.

For simplicity, we are going to use timestamps without treating them like nonces (e.g., checking for repeats). We'll update our protocol to include t_1 as Alice's timestamp:

$$A \rightarrow AS : A, t_1.$$

Let's update our AS to receive Alice's message and to send back an encrypted session key. For messages we've sent in previous examples and exercises, we've just concatenated data together with enough fixed-length pieces that we could break apart all of the individual elements.

This time, we're sending messages of less predictable length. When Alice transmits her username and timestamp, how will the AS be able to split out the two parts of the message? We could use a delimiter, such as a comma, and prohibit it from being part of a username, but we will be sending multiple *encrypted values*. How will we know where one ends and another begins? Delimiters can't be used directly on raw encrypted data because that data makes use of all possible byte values.

In real network communications, this problem is solved in many ways. For example, HTTP sends metadata using delimiters (e.g., key: value<newline>), and if any data is arbitrary (and might contain the delimiter), it is either escaped or converted to ASCII using some predefined algorithm, such as Base-64 encoding. Other network packets are created by serializing all values and including a length field as part of the binary packet.

To keep things simple for this exercise, we are going to use Python's json library to serialize and de-serialize dictionaries for us. We already used this once in a previous chapter for storing data to disk. Now we will use json to encode data transmitted over a network. However, json doesn't always play nice with byte strings. Listing 7-7 defines two quick methods for quickly dumping our dictionaries to JSON and reloading from them again. Make sure you have this code in all three of the Kerberos scripts we will create in this example (or import them from a common file).

Listing 7-7. Utility Functions for JSON Handling

```
1   # These helper functions deal with json's lack of bytes support
2   def dump_packet(p):
3       for k, v in p.items():
4           if isinstance(v, bytes):
5               p[k] = list(v)
6       return json.dumps(p).encode('utf-8')
7
8   def load_packet(json_data):
9       p = json.loads(json_data)
10      for k, v in p.items():
11          if isinstance(v, list):
12              p[k] = bytes(v)
13      return p
```

Real Kerberos calls the packet sent from Alice to the AS an "AS_REQ packet." We will use that notation as well. Alice's packet to our simple Kerberos AS will be a dictionary with the following fields:

- type: AS_REQ

- principal: Alice's username

- timestamp: A current timestamp

When the AS receives the data, it needs to check if the timestamp is fresh and if the user is in the database. Let's update our `data_received` method to handle this in Listing 7-8.

Listing 7-8. Kerberos AS Receiver

```
1   # Partial Listing: Some Assembly Required
2
3   class SimpleKerberosAS(asyncio.Protocol):
4   ...
5       def data_received(self, data):
6           packet = load_packet(data)
7           response = {}
8           if packet["type"] == "AS_REQ":
9               clienttime = packet["timestamp"]
10              if abs(time.time()-clienttime) > 300:
11                  response["type"] = "ERROR"
12                  response["message"] = "Timestamp is too old"
13              elif packet["principal"] not in USER_DATABASE:
14                  response["type"] = "ERROR"
15                  response["message"] = "Unknown principal"
```

Once the "packet" is restored, it is just a dictionary. We first check the type and make sure it is the type of packet we expected. Next, we check the timestamp. If the delta is greater than 300 seconds (5 minutes), we send back an error. Similarly, if the username is not in the password database, we also send back an error.

This error packet type is completely made up. Kerberos uses a different packet structure to report an error, but this will meet our needs.

Now we get to the fun part. Assuming the timestamp is recent and the username is in our database, we need to derive the user's key from their password, create a session key, and send back this session key encrypted under the user's key.

What algorithms and parameters should we use?

This is one area where the real Kerberos is significantly more complicated than what we're going to do. The real Kerberos, like many cryptographic protocols, actually defines a *suite* of algorithms that can be used for its various operations. When Kerberos v5 was first deployed, the DES symmetric encryption algorithm was widely used. Now, of course, that's largely been retired and AES has been added.

We know better by now than to think that "AES" is a complete answer. What *mode* of AES are we using? And where do we get the IV from?

Interestingly, Kerberos uses a mode of operation called "CTS" (ciphertext stealing). We aren't going to spend a lot of time on this mode of operation (which is typically built on top of CBC mode), but we will briefly mention that for many Kerberos cipher suites, they are not using an IV to differentiate the messages. Instead, they use a "confounder." A confounder is a random, block-sized plaintext message prepended to the real data. When using CBC mode, a random first block serves, in many ways, the same function as an IV.

We're not going to mess with these complexities. We will focus on the encryption process and how symmetric encryption is used in the protocol. So, for our simple Kerberos, we will use AES-CBC with a fixed IV full of zeros. We will also leave out the MAC operation for now. It should be obvious that this is not secure and should not be used in production environments.

Let's write helper functions for deriving keys from passwords, encrypting, and decrypting. These are found in Listing 7-9.

Listing 7-9. Kerberos with Encryption

```
1   # Partial Listing: Some Assembly Required
2
3   # Encryption Functions for Kerberos AS
4   def derive_key(password):
5       return HKDF(
6               algorithm=hashes.SHA256(),
7               length=32,
8               salt=None,
```

```
 9                info=None,
10              backend=default_backend()
11      ).derive(password.encode())
12
13  def encrypt(data, key):
14      encryptor = Cipher(
15          algorithms.AES(key),
16          modes.CBC(b"\x00"*16),
17          backend=default_backend()
18      ).encryptor()
19      padder = padding.PKCS7(128).padder()
20      padded_message = padder.update(data) + padder.finalize()
21      return encryptor.update(padded_message) + encryptor.finalize()
22
23  def decrypt(encrypted_data, key):
24      decryptor = Cipher(
25          algorithms.AES(key),
26          modes.CBC(b"\x00"*16),
27          backend=default_backend()
28      ).decryptor()
29      unpadder = padding.PKCS7(128).unpadder()
30      padded_message = decryptor.update(encrypted_data) +
        decryptor.finalize()
31      return unpadder.update(padded_message) + unpadder.finalize()
```

Notice that we used padding in order to satisfy the CBC requirements. As a side
note, one reason why Kerberos uses CTS mode is because it doesn't require padding. It's
called "stealing" because it steals some cryptographic data from the penultimate block to
fill in the last block's missing bytes.

The preceding three functions will be used in multiple scripts, so you may want to
save them in a separate file and import them.

Now we're ready to send our response from the AS, in Listing 7-10. Kerberos calls
this packet an AS_REP and we will do the same. Our response will be a dictionary that we
serialize before sending. For reasons that we will explain shortly, we are not encrypting
the entire packet; we are only encrypting a portion we call the user_data.

Listing 7-10. Kerberos AS Responder

```
1    # Partial Listing: Some Assembly Required
2
3    class SimpleKerberosAS(asyncio.Protocol):
4    ...
5        def data_received(self, data):
6            packet = load_packet(data)
7            response = {}
8            if packet["type"] == "AS_REQ":
9                if ... # check errors
10               else:
11                   response["type"] = "AS_REP"
12
13                   session_key = os.urandom(32)
14                   user_data = {
15                       "session_key":session_key,
16                       }
17                   user_key = derive_key(USER_DATABASE[packet["principal"]])
18                   user_data_encrypted = encrypt(dump_packet(user_data),
                         user_key)
19                   response["user_data"] = user_data_encrypted
20           self.transport.write(dump_packet(response))
21       self.transport.close()
```

That seems pretty reasonable. Now we need to write the client side of this, but before we do, it's time to explain how the next piece of the Kerberos protocol works.

Once Alice has logged in via the AS, she next needs to talk to a different entity called the Ticket-Granting Service (TGS). Alice will tell the TGS which service, or application, she would like to connect to. The TGS will verify that she is logged in and then provide her with the credentials to use for that service.

To enable Alice to convince the TGS that she is logged in, the AS also sends her what is called a Ticket-Granting Ticket (TGT). The TGT is information encrypted *under the TGS's key* that proves to the TGS that the AS has verified Alice's identity. This modifies our protocol thus:

$$\text{AS} \rightarrow A: \{K_{\text{sessoin}}\} K_A, \text{TGT}.$$

The TGT is opaque to Alice. She cannot decrypt or read it in any way; she can only pass it to the TGS. The TGT contains the very same session key sent to Alice, Alice's name (identity), and a timestamp. Real Kerberos includes additional data such as the IP address and a ticket lifetime, but the first three elements are the most critical for cryptography. This first phase of the Kerberos protocol is shown in Figure 7-1.

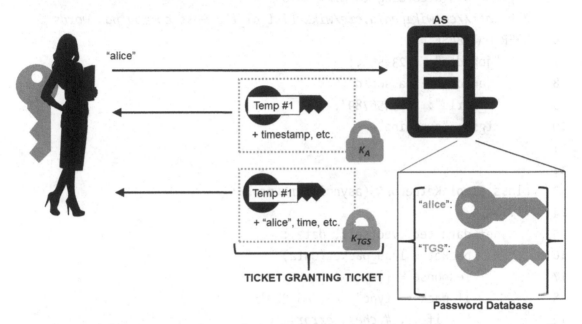

Figure 7-1. *Alice initiates the Kerberos login process with a clear text message of her identity. The AS looks up her key in its database and encrypts a session key for the TGS. It also sends the TGT to Alice encrypted under the TGS's key.*

As stated, the session key is sent both to Alice (under her key) and to the TGS within the TGT (encrypted under the TGS key). This key is a session key between Alice and the TGS that will allow them to communicate. We should rename $K_{session}$ to be $K_{A,TGS}$. If we expand TGT within our protocol notation, what we now have is

$$AS \rightarrow A : \{K_{A,TGS}\}K_A, \{K_{A,TGS}, A, t_2\}K_{TGS}.$$

We need to update our code to include the TGT. We also need to update our user database to have an entry for the TGS. In real Kerberos, the TGS's key is not necessarily derived from a password stored in the password database, but it will be easier for us to run the AS, TGS, and other services if the shared keys are all derived from passwords we can input at the command line. This is shown in Listing 7-11.

277

Listing 7-11. Kerberos Ticket-Granting Ticket

```
1    # Partial Listing: Some Assembly Required
2
3    # we used the most common passwords
4    # from 2018 according to wikipedia
5    # https://en.wikipedia.org/wiki/List_of_the_most_common_passwords
6    USER_DATABASE = {
7        "johndoe": "123456",
8        "janedoe": "password",
9        "h_world": "123456789",
10       "tgs": "sunshine"
11   }
12
13   class SimpleKerberosAS(asyncio.Protocol):
14   ...
15       def data_received(self, data):
16           packet = load_packet(data)
17           response = {}
18           if packet["type"] == "AS_REQ":
19               if ... # check errors
20               else:
21                   response["type"] = "AS_REP"
22
23                   session_key = os.urandom(32)
24                   user_data = {
25                       "session_key":session_key,
26                       }
27                   tgt = {
28                       "session_key":session_key,
29                       "client_principal":packet["principal"],
30                       "timestamp":time.time()
31                       }
32                   user_key = derive_key(USER_DATABASE[packet["principal"]])
33                   user_data_encrypted = encrypt(dump_packet(user_data),
                     user_key)
```

```
34                    response["user_data"] = user_data_encrypted
35
36                    tgs_key = derive_key(USER_DATABASE["tgs"])
37                    tgt_encrypted = encrypt(dump_packet(tgt), tgs_key)
38                    response["tgt"] = tgt_encrypted
39               self.transport.write(dump_packet(response))
40          self.transport.close()
```

Let's start working on the client now and create a protocol class for that side of the communication. First, our class (Listing 7-12) needs to be able to transmit the username to the AS, and it needs the password for deriving its own key. We'll pass these in as parameters to the class constructor.

We will also pass in a callback function on_login for receiving the session key and TGT when they are received.

Listing 7-12. Kerberos Login

```
1    # Partial Listing: Some Assembly Required
2
3    # Skeleton for Kerberos Client Code. Imports, initial class decl
4    # Dependencies: derive_key(), encrypt(), decrypt(),
5    #               load_packet(), dump_packet()
6    import asyncio, json, sys, time
7    from cryptography.hazmat.backends import default_backend
8    from cryptography.hazmat.primitives import hashes
9    from cryptography.hazmat.primitives.ciphers import Cipher, algorithms,
     modes
10   from cryptography.hazmat.primitives import padding
11   from cryptography.hazmat.primitives.kdf.hkdf import HKDF
12
13   class SimpleKerberosLogin(asyncio.Protocol):
14       def __init__(self, username, password, on_login):
15           self.username = username
16           self.password = password
17           self.on_login = on_login
18
```

```
19          self.session_key = None
20          self.tgt = None
```

The SimpleKerberosLogin class should transmit the user's identity as soon as the connection is made, so let's put that functionality into the connection_made method in Listing 7-13.

Listing 7-13. Kerberos Login Connection

```
1   # Partial Listing: Some Assembly Required
2
3   # Dependencies: derive_key(), encrypt(), decrypt()
4   class SimpleKerberosLogin(asyncio.Protocol):
5   ...
6       def connection_made(self, transport):
7           self.transport = transport
8           request = {
9               "type":      "AS_REQ",
10              "principal": self.username,
11              "timestamp": time.time()
12          }
13          self.transport.write(dump_packet(request))
```

There should be no surprises in there. We create our AS_REQ packet and send it along. When the server writes back to us, it will either be an error or an AS_REP packet. If it's the latter, we will need to decrypt the user_data to get our session key. The TGT is opaque to us and is not processed in any other way.

Listing 7-14. Kerberos Login Receiver

```
1   # Partial Listing: Some Assembly Required
2
3   # Dependencies: derive_key(), encrypt(), decrypt()
4   class SimpleKerberosLogin(asyncio.Protocol):
5   ...
6       def data_received(self, data):
7           packet = load_packet(data)
8           if packet["type"] == "AS_REP":
```

```
 9              user_data_encrypted = packet["user_data"]
10              user_key = derive_key(self.password)
11              user_data_bytes = decrypt(user_data_encrypted, user_key)
12              user_data = load_packet(user_data_bytes)
13              self.session_key = user_data["session_key"]
14              self.tgt = packet["tgt"]
15          elif packet["type"] == "ERROR":
16              print("ERROR: {}".format(packet["message"]))
17
18          self.transport.close()
19
20      def connection_lost(self, exc):
21          self.on_login(self.session_key, self.tgt)
```

The connection will close one way or another in Listing 7-14. When it does, we trigger our callback with the session key and TGT. If there were errors, these values will be None.

The code we've written so far should give us a client that can connect to the AS, send an identity, and receive back an encrypted session key and TGT. Now, it's time to create the TGS (Ticket-Granting Service)!

In many Kerberos systems, the AS and TGS are co-located on the same host. They serve similar purposes and have similar security requirements. In many cases, they may need to share database information. For our exercise, however, and in order to visualize the TGS as a separate entity, we have it run as a separate script.

When Alice is logged in and wishes to talk to a service S, Alice sends a message to the TGS with the TGT, the name of the service, and an "authenticator." The authenticator contains Alice's identity and a timestamp encrypted under $K_{A,TGS}$, the session key generated by the AS. That same session key is within the TGT. When the TGS decrypts the TGT and obtains $K_{A,TGS}$, the TGS will be able to decrypt the authenticator and verify that Alice also has the Key $K_{A,TGS}$. If Alice did not have that key, she would not have been able to create the authenticator. The fact that she has that key, and that the same key is in the TGT, means that the AS authorized her for this communication.

By way of protocol notation, here is the message that Alice sends to the TGS:

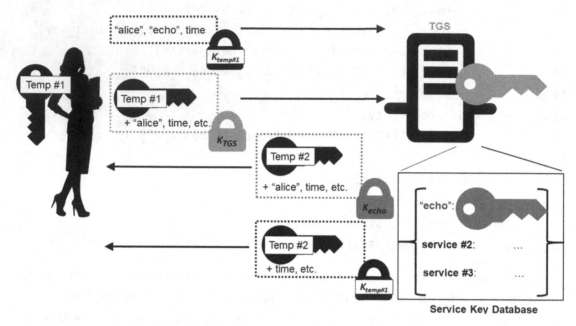

Figure 7-2. *Alice uses the TGT to prove her identity and asks the TGS for a session key to communicate with the echo service. Similar to the TGT, Alice will receive an encrypted message for the echo service that she cannot open but can forward.*

$$A \rightarrow \mathrm{TGS} : S, \{A, t_3\} \, K_{A,\mathrm{TGS}}, \{K_{A,\mathrm{TGS}}, A, t_2\} \, K_{\mathrm{TGS}}.$$

If the TGS validates the data and approves the request, it sends back a ticket and a new session key for Alice to communicate with the service *S*. Like the TGT, the ticket is opaque to Alice. It is encrypted under *S*'s key and contains authorization data related to Alice. Specifically, it contains Alice's identity, the service's identity, and a timestamp. Again, the real Kerberos ticket contains additional data not included here. The protocol notation for this transmission is

$$\mathrm{TGS} \rightarrow A : \{S, K_{A,S}\} \, K_{A,\mathrm{TGS}}, \{K_{A,S}, A, t_3\} \, K_S.$$

Figure 7-2 depicts this process.

Alice will use her session key with the TGS to decrypt the new session key for her to use with service *S*. But before we do that part, let's get the TGS written.

Much of the Ticket-Granting Service's operations are the same as the Authentication Service's, and we will not write out all the code again. However, it is worth noting that the TGS requires a database with keys for the various services it authorizes. We have, again, used a database with passwords to make things easier. Our sample code in Listing 7-15 has just one service: echo.

Listing 7-15. Kerberos Ticket-Granting Service

```
1   # Partial Listing: Some Assembly Required
2
3   # Skeleton for Kerberos TGS. Imports, initial class decl, Service DB
4   # Dependencies: derive_key(), encrypt(), decrypt(),
5   #               load_packet(), dump_packet()
6   import asyncio, json, os, time, sys
7   from cryptography.hazmat.backends import default_backend
8   from cryptography.hazmat.primitives import hashes
9   from cryptography.hazmat.primitives.ciphers import Cipher, algorithms,
    modes
10  from cryptography.hazmat.primitives import padding
11  from cryptography.hazmat.primitives.kdf.hkdf import HKDF
12
13  # we used the most common passwords
14  # from 2018 according to wikipedia
15  # https://en.wikipedia.org/wiki/List_of_the_most_common_passwords
16  SERVICE_DATABASE = {
17      "echo":"qwerty",
18  }
19
20  class SimpleKerberosTGS(asyncio.Protocol):
21      def __init__(self, password):
22          self.password = password
```

Notice that we also handed a password to the constructor. Our SimpleKerberosTGS needs to be able to derive its key; otherwise, it wouldn't be able to decrypt the TGT sent to it by the AS.

The meat of the TGS code is within data_received in Listing 7-16. We will jump right inside that method to where the TGS server receives a TGS_REQ packet (following Kerberos naming).

Listing 7-16. Kerberos TGS Receiver

```
1   # Partial Listing: Some Assembly Required
2
3   class SimpleKerberosTGS(asyncio.Protocol):
4   ...
5       def data_received(self, data):
6           packet = load_packet(data)
7           response = {}
8           if packet["type"] == "TGS_REQ":
9               tgsKey = derive_key(self.password)
10              tgt_bytes = decrypt(packet["tgt"], tgsKey)
11              tgt = load_packet(tgt_bytes)
12
13              authenticator_bytes = decrypt(packet["authenticator"],
                    tgt["session_key"])
14              authenticator = load_packet(authenticator_bytes)
15
16              clienttime = authenticator["timestamp"]
17              if abs(time.time()-clienttime) > 300:
18                  response["type"] = "ERROR"
19                  response["message"] = "Timestamp is too old"
20              elif authenticator["principal"] != tgt["client_principal"]:
21                  response["type"] = "ERROR"
22                  response["message"] = "Principal mismatch"
23              elif packet["service"] not in SERVICE_DATABASE:
24                  response["type"] = "ERROR"
25                  response["message"] = "Unknown service"
26              else:
27                  response["type"] = "TGS_REP"
28
```

```
29              service_session_key = os.urandom(32)
30              user_data = {
31                  "service":               packet["service"],
32                  "service_session_key": service_session_key,
33                  }
34              ticket = {
35                  "service_session_key": service_session_key,
36                  "client_principal":    authenticator["principal"],
37                  "timestamp":           time.time()
38                  }
39              user_data_encrypted = encrypt(dump_packet(user_data),
                tgt["session_key"])
40              response["user_data"] = user_data_encrypted
41
42              service_key = derive_key(SERVICE_
                DATABASE[packet["service"]])
43              ticket_encrypted = encrypt(dump_packet(ticket),
                service_key)
44              response["ticket"] = ticket_encrypted
45          self.transport.write(dump_packet(response))
46      self.transport.close()
```

Much of this looks very similar to the AS code, as we suggested it would. But there are a few key differences.

First, the TGS has to decrypt the authenticator to get the timestamp. It is not sent in the clear this time, but it ensures that the encrypted data (the authenticator) is at least somewhat fresh (within the last 5 minutes). In real Kerberos, timestamps would be stored and duplicates identified and discarded.

Also note that the TGS checks that the principal is the same in the authenticator as in the TGT. It must do this check to ensure that the identity authorized by the AS is the same identity asking for a ticket.

Finally, the user's data with the session key and so forth is not encrypted under a key derived from their password (which the TGS doesn't have anyway). Rather, it is encrypted under the session key $K_{A, TGS}$. The TGS encrypts with this key because only Alice should be able to decrypt it.

We need to update the client code to handle the TGS communications. This involves processing the login information received from the AS and triggering a new communication to the TGS. Let's first create the SimpleKerberosGetTicket class in Listing 7-17 to communicate with the TGS server we just created.

Listing 7-17. Get Kerberos Ticket

```
1    # Partial Listing: Some Assembly Required
2
3    # SimpleKerberosGetTicket is also part of the Client
4    # This class connects to the TGS to get a ticket
5    class SimpleKerberosGetTicket(asyncio.Protocol):
6        def __init__(self, username, service, session_key, tgt, on_ticket):
7            self.username = username
8            self.service = service
9            self.session_key = session_key
10           self.tgt = tgt
11           self.on_ticket = on_ticket
12
13           self.server_session_key = None
14           self.ticket = None
15
16       def connection_made(self, transport):
17           print("TGS connection made")
18           self.transport = transport
19           authenticator = {
20               "principal": self.username,
21               "timestamp": time.time()
22           }
23           authenticator_encrypted = encrypt(dump_packet(authenticator ),
             self.session_key)
24           request = {
25               "type":          "TGS_REQ",
26               "service":       self.service,
27               "authenticator": authenticator_encrypted,
28               "tgt":           self.tgt
29           }
```

```
30          self.transport.write(dump_packet(request))
31
32      def data_received(self, data):
33          packet = load_packet(data)
34          if packet["type"] == "TGS_REP":
35              user_data_encrypted = packet["user_data"]
36              user_data_bytes = decrypt(user_data_encrypted, self.
                session_key)
37              user_data = load_packet(user_data_bytes)
38              self.server_session_key = user_data["service_session_key"]
39              self.ticket = packet["ticket"]
40          elif packet["type"] == "ERROR":
41              print("ERROR: {}".format(packet["message"]))
42
43          self.transport.close()
44
45      def connection_lost(self, exc):
46          self.on_ticket(self.server_session_key, self.tgt)
```

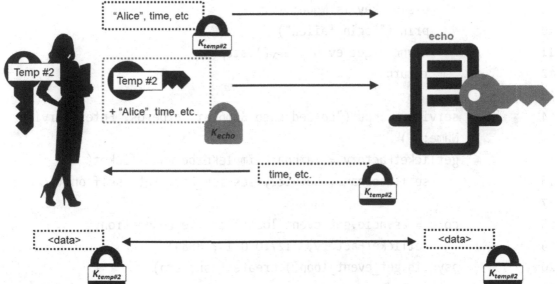

Figure 7-3. *Both Alice and the echo service end up with a shared symmetric key that they can use for secure communications*

This protocol, on connection, sends the TGS_REQ packet along with the encrypted authenticator, the service name, and the TGT. Remember, the TGT was transmitted by the AS, as was the session key. These pieces of data are passed to the constructor of this protocol. Once we receive the TGS_REP, we can extract the service's session key and the ticket to send to the service. We use another callback on_ticket to process this information.

Figure 7-3 shows the rest of the protocol.

To glue all of this together, we use a ResponseHandler class in Listing 7-18 to receive the callbacks on_login and on_ticket. The on_login will also trigger the call to the TGS.

Listing 7-18. Kerberos Client

```
 1   # Partial Listing: Some Assembly Required
 2
 3   # ResponseHandler is also part of the client. It connects to the service.
 4   class ResponseHandler:
 5       def __init__(self, username):
 6           self.username = username
 7
 8       def on_login(self, session_key, tgt):
 9           if session_key is None:
10               print("Login failed")
11               asyncio.get_event_loop().stop()
12               return
13
14           service = input("Logged into Simpler Kerberos. Enter Service
             Name: ")
15           getTicketFactory = lambda: SimpleKerberosGetTicket(
16               self.username, service, session_key, tgt, self.on_ticket)
17
18           coro = asyncio.get_event_loop().create_connection(
19               getTicketFactory, '127.0.0.1', 8889)
20           asyncio.get_event_loop().create_task(coro)
21
```

```
22      def on_ticket(self, service_session_key, ticket):
23          if service_session_key is None:
24              print("Login failed")
25              asyncio.get_event_loop().stop()
26              return
27
28          print("Got a server session key:",service_session_key.hex())
29          asyncio.get_event_loop().stop()
```

The only other part of this code worth pointing out is the use of input to get the name of the service to connect to. This is normally not the best way to use asyncio programs because it is a blocking call and prevents anything else from working. But, for our simplistic client, this is reasonable. It should be in between network communications anyway.

Note that the only service the TGS has in our example is "echo," so this should be the service name you enter, unless you want to test the error-handling code. We also hard-coded the IP address and port of the TGS to be local port 8889. You should adjust this accordingly.

When all is said and done, and if everything was done correctly, the on_ticket callback should have a service session key and a ticket.

In real Kerberos, this is where things get a little tricky. Each service that is going to use Kerberos for authentication has to be "Kerberized." This means that the service has to be modified to accept a Kerberos ticket instead of a username and password (or whatever other authentication methods it normally uses). However this is configured, Alice will send the ticket along with her identity and another timestamp under the service session key. Optionally, the service can respond with the timestamp under the same service session key. We can write this protocol exchange as

$$A \rightarrow S : \{A, t_4\} \, K_{A,S}, \{A, K_{A,S}, t_3\} \, K_S$$
$$S \rightarrow A : \{t_4\} \, K_{A,S}.$$

When this is finished, Alice and the service S know that they are communicating with the right parties (based on trust in the AS/TGT) and they have a session key to enable them to communicate.

You will notice that the session key is shown working in both directions. This is primarily for the actual authentication of the principals (Alice and service S) to one another. Once that is established, they can negotiate session keys further if necessary.

The Kerberos documentation has instructions about "subkeys" that can be sent or derived as necessary.

For the actual Kerberos authentication exchange, the messages will be unique if the confounder is used, even under the same key.

To repeat once more, Kerberos itself is far more complicated than what we have illustrated here. There are various extensions, for example, for enabling PKI authentication to the AS, AEAD algorithm support, extensive options, and additional details in the core specification.

Nevertheless, this walk-through should help Alice and Bob (and you!) have a better idea of how Kerberos works specifically and how symmetric keys can be used in general to establish identity between parties.

EXERCISE 7.5. KERBERIZE THE ECHO PROTOCOL

We didn't show any code for a Kerberized echo protocol. We've left that for you to figure out. We have already set up some of the pieces you need, however. In real Kerberos, a Kerberized service has to register with the TGS. We have already done that. Our TGS code has "echo" in the service database with a password "sunshine".

You will need to modify the echo client and echo server to use the session key from the TGS instead of deriving the session keys from a password. You can treat the session key from the TGS as key material and still use the HKDF to derive the write key and read key (two sub-session keys, as Kerberos would call them).

Many Kerberized implementations accept the ticket along with the request, and you can do the same here. In other words, send the Kerberos message along with the (encrypted) data to be echoed. Because you are sending a human-readable message, you can use the null terminator to indicate the end of the echo message and the beginning of the Kerberos message, if that's easiest. Alternatively, you could do something more complicated like transmit the Kerberos message first, prepended by its length, with the human-readable echo message as a trailer.

The server will also need to be modified to accept a password for deriving its key with the TGS. The server already has a password given as a parameter. You could simply change it to derive its Kerberos key instead of the read and write keys. Also, make sure to use the appropriate derivation function. The read and write keys will need to be derived in the data_received method after the ticket is received and decrypted. You can leave out the optional Kerberos response to the echo client.

Finally, you will have to figure out a way to get the Kerberos ticket data to the echo client. You can either build the echo client protocol directly into your Kerberos client or find some other way to transfer it.

EXERCISE 7.6. CONFOUNDER

Check to see if any part of your encrypted packets are repeating. This will happen if the data going into the encryption routine (with a fixed IV and key) is the same at the beginning. Because dictionaries do not necessarily order their data, the username may come after the timestamp, in which case the packets may be different each time. If your packets aren't repeating any bytes at all, perhaps fix the timestamp or otherwise force the encrypt function to encrypt the same data twice.

Once you have repeating bytes, introduce confounders into your code by prepending 16 bytes of random plaintext in front of the serialized bytes. Make sure to remove it upon decryption. Does that get rid of the repeating bytes? Would a confounder work for AES-CTR mode?

EXERCISE 7.7. PREVENTING SERVER REPLAY

The transmissions to the client from our AS and TGS do not include a timestamp. With no timestamp and no nonce, they can be completely replayed. Add timestamps into the user data structures transmitted by both servers and modify the client code to check them.

Additional Data

This section was a little simpler in terms of concepts and a little heavier in terms of engineering.

In the first place, we did introduce some new modes of operation for AES encryption and the new ChaCha encryption algorithm as well. AEAD algorithms (authenticated encryption with additional data) are largely seen as superior to doing encryption and MAC separately (e.g., using AES-CTR and HMAC). You should use these modes of operation whenever they are available.

We also introduced the Kerberos SSO service which is interesting because it is built from symmetric key algorithms. In a world where PKI is everywhere, it is nice to see that a 25-year-old (as of the time of this writing), symmetric-based system continues to be widely used.

Hopefully it was fun to get your hands dirty and actually write some client/server code. We hope so. Because the last chapter is coming up and network communications are what TLS is all about!

CHAPTER 8

TLS Communications

In this chapter, we will discuss one of the cornerstones of secure Internet communication: TLS. The topic, like so many things in cryptography, is a big one, filled with fiddly parameters, subtle pitfalls, and breathtaking logic. Let's find out more!

Intercepting Traffic

Eve is *very* proud of herself. She managed to get into computer rooms across East Antarctica and install "sniffing" software. Basically, she has managed to intercept HTTP (web) traffic and exfiltrate it for later analysis by the intelligence officers for her agency (the "West Antarctica Central Knights Office," or WACKO).

The HTTP protocol natively supports proxying. An HTTP client can connect to a server through an intermediary HTTP server (the proxy). When the client first connects to the proxy, it sends a special HTTP command called CONNECT that tells the proxy where the real destination is. Once the proxy has connected to the true server, it serves as a simple pass-through, forwarding the data from one party to the other.

Eve managed to install an HTTP proxy onto her enemy's computers. It was very similar to the code in Listing 8-1.

Listing 8-1. HTTP Proxy

```
1    import asyncio
2
3    class ProxySocket(asyncio.Protocol):
4        CONNECTED_RESPONSE = (
5            b"HTTP/1.0 200 Connection established\n"
6            b"Proxy-agent: East Antarctica Spying Agency\n\n")
7
```

© Seth James Nielson, Christopher K. Monson 2019
S. J. Nielson and C. K. Monson, *Practical Cryptography in Python*,
https://doi.org/10.1007/978-1-4842-4900-0_8

```
8       def __init__ (self, proxy):
9           self.proxy = proxy
10
11      def connection_made(self, transport):
12          self.transport = transport
13          self.proxy.proxy_socket = self
14          self.proxy.transport.write(self.CONNECTED_RESPONSE)
15
16      def data_received(self, data):
17          print("PROXY RECV:", data)
18          self.proxy.transport.write(data)
19
20      def connection_lost(self, exc):
21          self.proxy.transport.close()
22
23

24  class HTTPProxy(asyncio.Protocol):
25      def connection_made(self, transport):
26          peername = transport.get_extra_info('peername')
27          print('Connection from {}'.format(peername))
28          self.transport = transport
29          self.proxy_socket = None
30
31      def data_received(self, data):
32          if self.proxy_socket:
33              print("PROXY SEND:", data)
34              self.proxy_socket.transport.write(data)
35              return
36
37          # No socket, we need to see CONNECT.
38          if not data.startswith(b"CONNECT"):
39              print("Unknown method")
40              self.transport.close()
41              return
42
```

```
43              print("Got CONNECT command:", data)
44              serverport = data.split(b" ")[1]
45              server, port = serverport.split(b":")
46              coro = loop.create_connection(lambda: ProxySocket(self),
                    server, port)
47              asyncio.get_event_loop().create_task(coro)
48
49          def connection_lost(self, exc):
50              if not self.proxy_socket: return
51              self.proxy_socket.transport.close()
52              self.proxy_socket = None
53
54      loop = asyncio.get_event_loop()
55      coro = loop.create_server(HTTPProxy, '127.0.0.1', 8888)
56      server = loop.run_until_complete(coro)
57
58      # Serve requests until Ctrl+C is pressed
59      print('Proxying on {}'.format (server.sockets[0].getsockname()))
60      try:
61          loop.run_forever()
62      except KeyboardInterrupt:
63          pass
64
65      # Close the server
66      server.close()
67      loop.run_until_complete(server.wait_closed())
68      loop.close()
```

This HTTP proxy prints out everything it receives from either endpoint. Eve's real proxy doesn't do this. Instead, it sends the intercepted data over the network to a command and control server. Alternatively, she could have made it save the data to disk for later extraction.

Let's see what our network traffic looks like connecting to an unprotected HTTP server. First, copy the code for the HTTP proxy (it's only about 70 lines) and start it up.[1] It should be serving on localhost:8888. This is shown as follows in the Python shell.

```
>>> import http.client
>>> conn = http.client.HTTPConnection("127.0.0.1", 8888)
>>> conn.set_tunnel("www.example.com")
>>> conn.request("GET", "/")
>>> r1 = conn.getresponse()
>>> r1.read()
#SHELL# output_ommitted
```

Python's http.client module has some built-in methods for interacting with HTTP servers. It also has HTTP proxying capabilities. In the example code, the HTTPConnection object was configured with the proxy's IP address and port. The set_tunnel method re-configured the object to assume it is connecting to a proxy but will request "www.example.com" via the CONNECT method.

After it gets the response, the read method gets the output. You should see something akin to an HTML document as a result. This represents the data received by the WA user's browser when they navigate to www.example.com.

Note: Finding an HTTP Site

For this exercise to work, you need to browse to a web site that still supports HTTP. More and more web sites are disabling HTTP altogether, and you can only connect to them via HTTPS. At the time of this writing, www.example.com still supports both.

---

[1]If you are already comfortable using something like Wireshark, Fiddler, or tcpdump, you can use any of those tools instead. We are providing this proxy script for those that haven't done any traffic sniffing before. This script is lightweight, easy to use, and self-explanatory.

Meanwhile, Eve is watching. In the terminal where you have the HTTP proxy running, you should see something like this:

```
Got CONNECT command: b'CONNECT www.example.com:80 HTTP/1.0\r\n\r\n'
PROXY SEND: b'GET/HTTP/1.1\r\nHost: www.example.com\r\nAccept-Encoding:
identity\r\n\r\n'
PROXY RECV: b'HTTP/1.1 200 OK\r\nCache-Control: max-age=604800\r\nContent-
Type: text/html...
```

You will notice that they see the entire communications stream between the client (e.g., browser) and the web server. Eve has hit upon a fantastic source of intelligence.

Warning: Multiple Proxy Methods

Our proxy is using the CONNECT method. There are multiple ways to configure a web proxy, and our basic source code only supports this one method. Thus, it will not work with browsers or tools that attempt to make use of other methods.

Eve is happily collecting traffic on her enemies one day when suddenly everything stops working. To be clear, the proxy is still proxying data. In fact, the CONNECT method still appears, but almost all of the data that flows across the proxy is unreadable!

Looking carefully over the logs, Eve notices an interesting change.

```
Got CONNECT command: b'CONNECT www.example.com:443 HTTP/1.0\r\n\r\n'
```

Do you see the difference? Almost everything is the same except for one thing: the port. Eve used to see browsers connecting to www.example.com on port 80. Now it's on port 443. What is going on?

It turns out that the EA adversaries have switched to using HTTPS ("HTTP Secure"). While HTTP uses port 80 by default, HTTPS uses port 443. Just to be clear, it is not the port that is making things secure, it is the new protocol. The port difference is merely Eve's first clue that something has intentionally been changed.

To test this out for yourself, try the same exercise again but with one small difference, shown as follows.

```
>>> import http.client
>>> conn = http.client.HTTPSConnection("127.0.0.1", 8888)
>>> conn.set_tunnel("www.example.com")
```

```
>>> conn.request("GET", "/")
>>> r1 = conn.getresponse()
>>> r1.read()
#SHELL# output_ommitted
```

This code is literally different by just one character. Do you see it? We changed HTTPConnection to HTTPSConnection.

Take a look at your HTTP proxy sniffer. There will be *a lot* of output. A portion of it might look something like this:

```
Got CONNECT command: b'CONNECT www.example.com:443 HTTP/1.0\r\n\r\n'
PROXY SEND: b"\x16\x03\x01\x02\x00\x01\x00\x01\xfc\x03\x03\x81<\x06f...
...
PROXY RECV: b'\x16\x03\x03\x00E\x02\x00\x00A\x03\x03\xb1\xf0T\xd0\xc...
```

Eve, disturbed that she can no longer read the network traffic that she is intercepting, heads back to WA to do some research on HTTPS. She learns that HTTPS encapsulates HTTP traffic inside another protocol called TLS. This protocol allows a client to verify the identity of a server and for the two parties to establish a secret key between them. This key remains secret even if an eavesdropper (like Eve) is listening to the entire communication stream. TLS, in theory, will completely shut Eve out from snooping on Alice, Bob, and the EA!

Eve is frustrated by this discovery. But, being the determined person that she is, she decides to start searching for weaknesses. If there's one thing she's learned throughout this book, it's that cryptography is often done incorrectly and is therefore exploitable.

EXERCISE 8.1. WHAT'S IN WEB TRAFFIC?

Pretend to be Eve and examine some of your own encrypted traffic. That is, configuring your browser to use your proxy, navigate to some HTTP web sites and spy on your own data. Hint: Are there parts of the secure communications that are still in plaintext?

If you don't know how to configure your browser for proxying, please do some searching on the search engine of your choice! Be aware that you may not be able to configure your browser to use your proxy correctly for unencrypted (HTTP) traffic. We personally tested Chrome and found that it uses the CONNECT method for HTTPS but not for HTTP.

Digital Identities: X.509 Certificates

To start searching for weaknesses, Eve first turns to the authentication part of the TLS protocol.

She learns that TLS uses a public key infrastructure (PKI) to establish identities and secure communications. Parties that wish to have an identity for use with TLS (typically) require an X.509 certificate.

In Chapter 5, we introduced the concept of certificates. At the time, to keep things simple, we used fake certificates that were nothing more than dictionaries we serialized with the Python json library. Now it's time to dig into real X.509 certificates, the most common type of certificate used on the Internet today.

X.509 Fields

Somewhat similar to our dictionary-based certificates, X.509 is a collection of key/value pairs. These pairs could also be represented using a dictionary, although X.509's fields permit hierarchical subfields.

Specifically, version 3 of X.509 has the following hierarchical keys:

1. Certificate
    (a) Version Number
    (b) Serial Number
    (c) Signature Algorithm ID
    (d) Issuer Name
    (e) Validity Period
        i. Not Before
        ii. Not After
    (f) Subject Name
    (g) Subject Public Key Info
        i. Public Key Algorithm
        ii. Subject Public Key

        (h) Issuer Unique Identifier (optional)

        (i) Subject Unique Identifier (optional)

        (j) Extensions (optional)

  2. Certificate Signature Algorithm

  3. Certificate Signature

Versions 1 and 2 of X.509 are subsets. The most important addition of version 3 is the extensions. These extensions are used in making certificate-enabled PKI more secure by, for example, limiting what a certificate can be used for. Nevertheless, version 1 certificates still exist and are usable, as we will see in a moment when we start generating some samples.

The primary purpose of a certificate is to tie a subject's identity to a public key under the signature of an issuer. The fields that identify the subject, the public key, and the issuer are the most critical, but the other fields provide contextual information necessary to understand and interpret the data.

For example, the validity period is used to determine when a certificate should be considered valid. While the "Not Before" field is important and must be checked, in practice the "Not After" period usually gets the most attention. Certificates with a higher risk of compromise can be issued with a shorter validity period to mitigate the damage done if a compromise occurs.

Another important piece of context with an X.509 certificate is found in the fields for identifying the certificate creation algorithms used and the type of public key embedded within it. Unlike most of our toy examples in this book, real cryptographic systems make use of a wide range of algorithms, and certificates have to be flexible enough to support them.

Scanning through the preceding X.509 fields, there is a "Certificate:Signature Algorithm ID" field that identifies how the certificate is signed.[2] Because it specifies all the details for the actual signature embedded in the certificate, it includes both the signing algorithm (e.g., RSA) and the message digest (e.g., SHA-256).

---

[2]The "Certificate Signature Algorithm" that appears later is a duplicate, for reasons not relevant to our current discussion.

The "Certificate:Subject Public Key Info:Public Key Algorithm" field, on the other hand, specifies what type of public key is being used by the certificate owner.

The last contextual field we will mention is the serial number. This is a unique number (per issuer) that identifies the certificate uniquely. This number is useful for revocation purposes discussed later in the chapter.

Now let's go back to the real reason we have certificates in the first place: identifying the subject, the subject's public key, and the trusted third party that "proves" this.

Clearly, the fields "Issuer Name" and "Subject Name" describe the identities claimed by the issuer and the subject. In our fake certificates from previous chapters, these were just simple strings. In real certificates, these are not just raw text fields but have a structure and subcomponents. Called the "Distinguished Name," these two identity fields typically have the following subfields[3]:

1. CN: CommonName

2. OU: OrganizationalUnit

3. O: Organization

4. L: Locality

5. S: StateOrProvinceName

6. C: CountryName

So, for example, a "Subject Name" or an "Issuer Name" might look like this:

```
CN= Charlie, OU= Espionage, O=EA, L= Room 110, S=HQ, C=EA
```

Not all of these subfields have to be filled in, but CN (Common Name) is typically the critical subfield. Later, when we look to validate a certificate, the subject's common name is used as the primary identifier. Additionally, most modern certificates include a field called "Subject Alternative Name" (which is a version 3 to store alternative subject names. While in many of our examples we have been using agent (code) names (e.g., "Charlie") as the subject name, certificates associated with TLS-protected web servers have to identify the host name—such as google.com—as the subject's identity.

You may also have noticed that the certificate included "Issuer Unique Identifier" and "Subject Unique Identifier" fields, but these can usually be left out and are not discussed here.

---

[3]Other kinds of identifiers are used, but these fields are the "classic" identity definition.

With the subject and the issuer identified, the remaining fields are the public key and the signature computed on the certificate's contents. The signature is calculated over a binary encoding of the certificate called the "DER" ("Distinguished Encoding Rules"). The signature both proves that the certificate was signed by the true issuer and that it has not been modified.

Certificate Signing Requests

To create a certificate in real life, a party creates a certificate signing request (CSR) and transmits it to a certificate authority (CA). The CSR has almost all of the same fields as an X.509 certificate but is missing, for example, an issuer (since issuance is what we're trying to obtain with the request). Once the CA has the CSR, it uses its own certificate and associated private key to generate the finalized certificate, filling in fields as necessary. One of the most important fields is the "Issuer" field. The issuer of one certificate should be identical to the "Subject" field of the signer's certificate. Once all of the fields are populated, the CA signs the certificate with its own private key.

Note: Private Keys Are Still Private

The party requesting a certificate did *not* send its private key to the CA. It only sent a CSR with its *public* key! Nobody, not even the CA, should have the private key!

We mentioned earlier that certificates are encoded in a format known as DER before signing. The DER format is, as we said, a binary format. Most on-disk representations of certificates (and CSRs and private keys) are actually in a text (ASCII) format known as PEM ("Privacy-Enhanced Mail"). Because all of the binary data has been encoded as ASCII, it is easy to send these certificates by text-based transmission systems, for example, email.

Armed with this knowledge about certificates, Eve decides to create a certificate. Because Eve doesn't have a certificate authority (CA) to sign her certificate, she will experiment with two alternative approaches: self-signed and signed by a "fake" CA she creates herself.[4]

---

[4]The CA certificate will be self-signed.

One common method for generating an X.509 certificate is using `openssl` from the command line. As you're using the `cryptography` module (which uses OpenSSL libraries under the hood) for the exercises in this book, you should have OpenSSL installed. Eve does, so she is going to use it.

First, Eve needs to create a private key and an associated CSR ("certificate signing request"). She starts by creating a CSR with a 2048-bit-modulus RSA public key, and a SHA-256 message digest. A lot of the following commands can be combined together for a simpler command line, but we are breaking them up to emphasize the different steps that Eve takes:

1. Generate an RSA key.

2. Create a CSR from the key.

3. Send to a certificate authority for signing (or sign it herself).

Generate a Key

First, she generates an RSA key. We have done this from Python before, but to get some practice with OpenSSL, let's look at the command-line approach:

```
openssl genpkey -algorithm RSA -out domain_key.pem -pkeyopt rsa_keygen_
bits:2048
```

In the various instructions for generating RSA keys that litter the Internet, there are many guides and walk-throughs that use a different OpenSSL command called `genrsa`. Please note that `genpkey`, which is more general, has superseded `genrsa`. Eve's example command says to generate a 2048-bit private key using the RSA algorithm. The output will be saved in `domain_key.pem` (in PEM format).

Eve examines the key file in a text editor and sees something like this:

```
-----BEGIN PRIVATE KEY-----
MIIEvQIBADANBgkqhkiG9w0BAQEFAASCBKcwggSjAgEAAoIBAQCpQoVUe4POr8+l
6rX4qQGyNHD613X16sqeIW2x+PtkeE9pjAm6sNhFKAspHKa7nWgFoW/O9iiT8oiy
1ah7KbtJsAXceUEbj9Yt6fHPytGe+qIidI1/Rg7ah4k7cn6pbPrqaxGc8n8368pM
NzJZMnLZLOePVn/y2mTsGX5wR+Cm+imEFBWxL7jgnhYAyLRdOYsdGaZi5DJQaHl7
HqXaL7+6G6RAjhW+Hn34ImBufOvY9eV3dCRvOFCSWr4e5uHv5ofUyRWB2Emwm8u6
SM3zzI3O0Fb6zHWoBsccU8xJadhWgPXLq27rcSl3A5NK6y1p7KKHimqcp6WDUgMK
3NzCIXK9AgMBAAECggEAB2zfDry4ZjSMPHAWeYkYfPPV/PsUvqwFJXi78jHE/XxV
```

p4CwMJNveWEvVCdgnRxjotOZLxAXaZ4bJxU+ZeDHyYzCRRDArW/a6nq30/DGz12Z
XT+VsX6mSinl+Eimi9IvE7eMtODgGdjrL/q/56/R3/s1/XDC/ilcggsAQ/azQT/n
3cOxWooOHYQQdbMkoi7YDRKOC7F2sfV3XO2WMDq4PuWG6mFtLg4j8tpAaJRCOlEz
bNnJnbBS6Dj3RnU53nj5TKBObCIZWkgpYcGK9e2iIg5+kMgkmwY5uxv3hTB5QHZY
tKDOPM9wgvDIR6NrccOGQOJOcvJmMHDNS8apT2rewQKBgQDhjsS3M3qWT6lzhFx3
+w6NJv7i/uOA2eNd+KorOq5XYOTicT8XCShSO2gFT6Fg4HRrSvwcjaTpjacUIyjZ
IhfrIIcSEe8Bk1VoBbrcS2NEZ3hMpPrPQ/hZtzUchhA1ftMJOfnysYGtqjA4drpq
HS8rPGmcP8NN1zYnv29ptfkmzQKBgQDAG3W8gA/mqjpboOB/OeC1fMX7u6pJVWGj
f+Bahjj5FAwfOYHJ8ON1Om/NpUD7BnKKdsOdYyOwV287+hhLnQZ2c3glxM/zONUn
9uYIgAWNmOwjsCKOVY6r9nc6kWWO7IOkIm628K5OBPxiXC/GqsXVpKSPjSrDhKnQ
vG1xFN4bsQKBgA1kP5Os78NK2YGtQxwwgK2quglaHsHArfofUGMnsAgqDYzQMnG4
rncrZcKi9q7cxKy2F//N/ROMwHW2nK8/kfH4zWwqOml6iOCTLoPzyeH+zqqmROnX
XEBfWzzlTMMQU5FBqvBYz5Oy9If1rJ2uO+WyQYbwVjUh6Oo1OHUrQ66lAoGAXKti
aiHkicLID/dVFEpZKXMdFkf65xE23mYLVd+1kAGprO5QW5jri+SNZkg3RmBf1Idm
fqyaRLCIygfkvGTs/yrIZH/CSHO772FcqfEHvL2TRwvqP3rqLe3gqfIFe/c4RpwN
iFYl8XWOQexyZ4VtlZesgkr4vAQ83qJmsMv+MKECgYEAjRVzqXEAV8DB5nzN+1cf
2OvCrZxd1Ktgb/DUqRfZwpAWU5K9YFCHbLWTS96KiMFh45kuAUg/hSKJIktuY1eI
Pl+r3g9FwlnntIHaUiRstDGXuyZku//+gWZMAZU4t5DwvhIXXAG3AqSeOEsB/bi4
kdlstdXcN/HgthWvTQkVycY=
-----END PRIVATE KEY-----

Create a CSR from a Key

Now that Eve has her key, she creates a CSR for this key. The CSR generation process will extract the public key from the private key Eve created and put it into the request. Eve uses the openssl req command for this operation with the following parameters:

```
openssl req -new -key domain_key.pem -out domain_request.csr
```

This instructs OpenSSL to build a CSR from the private key and put the result in domain_request.csr. Running this command results in some interactive questions for filling in elements of the subject name. Only the "Common Name" is absolutely required for TLS to work, but many certificate authorities will require these fields to be filled in before they will be willing to sign it.

```
You are about to be asked to enter information that will be incorporated
into your certificate request.
```

```
What you are about to enter is what is called a Distinguished Name or a DN.
There are quite a few fields but you can leave some blank
For some fields there will be a default value,
If you enter '.', the field will be left blank.
-----
Country Name (2 letter code) [AU]: WA
State or Province Name (full name) [Some-State]:West Antarctic Shelf
Locality Name (eg, city) []:West Antarctic City
Organization Name (eg, company) [Internet Widgits Pty Ltd]:WACKO
Organizational Unit Name (eg, section) []:Espionage
Common Name (e.g. server FQDN or YOUR name) []:wacko.westantarctica.
southpole.gov
Email Address []:eve@wacko.westantarctica.southpole.gov
```

Once Eve enters all of these fields, OpenSSL produces the CSR file and saves it to disk (also in PEM format). Eve uses the same utility (openssl req) to load the CSR from disk and view the fields in a human-readable format.

Executing the command

```
openssl req -in domain_request.csr -text
```

results in the following output:

```
Certificate Request:
    Data:
        Version: 1 (0 x0)
        Subject: C = WA, ST = West Antarctic Shelf, L = West Antarctic City,
            \
        O = WACKO, OU = Espionage, CN = wacko.westantarctica.southpole.gov,
            \
        emailAddress = eve@wacko.westantarctica.southpole.gov
        Subject Public Key Info:
            Public Key Algorithm: rsaEncryption
                Public-Key: (2048 bit)
...
    Signature Algorithm: sha256WithRSAEncryption
        6d:ef:8c:91:cd:a0:5d:9f:56:42:44:7f:1a:06:94:3f:8e:e1:
...
```

You'll notice that the version of Eve's CSR is version 1 and not version 3. OpenSSL always assigns version 1 unless version 3 extensions are in use. But remember, this is just the *request*, not the actual *certificate*. When CAs generate the actual certificate, they may insert V3 extensions for security reasons, resulting in a certificate that is using X.509 version 3.

Additionally, some certificate fields are not present, such as "Serial Number." Those will also be added when the CSR is signed by the CA.

In looking over Eve's shoulder, you may also have been surprised to see that the CSR already has a signature (the data on the line following `Signature Algorithm`). Where did that come from? Aren't signatures created when the issuer signs the certificate?

CSRs are typically signed *by their own key* as a way of indicating that the private key is actually held by the requester. Anybody could throw anyone's public key into a CSR. By having it be self-signed, this proves to the CA that the requester is in control of the private key, sometimes called "proof of possession." The real signing by the CA to produce a certificate is a separate process, and the next step.

Signing a CSR to Produce a Certificate

To review, let's remember that a certificate always has to be *signed* by the CA/issuer. If Eve, for example, created a web site and wanted a TLS certificate for it, she would generate the CSR and send it to a CA for a signature as we discussed. This signature is their stamp of approval that Eve's certificate is valid and she is permitted to claim the requested identity. The CA is responsible for a certain level of verification. If Eve requests an identity within the East Antarctica government, for example, the CA should determine, as part of their verification process, that she can't claim that identity. They would then deny her request. On the other hand, she can claim an identity within her native West Antarctica and may need to provide the government with physical documentation and have an in-person meeting with a representative of the CA to prove it.

Eve does have another option besides sending her CSR to a CA. She could *sign the certificate herself* using the same private key. This is called generating a *self-signed* certificate. All root certificates (e.g., root certificates held by a CA) are self-signed. After all, the chain has to stop somewhere.

We're getting ahead of ourselves. What is a certificate chain anyway?

We mentioned the concept briefly in Chapter 5. If you recall, when we were using our simplified (not very real) certificates, we discussed having an issuer of an issuer chain that could be arbitrarily long. That is, a party's certificate (say Eve's certificate) could be signed by an issuer, that is in turn signed by a "higher" issuer, that is signed by an even higher issuer, until some root certificate is the highest level issuer for the entire chain. The root certificate is signed *by itself!* In fact, the subject and issuer sections of a root certificate are identical.

This is one reason why verifying a certificate requires great care. You have to ensure that your certificate chain ends with a root that is *trustworthy*. The entire security of the system rests on this requirement. Anybody, including Eve in West Antarctica, you, or a Mafia Mob Boss in America, can create a self-signed certificate for any identity (the West Antarctica government, Google, Amazon, your bank, etc.). The only reason your browser won't trust Eve's self-signed certificate is because it isn't signed by an issuer that it (the browser) already trusts.

How does a browser know which root certificates to trust? Most browsers are shipped with certain trusted root certificates baked in. In our hypothetical Antarctic example, East Antarctica and West Antarctica could produce browsers with only government-authorized CAs installed. This would literally prevent the two countries from communicating with each other (at least over HTTPS or TLS).

But let's get back to Eve. She cannot get a certificate signed by an EA root. Instead, a self-signed certificate can be useful, and generating one is instructive. It is also Eve's best option at present, so let's move her forward. Eve signs her CSR using the `openssl x509` command:

```
openssl x509 -req \
  -days 30 \
  -in domain_request.csr \
  -signkey domain_key.pem \
  -out domain_cert.crt
```

This command creates a certificate valid until 30 days from now. It is signed by `domain_key.pem`, which is the same key associated with the CSR. The self-signed certificate is saved in the file `domain_cert.crt`.

Using syntax similar to what we used for `openssl req`, Eve dumps the fields into a human-readable format for viewing. The command

```
openssl x509 -in domain_cert.crt -text
```

produces output similar to the following:

```
Certificate:
    Data:
        Version: 1 (0x0)
        Serial Number:
            a5:f5:15:a8:55:58:12:5e
    Signature Algorithm: sha256WithRSAEncryption
        Issuer: C = WA, ST = West Antarctic Shelf, L = West Antarctic City,
            \
        O = WACKO, OU = Espionage, CN = wacko.westantarctica.southpole.gov,
            \
        emailAddress = eve@wacko.westantarctica.southpole.gov
        Validity
            Not Before: Jan 6 01:13:18 2019 GMT
            Not After : Feb 5 01:13:18 2019 GMT
        Subject: C = WA, ST = West Antarctic Shelf, L = West Antarctic City,
            \
        O = WACKO, OU = Espionage, CN = wacko.westantarctica.southpole.gov,
            \
        emailAddress = eve@wacko.westantarctica.southpole.gov
        Subject Public Key Info:
            Public Key Algorithm: rsaEncryption
                Public-Key: (2048 bit)
                Modulus:
                    00:a9:43:45:54:7b:83:f4:af:cf:a5:ea:b5:f8:a9:
...
    Signature Algorithm: sha256WithRSAEncryption
        20:da:25:88:db:4e:ee:21:19:78:58:ed:b8:7b:3f:28:dd:83:
...
```

Now all of the fields are filled in. For example, Eve did not specify a serial number so one was automatically generated. The issuer field is also filled in and, as expected for a self-signed certificate, it has the same identity as the subject.

Eve decides to create a second certificate and sign it with *this* certificate. She sets about creating the new certificate and decides to assign it the identity of 127.0.0.1

(localhost). Eve decides it might be good to experiment with creating keys other than RSA keys, and she sets about creating an EC (elliptic-curve) key pair.

```
openssl genpkey \
  -algorithm EC \
  -out localhost_key.pem \
  -pkeyopt ec_paramgen_curve:P-256
```

This EC key is based on the P-256 curve which is a very popular and widely used curve and a reasonable choice.[5]

Eve generates a new CSR from the EC key using the same command line as before:

```
openssl req -new -key localhost_key.pem -out localhost_request.csr
```

Now Eve has a *request to create a certificate*, not a signed certificate. Not yet, anyway. To create the certificate, Eve needs to sign with domain_key.pem, as she is treating that key and certificate like a CA key/cert.

She is also going to add some X.509 V3 options. These options are used for limiting how a certificate can be used. For example, Eve wants to use her first certificate and private key (domain_cert.crt and domain_key.pem) to sign her second certificate. She wants her first certificate to be able to be used as a CA. She does not, however, want her second certificate (for localhost) to be able to sign other certificates. Using V3 extensions, it is possible for Eve to encode these limitations directly into the certificate itself.

To see why this is important, imagine if Eve is granted a certificate by a real CA for wacko.westantarctica.southpole.gov. If this certificate does *not* have limitations on its use, nothing stops Eve from using it to sign a *new* certificate granting her the identity of eatsa.eastantarctica.southpole.gov. This would give Eve a chain of authority back to the CA for an identity she shouldn't have. Thus, in order for certificate chains to mean something, Eve's certificate must deny her the right to create other certificates.

In Eve's experimentation, the two fields she cares most about are

- Key Usage

- Basic Constraints

---

[5]The SafeCurves organization lists certain concerns with a number of curves, including P-256. There are no known vulnerabilities against this curve, but there are questions about its parameters and whether it was designed with a "back door." Other curves, such as Curve 25519 might be better choices, but are not yet supported by the cryptography library for digital signatures.

Eve is going to use these fields to express that this new certificate should not be used as a CA. In fact, it will say so expressly in the "Basic Constraints" field. The "Key Usage" field will include normal key uses such as "Digital Signature" but it will leave out things like being used as signing "Certificate Revocation Lists" (CRLs).

To add these V3 features into her certificate, Eve creates an extension file called v3.ext. It contains the following two lines:

```
keyUsage=digitalSignature
basicConstraints=CA:FALSE
```

Now Eve is ready to sign the CSR.

```
openssl x509 -req \
  -days 365 \
  -in localhost_request.csr \
  -CAkey domain_key.pem \
  -CA domain_cert.crt \
  -out localhost_cert.crt \
  -set_serial 123456789 \
  -extfile v3.ext
```

When signing with a CA key and certificate, the signkey parameter is removed and CA option and CAkey parameters are added. The CA option specifies the certificate of the CA/issuer, and the CAkey specifies the associated private key used for signing. Eve plugs in the private key and self-signed certificate from her first experiment.

Although not required when creating a self-signed certificate, Eve now has to explicitly specify a serial number when signing with a CA key and certificate. A real CA must not reuse serial numbers and must keep a record of the serial numbers issued in case the certificate needs to be revoked.

Using her command line, Eve reviews this new certificate and identifies a few differences:

```
Certificate:
    Data:
        Version: 3 (0x2)
        Serial Number: 123456789 (0x75bcd15)
    Signature Algorithm: sha256WithRSAEncryption
        Issuer: C = WA, ST = West Antarctic Shelf, L = West Antarctic City,
```

```
            \
       O = WACKO, OU = Espionage, CN = wacko.westantarctica.southpole.gov,
            \
       emailAddress = eve@wacko.westantarctica.southpole.gov
       Validity
            Not Before: Jan 6 05:41:35 2019 GMT
            Not After : Jan 6 05:41:35 2020 GMT
       Subject: C = WA, ST = WhoCares, L = MyCity, O = Localhost,
            OU = Office, CN = 127.0.0.1
       Subject Public Key Info:
            Public Key Algorithm: id-ecPublicKey
                 Public-Key: (256 bit)
                 pub:
                      04:46:64:ca:95:0c:fc:dd:85:fb:cc:54:5a:9b:e9:
...
                 NIST CURVE: P-256
       X509v3 extensions:
            X509v3 Key Usage:
                 Digital Signature
            X509v3 Basic Constraints:
                 CA:FALSE
   Signature Algorithm: sha256WithRSAEncryption
       07:78:b5:1d:4a:2f:e4:33:a6:f6:a8:fb:e2:51:16:eb:c5:3b:
...
```

As you would expect, the issuer is not the same as the subject this time around. In fact, the issuer field from this certificate matches the subject field from the signing certificate. This is required for correct certificate chain validation.

Also, the public key algorithm is elliptic curve now instead of RSA, but the Signature Algorithm is still sha256WithRSAEncryption. That's because this certificate is signed by the domain_cert.crt Eve created earlier, and that is still RSA.

As you can see, the X.509 V3 extensions are present and the version of the certificate is now listed as "3" as well.

Eve made the subject identity 127.0.0.1 on purpose. She decides to test out her newly minted certificates and see how a web browser treats them. Using openssl s_server, Eve quickly sets up a test of the certificates she has generated.

```
openssl s_server -accept 8888 -www \
    -cert localhost_cert.pem -key localhost_key.pem \
    -cert_chain domain_cert.crt -build_chain
```

This command starts the server listening on port 8888 (for your own tests, make sure your HTTP proxy is turned off or else pick a different port). It uses the localhost cert as its identity certificate, but uses the domain cert file as a list of certificates for use in building chains. The build_chain option instructs the server to attempt to build a complete chain of certificates for transmission to clients. In other words, it sends the entire chain to the client, not just the identity certificate.

Once Eve has the server running, she points a browser at https://127.0.0.1:8888. She sees something like Figure 8-1.

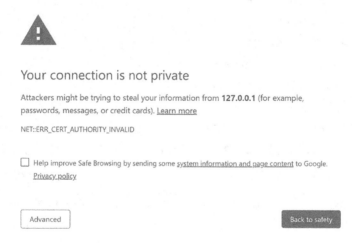

Figure 8-1. *Chrome's warning about an untrusted certificate*

That is an image from the Chrome browser reporting that it doesn't like the certificate Eve created. Note that what Eve received is the ERR_CERT_AUTHORITY_INVALID error. Using Chrome's developer tools, Eve gets more information on how the browser views this certificate and its chain, shown in Figure 8-2.

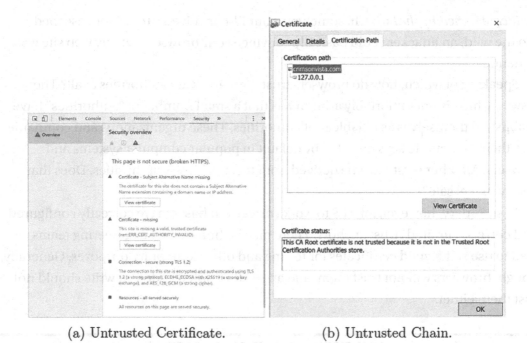

(a) Untrusted Certificate.   (b) Untrusted Chain.

Figure 8-2. *Chrome's warnings for untrusted situations*

Figure 8-2(b) is an image with details about the certificate chain, specifically. Notice that it received the chain (both the certificate and its issuing certificate). It recognizes that the domain certificate Eve created (identified in this figure by the common name wacko.westantarctica.southpole.gov) as a "root" certificate, because it is self-signed. But, it says that this root certificate is not a trusted certificate. If a root certificate is not trusted, then the entire security of the chain cannot be established.

There are ways to *add* a root certificate to a browser's trusted certificate store. Eve studies this concept very closely as she might be able to use this approach to defeat TLS. We are *not* going to include the details in this book, however, as it is actually a pretty bad and dangerous idea. It is probably the *most dangerous thing we have discussed so far*.[6] If you install a new root certificate into your browser, your browser will trust *any*

---

[6]Many companies, universities, and other organizations require their employees to do this. That is ill-advised *at best*. It undermines the security of everything those people do from within the corporate network, making them vulnerable in the same ways the company itself is, because their traffic, which should be encrypted end to end, isn't. This means that a company that represents an attractive target for motivated criminals is also placing their individual employees at risk of losing their data, which is traversing part of the company network unencrypted. This is **bad**.

certificate signed by that root. If, somehow, your ill-conceived trusted root escaped into the wild, an attacker could basically convince your browser that any web site was authentic.

Speaking of which, how do browsers trust any certificate authorities at all? The answer, which is uncomfortably arbitrary, is that a small number of "authorities" have established themselves as reliable root authorities. These organizations and companies have their root public keys installed by default in popular computer systems and browsers. All other trust must be derived from these arbitrary authorities. Does that make you feel safe?

In summary, however, for TLS to work correctly, it has to have correctly configured (and correctly limited) trust anchors. There may be times when engineering teams need to use self-signed certificates for testing and other temporary purposes. Generally, though, browsers will not trust them, and any TLS-enabled code you write should not trust them either.

EXERCISE 8.2. CERTIFICATE PRACTICE

Generate some different TLS certificates experimenting with different algorithms and parameters (such as key sizes).

EXERCISE 8.3. FANTASY CERTIFICATES

Create some "fantasy" certificates for some of your favorite organizations. Self-sign a certificate or two that reads amazon.com or google.com. You can't use these as nobody's browser will accept them.[7] But it is kind of a fun game.

Maybe you could print out a copy of Openssl's text representation and frame it. After all, how many of your friends have an Amazon TLS certificate?

---

[7]And seriously, don't be evil. This exercise is not meant to encourage fraud in any way.

Creating Keys, CSRs, and Certificates in Python

After getting done with her OpenSSL certificate tests, Eve explores creating these same objects programmatically using the Python cryptography library. Using this library, Eve can generate self-signed certificates, certificate requests, signed certificates, and keys. Alice, Bob, Eve, and you have already generated keys in previous chapters, so let's skip ahead to certificate requests.

The cryptography library has a "builder" class for constructing a CSR and a separate class for representing the CSR. When building a CSR using the builder, the only information required is the subject name data and the private key. All other fields can be derived or otherwise automatically populated. Extensions can optionally be added. The following code is taken from the cryptography module's documentation:

```
>>> from cryptography import x509
>>> from cryptography.hazmat.backends import default_backend
>>> from cryptography.hazmat.primitives import hashes
>>> from cryptography.hazmat.primitives.asymmetric import rsa
>>> from cryptography.x509.oid import NameOID
>>> private_key = rsa.generate_private_key(
...     public_exponent=65537,
...     key_size=2048,
...     backend=default_backend())
>>> builder = x509.CertificateSigningRequestBuilder()
>>> builder = builder.subject_name(x509.Name([
...     x509.NameAttribute(NameOID.COMMON_NAME, 'cryptography.io')]))
>>> builder = builder.add_extension (
...     x509.BasicConstraints(ca=False, path_length=None),
...     critical=True)
>>> request = builder.sign(
...     private_key,
...     hashes.SHA256(),
...     default_backend())
```

The CertificateSigningRequestBuilder follows the object-oriented "builder pattern" wherein each building method returns a new copy of the builder object. This is handy for when Eve decides to construct multiple CSRs with partially overlapping

315

parameters. One builder can be configured with the overlapping parameters, and then individual builders are created when the parameters diverge.

As a side note about X.509 extensions, you will note that the CSR created in our example set `ca=False`. As with our earlier OpenSSL example, we are explicitly marking this certificate as not being able to sign other certificates (e.g., act as a CA). In this example, it also sets `path_length=None`, but that's a superfluous piece of data because `path_length` only applies when `ca=True`. The `critical` flag indicates that this is a mandatory extension that must be processed by processing software.

When ready, Eve uses the `sign` method to build the actual CSR request object using a private key. Recall that CSRs are self-signed to ensure that the requester has the private key corresponding to the embedded public key. The `sign` method extracts the public key from the private key, inserts it into the CSR, and then signs with the private key. The object built by this method is an instance of `CertificateSigningRequest`.

To save a CSR to disk, Eve uses the `public_bytes` method in the `CertificateSigningRequest` object that returns the PEM serialization of the data.

```
>>> from cryptography.hazmat.primitives.serialization import Encoding
>>> csr.public_bytes(Encoding.PEM)
b'-----BEGIN CERTIFICATE REQUEST-----\
nMIICcDCCAVgCAQAwGjEYMBYGA1UEAwwPY3J5cHRvZ3JhcGh5LmlvMIIBIjANBgkq\
nhkiG9w0BAQEFAAOCAQ8AMIIBCgKCAQEAntx7bGVFlIaO/dlImzUHbN4xCQ8d8/if\
ng8GQaASN9oyfXUmOB8r+P8p4K6U8xoPXa+lc+KgexZrqibY5x1FEAvzQPanhmOw8\
nhS7Uo1Pqt3okP6zsdfzXcjgceud8JJhVTqZWpN1Q5e+RldYwuzIsJyxNUFMUZrpL\
nqZNQOS/KG5re7YIHJLy3iCx6a/KAW5BbqW9cq989sdTpOFo462+qCqoHaQO//hQM\
nTmWI/
IJIZ9mIcP4ggJrOsy8JLAw/RLzcrpMRut8e1/A9mozo+YZJDPt9d+WzXj5p\
nZvTkpFUfOB8HpogCdtbhPmc5jfgbN/rwOzSO8bQTdHAwTS/5fQjtAQIDAQABoBEw\
nDwYJKoZIhvcNAQkOMQIwADANBgkqhkiG9w0BAQsFAAOCAQEAR1E3c/aF1X41x4tI\
n2kUeCeV38C01ZFrCJADXKKl4k6wvHU81ZoDCV6F1ytCeJAlD1ShGS6DmlfH78xay\
nrefzaIjCpOtRs5R4rccoRNK3LhyBnxEqLY1LZx1fq2FOXiMHlG8jEcK/jjhWm7OB\
naKwBbvWwlHGgha5ZlOgvALOPSFUC9+6LvTStanSABtlBM4eA2izLG2hMek9S5xIw\
nK53WJG42Mz3PHDMUfYWdGtsJalAnGMkQtqbvR4yKi9o5y4RcvihQtitGFeYQmZc+\
nhmuVBOBGCe9LUBOiL9J3kUgL4avO2AviCFev48i9OYGD54G73vKrd5KODtY78own\
nVrbzMw==\n-----END CERTIFICATE REQUEST-----\n'
```

CSR objects cannot be constructed directly. They can be built by the builder class or loaded from disk. The class is a read-only style class that allows access to data fields but does not permit altering them. Eve uses the builder class to construct new CSRs when necessary. She also uses the `load_pem_x509_csr` method to load CSRs from disk. The following example code is taken from the `cryptography` documentation.

```
>>> from cryptography import x509
>>> from cryptography.hazmat.backends import default_backend
>>> pem_req_data = b'''------BEGIN CERTIFICATE REQUEST------\
nMIICcDCCAVgCAQAwGjEYMBYGA1UEAwwPY3J5cHRvZ3JhcGh5LmlvMIIBIjANBgkq\
nhkiG9w0BAQEFAAOCAQ8AMIIBCgKCAQEAntx7bGVFlIaO/dlImzUHbN4xCQ8d8/if\
ng8GQaASN9oyfXUmOB8r+P8p4K6U8xoPXa+lc+KgexZrqibY5x1FEAvzQPanhmOw8\
nhS7Uo1Pqt3okP6zsdfzXcjgceud8JJhVTqZWpN1Q5e+RldYwuzIsJyxNUFMUZrpL\
nqZNQOS/KG5re7YIHJLy3iCx6a/KAW5BbqW9cq989sdTpOFo462+qCqoHaQO//\
hQMnnTmWI/
IJIZ9mIcP4ggJrOsy8JLAw/RLzcrpMRut8e1/A9mozo+YZJDPt9d+WzXj5p\
nZvTkpFUfOB8HpogCdtbhPmc5jfgbN/rwOzSO8bQTdHAwTS/5fQjtAQIDAQABoBEw\
nDwYJKoZIhvcNAQkOMQIwADANBgkqhkiG9w0BAQsFAAOCAQEAR1E3c/aF1X41x4tI\
n2kUeCeV38CO1ZFrCJADXKKl4k6wvHU81ZoDCV6F1ytCeJAlD1ShGS6DmlfH78xay\
nrefzaIjCpOtRs5R4rccoRNK3LhyBnxCqLY1LZx1fq2FOXiMHlG8jEcK/jjhWm7OB\
naKwBbvWwlHGgha5ZlOgvALOPSFUC9+6LvTStanSABtlBM4eA2izLG2hMek9S5xIw\
nK53WJG42Mz3PHDMUfYWdGtsJalAnGMkQtqbvR4yKi9o5y4RcvihQtitGFeYQmZc+\
nhmuVBOBGCe9LUBOiL9J3kUgL4avO2AviCFev48i9OYGD54G73vKrd5KODtY78own\
nVrbzMw==\n------END CERTIFICATE REQUEST------\n'''
>>> csr = x509.load_pem_x509_csr(pem_req_data, default_backend())
```

For making certificates, Eve discovers that the `cryptography` library follows a similar pattern as it did for making CSRs. There is a builder class and a read-only certificate class that can also be serialized to and from disk.

Interestingly, there is no method for creating a certificate from a CSR. The `cryptography` documentation explicitly identifies that the purpose of the certificate builder class is to generate self-signed certificates. There is no reason to start from a CSR.

Even if Eve wanted to establish a CA (for her own West Antarctic colleagues), it would be better for her to not automate CSR signing. As we discussed earlier, CAs need to verify CSR information very carefully, and sometimes manually; correctness and validity must be established before signing.

Still, Eve finds that if she needs to create a certificate from a CSR, she can load the CSR and then use its data fields to fill in the certificate builder.

From the `cryptography` documentation, Listing 8-2 contains an example for building a self-signed certificate. After this code runs, the `certificate` variable has what we need.

Note: Dot Chaining

We take advantage of the fact that each operation on the builder returns itself. This allows the method "dot chaining" approach you see. Since the final call to "sign" returns a certificate, not a builder, we can assign this long operation to the certificate itself.

Listing 8-2. TLS Builder

```
1    from cryptography import x509
2    from cryptography.hazmat.backends import default_backend
3    from cryptography.hazmat.primitives import hashes
4    from cryptography.hazmat.primitives.asymmetric import rsa
5    from cryptography.x509.oid import NameOID
6
7    import datetime
8
9    one_day = datetime.timedelta(1, 0, 0)
10
11   private_key = rsa.generate_private_key(
12       public_exponent=65537,
13       key_size=2048,
14       backend=default_backend())
15
16   public_key = private_key.public_key()
17
18   certificate = x509.CertificateBuilder(
19   ).subject_name(x509.Name([
20       x509.NameAttribute(NameOID.COMMON_NAME, 'cryptography.io')])
21   ).issuer_name(x509.Name([
```

```
22        x509.NameAttribute(NameOID.COMMON_NAME, 'cryptography.io')])
23    ).not_valid_before(datetime.datetime.today() - one_day
24    ).not_valid_after(datetime.datetime.today() + (one_day * 30)
25    ).serial_number(x509.random_serial_number()
26    ).public_key(public_key
27    ).add_extension(
28        x509.SubjectAlternativeName([x509.DNSName('cryptography.io')]),
29        critical=False,
30    ).add_extension(
31        x509.BasicConstraints(ca=False, path_length=None),
32        critical=True,
33    ).sign(
34        private_key=private_key, algorithm=hashes.SHA256(),
35        backend=default_backend())
```

To modify this example to create the certificate from a CSR, Eve can extract the subject name, public key, and optional extensions directly from the CSR object and copy them into the certificate builder. To sign the certificate with a CA certificate/key pair, Eve needs to load the CA certificate and key, copy the "Issuer" field from the signing certificate into the certificate builder, and sign using the certificate's private key.

Certificates can be loaded using load_pem_x509_certificate, then serialized for storage or transmission using the public_bytes method.

EXERCISE 8.4. OPENSSL TO PYTHON AND BACK

Generate a CSR with Python and sign it with Openssl.

Generate a CSR with Openssl, open it in Python, and create a self-signed certificate from it.

EXERCISE 8.5. CERTIFICATE INTERCEPT IN THE MIDDLE

In the next section, we will talk about TLS, the security protocol that underlies HTTPS. TLS relies on the certificates you learned about in this section. Going back to your HTTP proxy, intercept some more HTTPS traffic and see if you can figure out when the certificate is being sent.

This is a tough exercise and more for those interested in experimentation and tinkering. As a hint, certificates are not sent in PEM format, but DER. This is a binary format. But it's not *encrypted*. You can try poking around for certain binary byte combinations. You could also use openssl to convert the certificates you've created into DER format and examine them in a hex editor to see if there are common bytes to look for.

EXERCISE 8.6. CERTIFICATE MODIFICATION IN THE MIDDLE

If you do manage to find when certificates are going over the wire, modify your HTTP proxy program to intercept and modify them. At the very least, you could just have a certificate of your own pre-loaded that you send instead. How does your browser feel about this?

An Overview of TLS 1.2 and 1.3

With a little bit of knowledge about X.509 certificates under her belt, Eve turns to studying the TLS protocol. As you follow along, you should recognize that the TLS protocol draws on cryptography components that we have studied through all the preceding chapters. This is a chance for you and Eve to see how all of the pieces are put together in a modern security protocol.

The goal of the TLS protocol is to provide transport security (TLS stands for "Transport Layer Security"). The TCP/IP protocol suite, upon which the Internet is built, does not have any security guarantees. It does not provide confidentiality, which is why Eve was able to use an HTTP proxy to read the data being sent between two parties.

At least as bad, if not worse, is the fact that TCP/IP does not provide authenticity either. Eve could have used her HTTP proxy with a few modifications to masquerade as the true destination (`example.com`), and Alice and Bob would have had no idea. The TCP/IP protocol suite also does not provide message integrity. The proxy could *change* the data and the change would not be detected.

TLS is designed to add these security features on top of TCP/IP. The protocol originated as the "Secure Sockets Layer" (SSL) protocol from Netscape in the mid-1990s. Version 2 was the first public release, followed by version 3 shortly thereafter.

Subsequently, it received a few changes and was renamed TLS 1.0.[8] The updated versions since that time have been released to update cryptography and alleviate problems with the cryptographic protocol. Version 1.2 has been around for a number of years and is still considered current. Recently, version 1.3 was also released, but is not currently being described as a replacement to 1.2 (both versions are considered current).

How does TLS work? It starts with a handshake. That handshake is extremely critical. Keep in mind that TLS has two major goals: first, establish identity[9] and, second, mutually derive session keys for secure transport. These two goals are typically achieved by a successful TLS handshake.

The handshake is also where the various TLS versions are most different from one another. For this section, we will review the TLS 1.2 handshake and then briefly discuss how TLS 1.3's handshake is different. The TLS 1.3 changes will make more sense after the TLS 1.2 handshake has been explained.

Please note that this section is somewhat academic. There isn't much in the way of programming for Eve to experiment with. This background will help her understand how TLS is supposed to work and places where it has gone wrong in the past. Eve can use this information to figure out which servers are going to be easier to crack than others.

At the same time, you, the reader, will benefit from watching Eve's attempts to break through the cryptography shield that TLS is supposed to provide. Throughout this entire book, we've been pounding it into your head that you shouldn't create your own algorithms and shouldn't create your own implementations whenever a well-tested library is present.

TLS is actually a protocol you can and should use, and there is plenty of library support for it in Python, which helps a lot. Still, you want to know what kinds of things Eve will be looking for if she wants to attack your system. Let's dive in.

---

[8]Old habits die hard. Many times the term "SSL" is still used, even when talking about TLS. Certificates, for example, are still often referred to as SSL certificates even if they're only used for TLS.

[9]In common practice, only the *server's* identity is verified, though there are increasing use cases for "Mutual TLS" (MTLS), where the client verifies the server and the server also verifies the client.

The Introductory "Hellos"

TLS 1.2 begins with a client sending a client "hello" message to the server. The client hello message includes information about its TLS configuration, as well as a nonce. One of those bits of configuration is the client's list of *cipher suites*. Possibly one of the most confusing characteristics of TLS to newcomers is that the TLS protocol is actually a combination of protocols that work together. And it supports a number of different algorithms and protocol combinations.

The hello message must, out of necessity, get the client and the server preparing to communicate using the same algorithms and component protocols. The client sends a list of cipher suites to indicate all the different ways that it is willing to talk and the server will select one in its response (presuming there is any overlap between the cipher suites they support).

A cipher suite for TLS typically includes one choice of algorithm each for key exchange, signing, bulk encryption, and hashing. As we said, TLS brings together all the different elements you have been learning about in this book, so these terms should look familiar!

One cipher suite used by TLS 1.2 is TLS_ECDHE_ECDSA_WITH_AES_256_CBC_SHA384. This cipher suite can be understood as follows:

- TLS: The protocol the cipher suite is meant for. Easy enough.

- ECDHE: As described in Chapter 6, the client and server will use ECDHE to create a symmetric key.

- ECDSA: Recall from learning about ECDHE that it is not authenticated. In order to be sure that the server is who it claims to be, it will use ECDSA signatures on some of the handshake data.

- AES_256_CBC: After the handshake is over, the client and server will send data protected by AES-256 in CBC mode.

- SHA_384: This parameter has to do with *two different* parts of the TLS operation. The SHA-384 algorithm will be used in a key derivation function during the handshake. Additionally, the bulk encryption messages sent after the handshake (encrypted by AES-256 in CBC mode) will be protected from modification by HMAC-SHA-384.

These elements will make more sense as we go through the rest of the TLS protocol. Meanwhile, it is a good introduction to the number of components that are a part of TLS operations.

Note: ECDH vs. ECDHE

Throughout this book, we have not made too much of a distinction between DH/ECDH and DHE/ECDHE. As a reminder, the "E" stands for "ephemeral." When DH/ECDH is used in ephemeral mode, the public/private key pair is used once and discarded.

The reason we haven't made an effort to say "DHE" instead of "DH" is that in many contexts DH is implicitly ephemeral.

This is *not* the case with TLS. There are modes of operation that are *not* ephemeral at all. Accordingly, we will use the full DHE/ECDHE term throughout this chapter to be explicit.

Notice that the strength of TLS depends greatly on its cipher suite. What is a little frightening is that two servers can be "using" TLS 1.2 where one server is strongly protected and the other is vulnerable to attack because of the choice of cipher suite. Don't ignore the hello part of the TLS handshake!

It is really important!

There are a few other fields in the client's hello. Figure 8-3 is an actual hello message intercepted by Wireshark (a network sniffer that can capture any kind of network traffic, not just HTTP like your proxy).

```
✓ TLSv1.2 Record Layer: Handshake Protocol: Client Hello
      Content Type: Handshake (22)
      Version: TLS 1.0 (0x0301)
      Length: 512
   ✓ Handshake Protocol: Client Hello
         Handshake Type: Client Hello (1)
         Length: 508
         Version: TLS 1.2 (0x0303)
      > Random: ab57c7b478cb1dddacba15597846c25d02a707cc25ddacbc...
         Session ID Length: 32
         Session ID: 732544558f5d80a02901aeecc6a5b1eaad1132ff2dc2f42a...
         Cipher Suites Length: 34
      > Cipher Suites (17 suites)
         Compression Methods Length: 1
      > Compression Methods (1 method)
         Extensions Length: 401
      > Extension: Reserved (GREASE) (len=0)
      > Extension: server_name (len=16)
      > Extension: extended_master_secret (len=0)
      > Extension: renegotiation_info (len=1)
      > Extension: supported_groups (len=10)
      > Extension: ec_point_formats (len=2)
      > Extension: SessionTicket TLS (len=0)
      > Extension: application_layer_protocol_negotiation (len=14)
      > Extension: status_request (len=5)
```

Figure 8-3. *Wireshark decoding of a TLS 1.2 hello message*

Notice that there is a whole section for cipher suites! In Figure 8-4 we see the expanded list. That's quite a list of cipher suites! Remember, this is a hello message from the client to the server, and this list is all of the cipher suites the client is willing to use.

```
v TLSv1.2 Record Layer: Handshake Protocol: Client Hello
      Content Type: Handshake (22)
      Version: TLS 1.0 (0x0301)
      Length: 512
   v Handshake Protocol: Client Hello
         Handshake Type: Client Hello (1)
         Length: 508
         Version: TLS 1.2 (0x0303)
       > Random: ab57c7b478cb1dddacba15597846c25d02a707cc25ddacbc...
         Session ID Length: 32
         Session ID: 732544558f5d80a02901aeecc6a5b1eaad1132ff2dc2f42a...
         Cipher Suites Length: 34
       > Cipher Suites (17 suites)
         Compression Methods Length: 1
       > Compression Methods (1 method)
         Extensions Length: 401
       > Extension: Reserved (GREASE) (len=0)
       > Extension: server_name (len=16)
       > Extension: extended_master_secret (len=0)
       > Extension: renegotiation_info (len=1)
       > Extension: supported_groups (len=10)
       > Extension: ec_point_formats (len=2)
       > Extension: SessionTicket TLS (len=0)
       > Extension: application_layer_protocol_negotiation (len=14)
       > Extension: status_request (len=5)
```

Figure 8-4. *Wireshark decoding of the cipher suites component of a TLS 1.2 hello message*

When the server receives the client's hello, it will see if it is willing to use on of the client's proposed cipher suites. If so, it sends back a response with multiple elements:

- Hello: The server's hello message includes its own random nonce.

- Certificate: The server's TLS certificate or certificate chain, the details of which we covered earlier in this chapter.

- Key exchange: If the cipher suite uses DHE or ECDHE, the server will also transmit its portion of the Diffie-Hellman exchange along with the hello. For RSA key transport, the server does not send this element.

- Finished: An end-of-message kind of marker.

The TLS specification actually gives specific names to each kind of message sent in the handshake. So while we've been informally referring to a client hello message, TLS 1.2 actually specifies that the name of the message is ClientHello. The exchange of the ClientHello and ServerHello, along with the official message names, is shown in Figure 8-5.

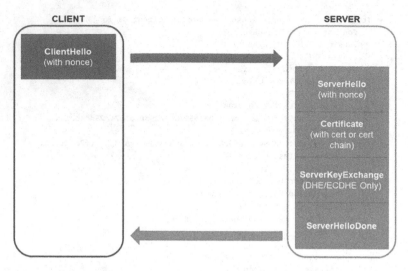

Figure 8-5. *TLS 1.2 client and server hello exchange*

EXERCISE 8.7. WHO GOES THERE?

If you've been practicing with your HTTP proxy (specifically in the previous exercise), you should already be getting a feel for the back and forth exchanges in TLS. So, now that you know how a TLS handshake starts with the initial hellos, try to reverse engineer it a little. Remember, this part of the communication is clear text!

Can you figure out whether you're looking at a TLS 1.2 or 1.3 handshake? That's a great start!

Client Authentication

The most popular configuration of TLS today authenticates only the server when the server's certificate is sent with the ServerHello. Unless explicitly requested by the server, the client will not send a certificate to authenticate itself.

For a lot of Internet applications, this is sufficient. The servers are running on the Internet, broadcasting their information to the world. They want to prove to the world that they are who they say they are. Anyone is welcome to come and visit without proving their identity. Plus, exactly what a client's identity should be is less clear. A server's identity is usually tied to a domain name (e.g., google.com) or an IP address. But when you are browsing the Internet, what should *your* computer's identity be?

For circumstances where the server needs to identify the client, like bank transactions, or any other kind of account access, the user's identity (rather than the machine's) is what really matters. Usernames and passwords (or other kinds of personal identification) are what the server concerns itself with in those cases. Conceptually, by first authenticating the server and creating a shared key with it, the user can then safely identify themselves to the server using something like a password without worrying about disclosing their confidential information to the wrong party.

There are times, however, when security policy dictates that the client device must also be authenticated. When TLS is thus configured, it is referred to as "Mutual TLS" (MTLS). In this mode, the server lets the client know that it requires a certificate and proof of certificate ownership.

EXERCISE 8.8. CLIENT AUTHENTICATION RESEARCH

Mutual TLS is not used very frequently, but it is used. The authentication of clients, even when certificates are used, is often a little different. Do a little Internet search about how to configure a browser with a client certificate, how one obtains such a certificate, and what kind of identifier is chosen for the subject.

Deriving Session Keys

Recall from Chapter 6 that a very common configuration for cryptography is to have asymmetric operations used to exchange or generate a symmetric session key. In that same chapter, we discussed two different ways of doing that: key transport and key agreement.

In the TLS 1.2 handshake, the goal is to get both the client and the server the same copy of a symmetric key. Actually, that's not completely true. The goal is to get what is called the "pre-master secret" (PMS). The PMS, along with some other non-secret data, will be used to generate the "master secret." The master secret will be used to generate all the necessary session keys for bulk data communications.

TLS 1.2, through its various cipher suites, provides both key transport and key agreement approach to provisioning the PMS.

TLS cipher suites that begin with TLS_RSA refer to TLS suites that use RSA encryption for key transport. For example, the cipher suite TLS_RSA_WITH_3DES_EDE_CBC_SHA.

You might notice that for ECDHE in our previous example we *also* required ECDSA signatures. Why do we not need RSA or ECDSA signatures with RSA key transport?

As we said in the previous section, if ECDHE or DHE is being used for key exchange, the server sends those parameters along with the server hello. But if RSA key transport is used, it sends nothing. Instead, in RSA key transport mode, the client receives the server's certificate that was sent with the server's hello, extracts the public key, and encrypts the PMS with the public key. It transmits the encrypted PMS to the server and only the server can subsequently decrypt it. Now both client and server have the same PMS.

The reason no signatures are required is because RSA encryption can only be opened by the party with the corresponding private key. If the server is able to use the session key derived from the PMS to communicate, it must be in possession of the private key and must be the owner of the certificate. This process is depicted in Figure 8-6.

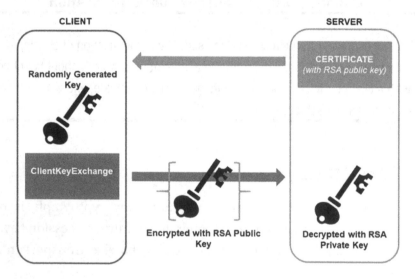

Figure 8-6. *TLS key exchange using RSA key transport*

DHE and ECDHE behave differently. They are called key agreement protocols because the PMS is not transmitted. Instead, both sides exchange DH/ECDH ephemeral public keys that can be used to simultaneously derive the PMS on both sides. As a reminder, exchanged DH/ECDH public keys are *not* like RSA or ECDSA public keys in the certificate. The DH/ECDH public keys are generated *on the spot and are used only once.* That's what makes them ephemeral.

That is also why they can't be trusted. If the public key was just made up on the spot, how does the client know that the public key really came from the server? How does the server know that the public key it received really came from the client?

The *long-term* RSA or ECDSA private key is used by the server to sign its DHE or ECDHE public key and parameters (e.g., curve). When the client receives them, it can use the server's public key in the certificate to verify that the DHE or ECDHE data came from the proper source. As discussed in the previous section, usually the client does not sign anything.

The DHE/ECDHE version of key exchange for the TLS handshake is depicted in Figure 8-7.

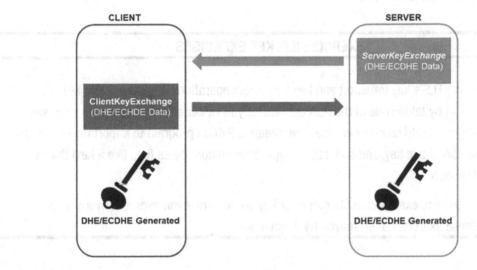

Figure 8-7. *TLS key agreement using DHE/ECDHE*

The security of these two approaches is very different. As we have already discussed in Chapter 6, the DH/ECDH approach provides perfect forward secrecy, while the RSA encryption approach does not. Furthermore, the RSA encryption approach has the pre-master secret generated entirely by the client. The server has to trust that the client is not reusing the same pre-master secret (or generating them from poor sources of randomness).

Even though the session key derivation from the pre-master secret depends on additional data—including the `ClientHello` nonce and the `ServerHello` nonce—that prevents a trivial replay attack, reusing the pre-master secret is suboptimal and potentially reduces the security of the system. On the other hand, when using

DH/ECDH the server and the client both contribute to the generation of the key material, ensuring that the server is not wholly dependent on the client for this value.

The RSA encryption scheme is problematic for one other reason: it uses PKCS 1.5 padding. You found that this scheme was vulnerable to a padding oracle attack in Chapter 4. TLS 1.2 has "countermeasures" designed to eliminate the oracle (remember, for the attack to work, the attacker needs to know when the padding was accepted), but unfortunately they aren't always successful. As described in more detail later in this chapter, this attack is still a threat.

For these reasons and others, most security experts are encouraging TLS servers to stop using RSA encryption for key transport. At the very least, this form of key exchange should be an option of last resort.

EXERCISE 8.9. KEY EXERCISES

Try re-creating TLS's key transport and key agreement operations. Let's start with key transport. Start by taking one of the RSA certificates you've generated. If you were a browser, this is what you would receive over the wire. Create a Python program to import the certificate, extract the RSA public key, and use it to encrypt some random bytes (i.e., like a key) that you write back to disk.

There were already exercises in Chapter 6 for key agreement, even over a network. If you didn't do those exercises, then maybe try it again now.

Switching to the New Cipher

Once the client has finished sending the key exchange information (either using RSA encryption or DHE/ECDHE), it no longer needs to send data in the clear. All subsequent information should be sent encrypted and authenticated.

To signal this, the client sends a message called a `ChangeCipherSpec` message to the server. This basically says that everything else sent from the client from this point forward will be sent using the negotiated cipher. Once the server has received the client key exchange data, it can also derive the session keys. As with the client, there is no further reason to communicate in the clear and the server sends its own `ChangeCipherSpec` message.

Each side then sends a Finished message to complete the handshake. The Finished message has a hash of all the handshake messages sent thus far, and because it is sent after the ChangeCipherSpec message, it is encrypted and authenticated under the new cipher suite.

The whole handshake, excluding a few less common messages, is visualized in Figure 8-8.

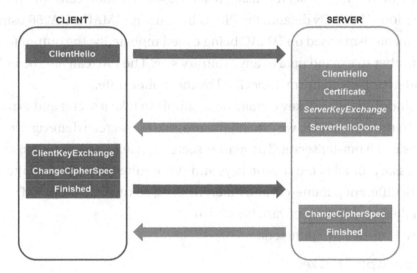

Figure 8-8. *TLS 1.2 handshake*

The purpose of this hash of handshake messages is to prevent an attacker from altering any of the messages sent in the clear before the changed cipher spec. For example, if an attacker intercepted and altered the client hello message, they could eliminate tougher ciphers and leave weak ones enabled, decreasing the difficulty of cracking the system. However, both sides keep a record of the messages sent and transmit a hash over all of these messages under the new cipher suite. If the hashes don't match, then what one side sent is not what the other side received. The communications channel is considered compromised in this case and is immediately closed.

Deriving Keys and Bulk Data Transfer

At this point, the TLS 1.2 handshake is over. The client has verified the server's identity using public key certificates, and both sides share a pre-master secret.

Regardless of how the pre-master secret is generated, both client and server derive keys using it. These keys are to create a secure authenticated channel using symmetric encryption and message authentication. Application data is set using this channel. But first, let's talk about these derived keys.

In this book, we've derived keys from data using a number of methods. Many are built in one form or another around hashing. In TLS 1.2, the pre-master secret is expanded into the "master secret" using what the specification calls the "pseudo-random function" (PRF). By default, the PRF is built using HMAC-SHA256 using an expansion mechanism based on HMAC being called repeatedly; the output from one call is fed into another to expand data to any arbitrary size. The PRF can also be built using a different underlying mechanism if specified by the cipher suite.

As a reminder, the idea of key expansion is simply to take a secret and expand it into more bytes. In the case of TLS, we expand the pre-master secret, whatever size it is, into 48 bytes. This is the master secret. The master secret is, itself, expanded into as many bytes as necessary for all of the session keys and IVs required by a cipher suite. Different suites require different parameters and different sizes, so the final output of the master suite, called the key_block, is of variable length.

There are at most six parameters:

- client write MAC key

- server write MAC key

- client write key

- server write key

- client write IV

- server write IV

It can be a little confusing to think about expanding the PMS to the master secret and the master secret to the key_block. To illustrate all of these moving parts, take a look at Figure 8-9.

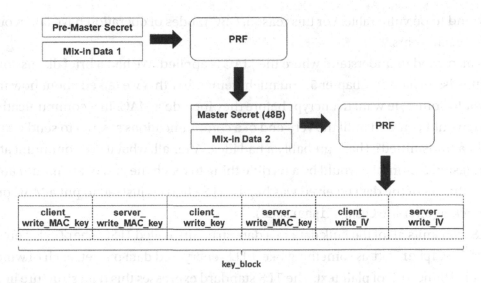

Figure 8-9. TLS key derivation. The pre-master secret is expanded to the master secret, which is expanded into the key_block. The final output is divided up as needed into individual keys and IVs.

You will notice that there are no *read* keys listed. That's because these are symmetric keys. In other words, the server's write key is the client's read key.

EXERCISE 8.10. IMPLEMENT THE PRF

Look in RFC 5246, available online, and look up the PRF. There is a description of how it works on pages 13 and14. Implement the PRF for HMAC-SHA256 and try out some key expansion. Generate a hundred bytes or so and divide some up for different keys.

Not all of these parameters are used for every cipher suite either. AEAD algorithms such as AES-GCM and AES-CCM do not need a MAC key. Even so, *every* cipher suite provides both confidentiality and authentication.[10] This either involves encrypting and applying a MAC or using AEAD encryption.

Speaking of which, the AES-CBC modes in TLS 1.0 are vulnerable to a padding oracle attack because they apply MAC first, then encrypt. This is vulnerable to the same attack you performed as an exercise in Chapter 3. While TLS 1.2 should theoretically not be vulnerable to this, some implementations did not follow the specification correctly and

---

[10]There are a few rare algorithms that are used for authentication only.

were found to be vulnerable. For this reason, CBC modes of operation have fallen out of favor in recent years.

It's also good to understand where the MAC is applied. We had a brief discussion about this issue back in Chapter 5. You might remember that we talked about how much data would someone want to encrypt before they include a MAC. In a communications context, would you wait until the very end of a communications session to send a MAC of all data transmitted? That's probably a bad idea. After all, what if the communications session lasted a month! It would be a terrible thing to reach the end of the month and find out that all of the data received was bogus. TLS chooses instead to put a MAC on every packet (after the ChangeCipherSpec).

TLS transmits all of the bulk data in a data structure called TLSCipherText. You can think of TLSCipherText as something like a TLS-encrypted data packet, each of which can hold around 16K of plaintext. The TLS standard expresses this data structure like a C-style struct:

```
1    struct {
2         ContentType type;
3         ProtocolVersion version;
4         uint16 length;
5         select (SecurityParameters.cipher_type) {
6              case stream: GenericStreamCipher;
7              case block: GenericBlockCipher;
8              case aead: GenericAEADCipher;
9         } fragment;
10   } TLSCiphertext;
```

If you're not familiar with C-style structs, this is really just a raw data structure. It's kind of like a class in Python but without any methods. The structure has type, version, and length fields that are reasonably straightforward. The exact types of ContentType and ProtocolVersion are defined elsewhere in the document, but the intent is clear even without looking them up.

The select statement is perhaps a little more confusing. What this part of the struct is expressing is that there is a fragment field, but its type is one of three options: GenericStreamCipher, GenericBlockStream, and GenericAEADCipher. Each of these three options represents a different kind of cipher.

Just to be clear, the struct shown here is conceptual. This struct shows how data is laid out and concatenated in binary form in a way that is easy to understand, as well as hierarchical (data structures within data structures). When sending data, TLS constructs a stream of binary data with these pieces in it, in this order.

The stream and block cipher types both include MACs as part of the cipher type. The subtypes are defined thus:

```
1    stream-ciphered struct {
2          opaque content[TLSCompressed.length];
3          opaque MAC[SecurityParameters.mac_length];
4    } GenericStreamCipher ;
5
6    struct {
7          opaque IV[SecurityParameters.record_iv_length];
8          block-ciphered struct {
9                opaque content[TLSCompressed.length];
10               opaque MAC[SecurityParameters.mac_length];
11               uint8 padding[GenericBlockCipher.padding_length];
12               uint8 padding_length;
13         };
14   } GenericBlockCipher;
```

The content field for both of these types is the plaintext (potentially compressed). The stream-ciphered and block-ciphered keywords in front of the respective structs indicate that the binary data is encrypted. The MAC for both of these cipher types is within the enciphered structure. The documentation states that these MACs are computed over the content which includes the content type, version, length, and the plaintext itself. Obviously, this is a MAC-Then-Encrypt scheme.

AEAD algorithms work just a little differently. The conceptual struct defined in the protocol looks like this:

```
1    struct {
2          opaque nonce_explicit[SecurityParameters.record_iv_length];
3          aead-ciphered struct {
4                opaque content[TLSCompressed.length];
5          };
6    } GenericAEADCipher ;
```

There is no MAC for this because the MAC is included by default in the output. Recall from Chapter 7 that the "AD" in AEAD means "additional data" that is authenticated, but not encrypted. In the case of TLS AEAD ciphers, the AD includes the same data—to which the MAC is applied—in the stream and block ciphers, namely, the content type, version, and length. By inserting this AD directly into the decryption process, the algorithm will not decrypt the plaintext unless the contextual data is correct. This helps reduce errors and ensure correctness.

Importantly, because there is a MAC for each record, the AEAD encryption is finalized for each TLSCiphertext chunk. In Chapter 7, we discussed the idea of not wanting to wait for gigabytes of data before determining that the ciphertext has been modified. Accordingly, the AEAD algorithm is run with an individual key and IV (nonce) on each one of these TLSCiphertext structures (the same key and IV *must not* be reused after finalizing an encryption and producing a tag).

In the GenericAEADCipher struct defined for TLS, it includes a nonce_explicit field that carries a certain amount of IV/nonce data. For AEAD algorithms, it is common to have an implicit part of the IV and an explicit part of the IV. The implicit part is calculated. For TLS 1.2, the server (or client) IV derived in the key derivation operation is the implicit part. Both parties calculate this internally without sending it over the network. The explicit part included in the fragment makes up the rest of the IV/nonce, permitting the nonce to be unique for each packet.

EXERCISE 8.11. THE TLS 1.2 PIECES

Try stringing together something similar to TLS 1.2 from the other exercises in the chapter so far. Exchange a certificate over the network (you can leave it in PEM format if it's easier). Once you get the server's certificate, have the client either send back a PMS encrypted or use ECDHE to generate the PMS on both sides.

You can leave out all of TLS's complicated stuff. You don't need to negotiate cipher suites, create an underlying record layer, or do the hash over all messages at the end. Exchange a certificate, get a PMS, and derive some keys. For "packet" structure, you can use the same JSON dictionaries you did for the Kerberos exercises.

TLS 1.3

The TLS 1.3 protocol represents the biggest change to the handshake process in the history of TLS.

First, TLS 1.3 gets rid of almost all of the ciphers included in TLS 1.2. There are only five ciphers available and all of them are AEAD ciphers:

- TLS_AES_256_GCM_SHA384

- TLS_CHACHA20_POLY1305_SHA256

- TLS_AES_128_GCM_SHA256

- TLS_AES_128_CCM_8_SHA256

- TLS_AES_128_CCM_SHA256

Basically, TLS 1.3 supports AES-GCM, AES-CCM, and ChaCha20-Poly1305. You have seen all three of these algorithms in this book. By reducing the cipher suites available and requiring AEAD, TLS 1.3 makes it much harder for servers to accidentally or unknowingly secure their web site with weak encryption or authentication.

RSA encryption is also no longer available as a key transport mechanism.

An even bigger change for TLS 1.3 is that the handshake is now a single round trip. This *significantly* reduces the latency for setup. The new handshake is depicted in Figure 8-10.

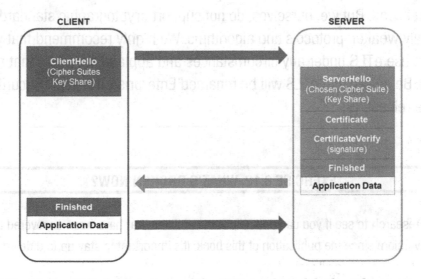

Figure 8-10. *A simplified depiction of the TLS 1.3 handshake. The entire handshake is designed to work in a single round trip.*

Technically, there is a second message from the client in the form of a "finished" message, but as shown in the figure, it can be piggybacked with the client's first application message. The server may have already transmitted application data piggybacked with its handshake message as well.

This speedup is especially important for stateless protocols like HTTP. Most HTTP messages are single-shot, one-time transmissions. Setting up a *new* TLS 1.2 tunnel for every single message really slows down a web site's speed and responsiveness. Cutting that latency in half makes a big difference for web communications.

More importantly, weak ciphers and modes have been removed. By eliminating RSA key transport, for example, TLS 1.3 makes forward secrecy *mandatory*! Limiting algorithms to AEAD is also an important improvement.

There are other differences and details for both protocols not covered here, but this is sufficient for an introduction.

Warning: Extra Terrible Lacking Security (eTLS)

There is a "variation" of TLS 1.3 being promoted called eTLS. We put variation in quotes because it is not a standard developed by the IETF, the standards body behind TLS. It takes TLS 1.3 and removes some of its most important security features including forward secrecy.

The purported motivations are data loss prevention (DLP), performance, and other usability reasons. But we, ourselves, do not support cryptographic standards that intentionally weaken protocols and algorithms. We highly recommend that you should not use eTLS under any circumstances and applaud browsers that refuse to support it. Be aware that eTLS will be renamed Enterprise Transport Security (ETS) in a future release [9].

EXERCISE 8.12. WHAT'S BROKEN NOW?

Do some research to see if you can find new vulnerabilities that have been uncovered in TLS (any version) since the publication of this book. It's important to stay up to date on vulnerabilities happening all around you and a mitigation path forward. It's a terrible thing when bad guys find out you're vulnerable before they do.

Certificate Verification and Trusting Trust

Eve is done reading about TLS. She has already collected a few possibilities for attacking TLS:

- Padding oracle attack against RSA encryption in some versions and implementations of TLS.

- Padding oracle attack against AES-CBC encryption in some versions and implementations of TLS.

- Attempting to coerce the client and server into using a weak cipher suite.

There are defenses to all of these, but they are areas that Eve can examine. Maybe she'll get lucky and find a poorly configured server. We will explore these attacks, and a few others, shortly. But first, Eve decides to look at one other potentially massive vulnerability: *certificate checking*.

In the preceding section, we made only the briefest of references to certificate verification. When a client receives a server's certificate, the client must ensure that the certificate is valid and trusted. The client certificate may rely on a chain of CAs, and the verification process is said to follow a certificate path. The path must terminate with a trusted root.

A high-level overview of this process is

- The client certificate's subject name must match the expected host name from the URI (e.g., if we navigated to `https://google.com`, then `google.com` needs to be the subject of the TLS certificate).

  - The host name can match the subject's common name, or

  - The host name can match one of the subject's alternate names (V3 extension).

- None of the certificates in the path can be expired.

- None of the certificates in the path can be revoked.

- The issuer of a certificate must be the subject of the next certificate in the chain until the root is reached.

- Certificate limitations (such as `KeyUsage` and `BasicConstraints`) are enforced.

- Policies are enforced related to maximum path length, name constraints, and so forth.

Eve realizes that this is a complicated process. There are a lot of checks to be made, and an error in any one of them might grant her access. Many TLS exploits have less to do with the protocol and more to do with programmer or user errors.

The entire security of TLS depends on certificates being issued to *authorized parties*. If Eve can get an unauthorized certificate, steal a private key, or convince Alice or Bob (or you) that she has an authorized certificate, the rest of the security breaks down. The most powerful certificate attack Eve could attempt is to convince Alice or Bob (or you) to install an evil root certificate! If that happens, TLS will accept any certificate Eve chooses to send!

Certificate Revocation

We mentioned in Chapter 5 that certificates have a big weakness in the realm of revocation. Unfortunately, revoking a certificate is a major pain, and Eve is looking closely at how she can exploit this.

There are two classic approaches to revoking certificates. The first is a certificate revocation list (CRL). As the name suggests, this is just a static record of certificates that have been revoked. To keep the size of the CRL manageable, the certificate is identified by its serial number. CRLs are often CA-specific and are signed by the CA, so it is important that the CA keep track of issued serial numbers. It must ensure that no serial number is used more than once, and it must ensure that the serial number matches the expected owner information. CRLs tend to be published on a fixed schedule (e.g., once per day).

Certificate verification systems, such as one used in TLS, must keep a list of all revoked certificates so that any such detected certificates can be invalidated during the verification process.

The other classic approach to checking for revocation is to use the Online Certificate Status Protocol (OCSP). As with CRLs, this protocol is used to check the validity of a certificate by serial number lookup. Unlike CRLs, however, this protocol is used with an online server in real time and can be executed during the certificate validation process. Once again, the issuing CA is often the OCSP responder for certificates that they have issued.

Obviously, OCSP will have more up-to-date information than static CRLs. OCSP, however, introduces additional latency into a TLS handshake setup. Worse, what should a client, like a browser, do if the OCSP responder *doesn't respond?* Should it *not* connect? Should it tell the user that "I'm sorry, I can't let you do online banking today because the OCSP server is down?"

Most browsers refuse to take this hard line. If the browser can't get an OCSP response, it just moves forward and assumes that the certificate isn't revoked. This makes Eve super excited. If she can get a revoked certificate (or a certificate that is immediately revoked once her theft is discovered), she can use it against Alice's and Bob's browsers. If the browsers try to reach out to OCSP servers, she will just execute a denial-of-service attack and ensure that the OCSP responses are never received. It's an easy way around the security measure.

For these and many other reasons, CRLs and OCSPs are considered obsolete. Many browsers, such as Google Chrome, don't even have an option to turn these features on.[11]

The truth is, revocation is *still* a hard problem and Eve is going to do everything she can to exploit this fact.

The good news is, new forms of certificate revocation are being explored right now including mandatory OCSP stapling. The concept for this is that a server *includes* an OCSP response along with their certificate. The OCSP response is only good for a relatively short period of time, so the server has to refresh regularly. The full details of this approach are beyond the scope of this book, but this might be a good topic of research for Alice and Bob.

Untrustworthy Roots, Pinning, and Certificate Transparency

Unfortunately for us (and to Eve's delight), as with all known approaches to establishing trust, TLS requires a trusted third party. And, as the Roman poet Juvenal would say, "Quis custodiet ipsos custodes?" ("Who guards the guards?" or "Who watches the watchmen?")

What is problematic about CAs is that if a CA private key is compromised, the thief can generate certificates for themselves for *any domain*. This is *not* a theoretical problem. By way of example, there was a successful attack on the now defunct DigiNotar

---

[11]Google Chrome and Firefox actually create their own lists of "bad" certificates and send them out to the browsers as part of software updates. They're essentially creating a proprietary CRL of sorts. This has actually been reasonably good in practice for certain kinds of certificates.

CA in 2011 [8]. The attacker infiltrated their servers and managed to generate forged certificates including a "wild card" certificate for google.com, plus additional certificates for Yahoo, WordPress, Mozilla, and TOR. The DigiNotar CA had to be removed from the trusted CA list of browsers and mobile devices. Unsurprisingly, DigiNotar went out of business almost immediately after the attack was uncovered.

For a more recent, and in some ways more disturbing, example, Trustico, a TLS certificate reseller, asked DigiCert to revoke more than 20,000 certificates. That, by itself, was not problematic. The certificates were being revoked because of a loss of trust in the issuer. What *was* shocking was the admission that Trustico had the *private keys* for these certificates and had sent them to DigiCert by *email* [4]! This means that the reseller was generating the key pairs for their customers and holding on to the private key. Although reportedly kept in "cold storage," in theory the reseller, an employee of the reseller, or a disgruntled former employee of the reseller could have taken a customer's private key and assumed their digital identity.

This particular problem of a CA keeping customer private keys cannot be solved technologically. If a party gives up their private key, there are no mechanisms for keeping them secure. All cryptography rests on keeping secrets secret.

The issue of fraudulent and misused certificates is more serious and more common. Eve desperately wants to compromise a CA or a CA's cert if she can (specifically one trusted by Alice or Bob). Stealing one cert only gives her one fraudulent identity. Stealing a CA cert gives her an unlimited number of fraudulent identities.

Fortunately, there are methods that Alice and Bob can use to protect themselves. Let's look at two of them.

The first is "certificate pinning." The term is used in a number of different ways, so make sure you are careful in your research. The basic concept is that a client like Alice or Bob has, one way or another, an expectation of what a certificate should be before receiving it. When the certificate is received, it is compared to the expected version—the "pinned" version—and a policy is invoked if there is a mismatch. It is assumed that a mismatch means, with high probability, that Eve is using a fraudulent certificate.

Although pinning is more general, some sources treat the more specific HTTP Public Key Pinning (HPKP) as a synonym. Perhaps this is because there was a time when some parties, including Google, were pushing for this technology as a general solution to identifying and rejecting compromised certificates. Since then, there has been a general consensus that this approach is insufficient and the new move is toward "certificate transparency" (CT).

Pinning (as a general concept) continues to have its uses even so, especially in mobile applications. An app on a phone, for example, can have its author's certificate baked into the app itself. This pinned version of the cert is always compared against the cert received in the TLS handshake. If it doesn't match, something is wrong. Should the company need to change out their certificate or rotate a key, they can push a new pinned version in an app upgrade. Mobile applications aside, Google and Firefox do this kind of static pinning in their browsers.

This is effective. Google actually discovered the issue with the compromised DigiNotar-issued Google certificate because of static pinning.

EXERCISE 8.13. MONITOR CERTIFICATE ROTATION

Assuming you successfully intercepted TLS certificates in your HTTP proxy program, visit a site multiple times and see if you receive the same certificate every time. How often do you expect a server's certificate to change?

HPKP, on the other hand, is a general purpose, dynamic pinning technology that relies on trust-on-first-use (TOFU) principles. Basically, the first time a client visits a web site, that web site can request that the client pin the certificate for a certain period of time. Should the certificate change within that period of time, it should treat the modified certificate as an imposter. The idea is interesting and reasonable, but it introduces a number of problems and can still be exploited by attackers in unhappy ways. Hence, the idea is already dying out.

Instead, the aforementioned certificate transparency (CT) is a second method of addressing certificate issues that is gaining momentum. The basic idea is in some ways similar to blockchain and distributed ledgers. Whenever a certificate is issued, it is also submitted to a public log. The public log is hosted by a third party, perhaps even the CA that issued the certificate, but it is verifiable so that the third party does not have to be trusted.

The purpose of the log is transparency: CAs are thus essentially audited for the certificates they produce. The goal is to have all issued certificates publicly available for inspection in a cryptographically verifiable way.[12] Browsers will eventually be configured to not accept any certificate that is not found in such a log.

---

[12]The name of one of the original projects behind this was called "Sunshine" and was started after the DigiNotar hack.

What do we get from using CT logs? It's deceptively simple but surprisingly helpful. Suppose that Eve attempts to create a fake certificate to an EA server. If EA browsers will not accept the cert unless it is published, Eve will have to submit it to one of the public logs. If that happens, EA can immediately detect that a forged certificate has been generated. While this does require that EA be monitoring the logs, it is easy to deploy an automated system that checks to see if any new certificates have been issued that shouldn't have been. The EA knows (or should know) which certs it has legitimately issued and can flag ones that aren't.

Even if Eve is so clever as to somehow interfere with East Antarctica's auditing system and does manage to get away with some subterfuge, once the attack is detected, the public logs will enable a thorough investigation of the problem and an accurate assessment of the damage. It is terrifying that in the DigiNotar hack, investigators were unable to even fully identify all the certificates that had been generated! To this day, *nobody knows* exactly how many certificates the attacker created. That is one reason why DigiNotar had to completely shut down. It was impossible to identify all of the certificates that needed to be revoked.

CT is still somewhat new, so it may continue evolving over time. It does not, for example, provide a mechanism for verifying revocation, and there is already a proposal for "revocation transparency" to be added to it. This is definitely the technology to watch and to start using as soon as possible.

Known Attacks Against TLS

Eve will always be trying to break certificates in some way or another. If she gets past that gate, everything else is broken. Of course, if Alice and Bob are using DHE or ECDHE with forward secrecy, everything else in the future is broken, but at least not the past.

Beyond certificates, there are some other contemporary attacks against TLS to be aware of. The following is a brief overview of well-known attacks against TLS and how to prevent them.

POODLE

POODLE stands for "Padding Oracle On Downgraded Legacy Encryption." TLS 1.0, as we've discussed, could be exploited when using CBC mode. At the time, the block cipher was DES, but the attack works on DES or AES so long as the mode of operation is CBC.

TLS 1.1 and 1.2 were supposed to fix this problem by changing how the CBC encryption was padded. But the POODLE attack showed that, even for servers running 1.1 and 1.2, they could be re-negotiated down to TLS 1.0 in order to be attacked.

Worse, it was later discovered that some TLS 1.1 and 1.2 implementations were using the same padding as TLS 1.0 (contrary to specifications). This kind of error caused no problem with normal communications because the two padding schemes are compatible for legitimate traffic. It is only when the data is attacked that it becomes clear that the padding is wrong. For the implementations that had the faulty implementation, they were vulnerable without the downgrade.

Defenses include

1. Disable TLS 1.0 (and 1.1 really).

2. Verify that TLS 1.2 is not vulnerable using an auditing tool.

FREAK and Logjam

The Logjam attack, like POODLE, relies on forcing a downgrade to earlier versions of TLS. Actually, the goal is to downgrade the cipher suites.

In the 1990s, the US government had a policy of now allowing strong cryptography to be exported to foreign countries. The government's policy treated these kinds of algorithms as *weapons*.[13] Security software still bears the scars of this policy, and there were specific TLS cipher suites that were called EXPORT algorithms. These algorithms were, in fact, very weak.

In Logjam, an attacker intercepts the client's message and removes all of the proposed cipher suites and replaces them with EXPORT variants of Diffie-Hellman (DH). The server picks weak parameters accordingly and sends them back to the client. The client doesn't know that anything is wrong and just accepts the server's poorly chosen configuration.

The resulting keys are easily broken.

Notice that the Finished message of the TLS protocol should detect this attack. The whole point of sending a message with a hash of all messages exchanged during the handshake was to reveal this kind of manipulation.

The problem is that the Finished message is sent encrypted under the new (weak) key. If Eve is attempting this attack, she can intercept the real message while still

---

[13]Maybe that's why East and West Antarctica are so far behind the times?

cracking the key. Once the key is cracked, she can create a false `Finished` message and encrypt it now using the cracked session key. Unless the time it takes to get the key cracked is longer than internal timeouts, Eve can succeed.

FREAK is a very similar attack to Logjam, but uses "export" RSA parameters instead. Defenses for both Logjam and FREAK include

1. Disable weak cipher suites—especially "export" ciphers—on the sever.

2. Use clients that unconditionally refuse to accept weak parameters (e.g., DH/ECDH or RSA parameters that are weak).

Sweet32

The Sweet32 attack is a little different from the ones we've seen before. It is designed specifically for block ciphers that have a block size of 64 bits. For most TLS 1.2 installations, there is only one cipher in use that has such a block size: 3DES.

Although a full explanation of 3DES is beyond the scope of this book, it uses DES underneath. It is slow, but it at least isn't as weak as DES. DES keys can be compromised in fairly reasonable time; 3DES cannot, yet.

Nevertheless, 3DES is using a 64-bit block size. The block size of an algorithm impacts how much data should be encrypted under a single key before rotation. The math is outside the scope of this book, but cryptography breaks down once more than $2^{n/2}$ blocks have been encrypted. For 64-bit block sizes, the limit is about 32GB of data, which is easily generated on modern computers. Even worse, $2^{n/2}$ is an *upper* bound! Vulnerabilities creep in much sooner in practice.

Sadly, many TLS implementations do not enforce maximum data limits with a key. The Sweet32 attack exploits this to send enough data to force collisions and recover data.

Defenses include

- Disable 3DES-based cipher suites (and any other 64-bit ciphers if any happen to be present).

ROBOT

Recall that in Chapter 4 we spent a lot of time beating up on RSA. We showed that it was trivially defeated when used without padding. We also showed that certain forms of padding could be exploited as well. In particular, PKCS 1.5 is vulnerable to a padding oracle attack. This is the very padding that is used for RSA encryption in TLS, up to and including version 1.2.

Bleichenbacher discovered the attack against PKCS 1.5 in 1999. Obviously, that was long before TLS version 1.2. Why wasn't it changed?

For compatibility reasons, the designers behind TLS decided to keep the same padding scheme and insert countermeasures. As we mentioned earlier in the chapter, the padding oracle attack requires an oracle! If the TLS protocol can keep from revealing the success or failure of padding, it should eliminate the attack.

Unfortunately, it isn't that simple. ROBOT stands for "Return Of Bleichenbacher's Oracle Threat." What the researchers behind ROBOT found is that TLS countermeasures aren't always successful. They also found new ways to extract oracle information from TLS, and they were able to demonstrate that their attack was practical. They could, for example, sign messages for Facebook without access to the appropriate private keys.

Defenses for ROBOT include

- Disable all cipher suites that use RSA encryption for the key exchange (any cipher that starts with `TLS_RSA`).

CRIME, TIME, and BREACH

TLS version 1.2 provides for compression of data before encryption. This has been disabled in TLS 1.3. The problem with compression is that it leaks information to people like Eve. That information can be used to recover information within the ciphertext.

CRIME, which stands for "Compression Ratio Info-leak Made Easy," was first demonstrated in 2012. The problem with compression is that it really only works well if data is *repeated*. So, even if you only have the ciphertext of some compressed plaintext, if you can insert or partially insert messages, a drop in the ciphertext size strongly suggests that there was some repeated data resulting in a better compression ratio. This information can be used to recover small numbers of bytes. Any loss of data, no matter how small, is unacceptable. But if the data being attacked is already small (e.g., a web cookie with authentication information), a small number of bytes lost can be catastrophic.

CRIME was followed by TIME, which was slightly more effective. It also inspired BREACH, which is a different attack, but also uses compression to reveal information.

Defenses include

- Disable compression.

Heartbleed

Heartbleed is a special mention in our list because it is not a vulnerability in TLS itself. Rather, it was a bug in OpenSSL's implementation (yes, the library you've been using). Specifically, it was a bug in an extension to TLS that enables heartbeats for detecting dead connections. Although an extension, it is a commonly used one.

The problem with OpenSSL's implementation was that they were not doing bounds checking on heartbeat request received from the other side. A typical heartbeat request included some data to echo back and the length of the data. If the length was longer than the data to echo, the incorrect implementation simply read contents out of memory. Although there were no guarantees on what would be included in those contents, it might include private keys and other secrets.

The point of this vulnerability is to indicate that not all attacks are on the protocols themselves but sometimes on the implementations. It is important to watch for both kinds of issues.

Defenses include

- Keep TLS libraries and applications up to date.

Using OpenSSL with Python for TLS

We have done a lot of talking in this chapter, but not a lot of programming. This background was helpful to Eve, though, and hopefully helpful to you. Let's get our hands dirty just a little bit to wrap up.

Many of Python's built-in networking operations have TLS support (often under parameter names referencing SSL because that name has persisted even after 20 years of TLS). Eve is concerned about TLS keeping her from sniffing traffic. From what she's learned in this chapter, however, she has seen that there are a lot of ways to do things wrong. Eve decides to walk through some examples to see what she might exploit.

She begins by connecting to a TLS server like Alice and Bob might do. Execute the code from the beginning of this chapter but, for simplicity, this time without the HTTP proxy snooping in the middle.

The bad news for Eve (and the good news for you) is that Python is trying to make sure programmers don't shoot themselves in the foot. This code, by default, tries to do a number of things reasonably correct where SSL is concerned. The default parameter loads the system's trusted certificates, validates the host name, and verifies the certificate. These things might sound obvious, but some APIs require the programmer to implement all of these checks on their own increasing the risk of leaving something out or implementing it incorrectly.

Eve decides to see how well TLS checks are enforced. She starts up the openssl s_server again using the certificates she created. She tries to connect with Python and encounters the following error (slightly truncated):

```
>>> import http.client
>>> conn = http.client.HTTPSConnection("127.0.0.1", 8888)
>>> conn.request("GET", "/")
#SHELL# output_match: '''certificate verify failed'''
Traceback (most recent call last):
  File "<stdin >", line 1, in <module>
  File "/usr/lib/python3.6/http/client.py", line 1239, in request
    self._send_request(method, url, body, headers, encode_chunked)
...
  File "/usr/lib/python3.6/ssl.py", line 689, in do_handshake
    self._sslobj.do_handshake()
ssl.SSLError: [SSL: CERTIFICATE_VERIFY_FAILED] certificate verify failed
(_ssl.c:841)
```

It rejected Eve's certificate, as is to be expected. After all, it has no reason to trust it. The certificate sent by the server (s_server) is not rooted in a valid certificate authority. The Python code, by default, did the right thing. Eve curses under her breath.

Still, after searching through Python documentation, Eve discovers that Python *will* let you shoot yourself in the foot if you really, really want to.

The HTTPSConnection class can take a parameter called context. It expects an instance of a class called SSLContext.[14] Eve experiments by plugging in her own version, shown in the following code block and runs the test again.

```
>>> import http.client
>>> import ssl
>>> evil_context = ssl.SSLContext()
>>> conn = http.client.HTTPSConnection("127.0.0.1", 8888, context=evil_
    context)
>>> conn.request("GET", "/")
>>> r1 = conn.getresponse()
>>> r1.read()
#SHELL# output_ommitted
```

Eve is pleased! She successfully received a response from s_server. Why?

The SSLContext object contains TLS configuration parameters and controls (at least partially) the processing of the TLS handshake including certificate checking. An empty SSLContext does *no* checking on certificates.

In fact, the Python documentation recommends not creating an SSLContext in this way. Instead, programmers should typically use SSLContext. create_default_context(). This method creates an SSLContext that performs the default checks Eve encountered earlier that resulted in a rejected certificate.

But using this manual method, Eve can have greater control over how certificate verification works. Rolling up her sleeves, Eve configures her evil_context to *trust* her domain certificate that is the issuer of her localhost certificate. She uses the load_verify_locations method to specify her domain certificate as a trusted CA file.

```
>>> import http.client
>>> import ssl
>>> evil_context = ssl.SSLContext()
>>> evil_context.verify_mode = ssl.CERT_REQUIRED
>>> evil_context.load_verify_locations("domain_cert.crt")
```

---

[14]The following examples all use HTTPSConnection class, but the SSLContext objects are used throughout Python in various network operations, so this information is more general than the examples we're using.

```
>>> conn = http.client.HTTPSConnection("127.0.0.1", 8888, context=evil_
    context)
>>> conn.request("GET", "/")
>>> r1 = conn.getresponse()
>>> r1.read()
```
#SHELL# output_ommitted

To verify that the trust system is working, Eve re-runs this test with the `verify_mode` = `ssl.CERT_REQUIRED` left in but the `load_verify_locations` left out. It results in the failed certificate check she saw earlier. Only by telling her context where her roots of trust are was she able to get her certificates validated.

There's yet another check that is currently disabled: host name checking. Recall that when validating a certificate, the certificate should have the same subject name (either in the distinguished name's Common Name or in the subject's Alternative Name) as the host URI. Eve created this localhost certificate with the common name of `127.0.0.1` on purpose so she could run host name matching tests. When she browses to `https://127.0.0.1`, she wants the certificate's subject name to match.

To see if host name checking is working, Eve first stops the `openssl s_server` and restarts it with new parameters. This time, she uses her *domain* certificate as the server's certificate (instead of as the issuer). Because she is using a self-signed cert, she won't need the command-line parameters related to chains. Her command looks something like this:

```
openssl s_server -accept 8888 -www -cert domain_cert.crt -key domain_key.pem
```

She re-runs the test code and it still works. Even though the URI is `https://127.0.0.1` and the subject common name is `wacko.westantarctica.southpole.gov`, the data was permitted. Without host checking enabled, this mismatch doesn't result in an error.

Eve now repeats her test after turning on host checking.

```
>>> import http.client
>>> import ssl
>>> evil_context = ssl.SSLContext()
>>> evil_context.verify_mode = ssl.CERT_REQUIRED
>>> evil_context.load_verify_locations("domain_cert.crt")
>>> evil_context.check_hostname = True
```

```
>>> conn = http.client.HTTPSConnection("127.0.0.1", 8888, context = evil_
    context)
>>> conn.request("GET", "/")
#SHELL# output_match: '''doesn't match'''
Traceback (most recent call last):
  File "<stdin>", line 1, in <module>
  File "/usr/lib/python3.6/http/client.py", line 1239, in request
    self._send_request(method, url, body, headers, encode_chunked)
...
  File "/usr/lib/python3.6/ssl.py", line 331, in match_hostname
    % (hostname, dnsnames[0]))
ssl.CertificateError: hostname '127.0.0.1' doesn't match'wacko.
westantarctica.southpole.gov'
```

As you can see in our truncated exception trace, TLS complained that the host name (127.0.0.1) didn't match the subject name (wacko.westantarctica.southpole.gov).

In general, programmers that don't want Eve getting fake certificates past them shouldn't be messing around with these parameters. The default context with its default checking is a good start.

EXERCISE 8.14. SOCIAL ENGINEERING

This is a thought exercise; there is no programming involved. How might Eve try to get others using less secure software? What could she do to convince them to use a poorly configured SSL context?

The additional functionality does have important uses, though. What if Alice and Bob would like to do static certificate pinning. Maybe Bob is running a command and control server, and Eve is in the field with a Python program that needs to securely communicate with it. How can Alice pin the certificate to Bob's server? There isn't an API for the SSLContext to do this. It can only specify trusted CA certificates. It has no method for specifying a trusted *server* certificate.

There are fortunately other Python APIs for getting the peer's certificate after connecting. For example:

```
>>> import http.client
>>> import hashlib
>>> conn = http.client.HTTPSConnection("google.com", 443)
>>> conn.request("GET", "/")
>>> conn.sock.getpeercert(binary_form=True)
#SHELL# output_match: ''''''
b'0\x82\x02\xdb0\x82\x01\xc3\xa0\...
>>> peer_cert = conn.sock.getpeercert(binary_form=True)
>>> hashlib.sha256(peer_cert).hexdigest ()
#SHELL# output_match: ''''''
'bf52e8d42812c7a09586aa19219b0c15a92de6664aad380ed4c66dea7c6a5b3a'
```

The hash can be compared against a pinned value to ensure that it's the expected certificate. Certificate pinning, especially static certificate pinning, might be a good idea in certain contexts.

Unfortunately for Alice and Bob, there isn't yet an API for using CT logs. The Python cryptography library is starting to add support, but it appears right now to be limited to extensions in X.509 certificates. There is no API for submitting a serial number to get a CT response nor a mechanism for submitting a certificate to a log for insertion.

Again, keep your eyes on this (Eve certainly will). There will probably be new additions to Python libraries soon.

If Eve had her way, she would love to see Alice and Bob writing their own certificate-checking algorithms. She wishes they would do something like that instead of using Python's built-in checker.

Alice and Bob could, for example, get the entire chain of certificates and try to manually verify each one. The cryptography module does have certificate "validation" using the issuer's public key, shown as follows.

```
1   from cryptography.hazmat.primitives.serialization import load_pem_
    public_key
2   from cryptography.hazmat.primitives.asymmetric import padding
3   from cryptography.hazmat.backends import default_backend
4   from cryptography import x509
5
```

```
 6   import sys
 7
 8   issuer_public_key_file, cert_to_check = sys.argv[1:3]
 9   with open(issuer_public_key_file,"rb") as key_reader:
10       issuer_public_key = key_reader.read()
11
12   issuer_public_key = load_pem_public_key(
13       issuer_public_key,
14       backend=default_backend())
15
16   with open (cert_to_check,"rb") as cert_reader:
17       pem_data_to_check = cert_reader.read()
18   cert_to_check = x509.load_pem_x509_certificate(
19       pem_data_to_check,
20       default_backend())
21   issuer_public_key.verify(
22       cert_to_check.signature,
23       cert_to_check.tbs_certificate_bytes,
24       padding.PKCS1v15(),
25       cert_to_check.signature_hash_algorithm)
26   print("Signature ok! (Exception on failure!)")
```

Note that the tbs_certificate_bytes are the DER-encoded (not PEM-encoded) bytes that are hashed for signing the certificate. So, in the sample code, the issuer's public key is used to check the signature in the certificate over those bytes. To repeat, the signature is *not* over the PEM data.

The reason Eve *wants* Alice and Bob to do this is because this is just a small part of real certificate validation![15] In the preceding code, there are no checks for valid data, no checks against revocation lists, and not even checks that the client certificate's issuer matches the subject line for the issuing certificate. There are a lot of ways to get this wrong, and Eve is far more likely to find a vulnerability if Alice and Bob use their own methods.

---

[15]Hence, the reason we put "validation" in quotes.

If you are smarter than Alice and Bob, leave certificate verification up to library operations. If you really feel that you want to do some specialized verification, do it *in addition* to, not in place of, these widely deployed and widely tested library functions.

Finally, beyond correct certificate checking, there is one other set of parameters that Eve decides to investigate: the supported TLS versions and supported cipher suites.

With respect to versions, even though TLS 1.0 and 1.1 are deprecated, most TLS implementations continue to support them for backward compatibility and legacy operations. This is almost always the wrong thing to do. Servers and clients should be disabling TLS 1.0 and 1.1 by default and only re-enabling them if this causes some kind of real, concrete, unresolvable problem. Eve hopes to find that she can use attacks like POODLE, Logjam, and FREAK against servers that still support these legacy versions.

Happily for Eve, she finds out that these vulnerable versions are still very much present. SSLv3 and SSLv2 are disabled, but this isn't enough. TLS 1.0 absolutely must be disabled and TLS 1.1 should be as well.

Python does permit turning them off, however, and perhaps we should show Alice and Bob how to do so. The following code turns off TLS 1.0 and 1.1 for a specific SSLContext object.[16]

```
>>> import ssl
>>> good_context = ssl.create_default_context()
>>> good_context.options |= ssl.OP_NO_TLSv1
>>> good_context.options |= ssl.OP_NO_TLSv1_1
```

After checking Python to see which versions of TLS are enabled, Eve now turns her attention to default cipher suites. She runs the following code to see all the ciphers installed on her test system.

```
>>> default_ctx = ssl.create_default_context()
>>> for cipher in default_ctx.get_ciphers():
...    print(cipher["name"])
...
ECDHE-ECDSA-AES256-GCM-SHA384
ECDHE-RSA-AES256-GCM-SHA384
```

---

[16]Version 3.7 introduced a new API for specifying a minimum version and a maximum version. However, not only was this book written for Python 3.6 but the new API also requires a certain version of the underlying OpenSSL. We have decided to stick with the 3.6 API for the time being.

```
ECDHE-ECDSA-AES128-GCM-SHA256
ECDHE-RSA-AES128-GCM-SHA256
ECDHE-ECDSA-CHACHA20-POLY1305
ECDHE-RSA-CHACHA20-POLY1305
DHE-DSS-AES256-GCM-SHA384
DHE-RSA-AES256-GCM-SHA384
DHE-DSS-AES128-GCM-SHA256
DHE-RSA-AES128-GCM-SHA256
DHE-RSA-CHACHA20-POLY1305
ECDHE-ECDSA-AES256-CCM8
ECDHE-ECDSA-AES256-CCM
ECDHE-ECDSA-AES256-SHA384
ECDHE-RSA-AES256-SHA384
ECDHE-ECDSA-AES256-SHA
ECDHE-RSA-AES256-SHA
DHE-RSA-AES256-CCM8
DHE-RSA-AES256-CCM
DHE-RSA-AES256-SHA256
DHE-DSS-AES256-SHA256
DHE-RSA-AES256-SHA
DHE-DSS-AES256-SHA
ECDHE-ECDSA-AES128-CCM8
ECDHE-ECDSA-AES128-CCM
ECDHE-ECDSA-AES128-SHA256
ECDHE-RSA-AES128-SHA256
ECDHE-ECDSA-AES128-SHA
ECDHE-RSA-AES128-SHA
DHE-RSA-AES128-CCM8
DHE-RSA-AES128-CCM
DHE-RSA-AES128-SHA256
DHE-DSS-AES128-SHA256
DHE-RSA-AES128-SHA
DHE-DSS-AES128-SHA
ECDHE-ECDSA-CAMELLIA256-SHA384
ECDHE-RSA-CAMELLIA256-SHA384
```

```
ECDHE-ECDSA-CAMELLIA128-SHA256
ECDHE-RSA-CAMELLIA128-SHA256
DHE-RSA-CAMELLIA256-SHA256
DHE-DSS-CAMELLIA256-SHA256
DHE-RSA-CAMELLIA128-SHA256
DHE-DSS-CAMELLIA128-SHA256
DHE-RSA-CAMELLIA256-SHA
DHE-DSS-CAMELLIA256-SHA
DHE-RSA-CAMELLIA128-SHA
DHE-DSS-CAMELLIA128-SHA
AES256-GCM-SHA384
AES128-GCM-SHA256
AES256-CCM8
AES256-CCM
AES128-CCM8
AES128-CCM
AES256-SHA256
AES128-SHA256
AES256-SHA
AES128-SHA
CAMELLIA256-SHA256
CAMELLIA128-SHA256
CAMELLIA256-SHA
CAMELLIA128-SHA
```

The default list on Eve's test computer is very bad for her (good for us!). No RSA encryption for key exchange, no AES-CBC mode ciphers, and no 3DES. It doesn't look like Alice and Bob need to make any changes. According to the Python documentation, most of the weak ciphers have already been disabled. Still, it doesn't hurt to check.

If Alice and Bob do have any ciphers that use RSA encryption for key exchange (e.g., TLS_RSA_WITH_AES_128_CBC_SHA), they should remove them from the cipher suites by curating the list returned by get_ciphers and then update the SSLContext using the set_ciphers method.

Eve sighs and then leaves the room. She's on her way back to East Antarctica to try some new approaches to stealing information. She might try to fake a certificate, or she might try to find a vulnerable TLS implementation. It might be a challenge; it might take some time, but Eve is patient, crafty, and persistent. And she's always listening.

EXERCISE 8.15. LEARN TO POKE AROUND

One of the best things you can do with your newly acquired (or improved) cryptography knowledge is learn to poke around. Most of the example code for this chapter was written as if executed in a Python shell on purpose. Get comfortable using the shell to poke a server or test a connection. There are many tools for testing publicly accessible TLS servers, but what about internal ones? If you find that your company is using poor security for internal TLS connections, let IT know. It's important to be aware of what's going on around you.

With that in mind, write a diagnostic program in Python that connects to a given server and looks for weak algorithms or configuration data. For example, you have seen that the SSLSocket class has the getpeercert() method to get the remote certificate. Write a program that, upon connecting to a server, obtains the certificate and reports if the signature on the certificate uses a SHA-1 hash (very broken and unlikely) or still supports RSA encryption (more probable).

You can also use the SSLSocket object to check the current cipher using cipher(). Which cipher suite is the server picking out of all the ones proposed? Is that a good choice?

Building on this cipher check, change your Python SSLContext to *only* support weak ciphers. That is, create a context that disables strong ciphers and re-enables weak ones. You can set a context's ciphers using the SSLContext.set_ciphers() function. The list of available cipher suites, for each version of TLS, can be found at www.openssl.org/docs/manmaster/man1/ciphers.html. The goal of this test is to see if a server is still supporting older, deprecated ciphers.

Should your analysis tool uncover any weaknesses, report them to the appropriate IT or administrative staff with recommendations for remediation.

The End of the Beginning

Well, reader, this is the end of this book. Hopefully it's a beginning for you. There is a lot to learn about cryptography and, to repeat for the thousandth time, this is just an introduction. You have learned much, but you are not a (crypto) Jedi yet!

Eve, representative of the EVEr listening EaVEsdropper, is not to be underestimated. Eve, along with Alice and Bob, was sometimes made out to be a little behind the times throughout most of this book. The truth is that Eve is always on the forefront of technology. There are still a lot of ways TLS servers get successfully attacked on a regular basis. Keep an eye out for news and updates about TLS. Unfortunately, new vulnerabilities and weaknesses are discovered more often than we'd like, and there are many who love to see and exploit them.

The good news is that, with strong cipher suites in use and legacy versions of TLS disabled, you already have a lot of good security in place. This chapter is an introduction to TLS security in Python programming. If you can understand the concepts in this chapter, it will be a good foundation to build on, but keep learning! Eve's most effective weapon against us is ignorance.

Python aside, if you're running a TLS-enabled web site, take time to occasionally have your site reviewed by a TLS audit program. For example, Qualys SSL Labs currently runs a free project to report on a site's TLS hygiene. You can try it out free here: `www.ssllabs.com/ssltest/index.html`.

Also, check in on the `cryptodoneright.org` web site as well. This project aims to keep crypto users as informed and well advised as possible.

In short, let's make Eve's life as difficult as possible. There will always be risks, but don't give her any easy wins. Make any victories painful and short-lived. After all, she is always keeping us on our toes, so we should return the favor!

EXERCISE 8.16. THREE CHEERS!

This is the last exercise in the book! Give yourself a round of applause for reaching this point.

And as you close the cover, please feel free to send the authors feedback, good or bad. And especially if you let us know if we've missed anything!

Bibliography

[1]   R. J. Anderson. *Security Engineering: A Guide to Building Dependable Distributed Systems*. Wiley Publishing, 2nd edition, 2008.

[2]   D. Bleichenbacher. Chosen ciphertext attacks against protocols based on the rsa encryption standard pkcs #1. In *Proceedings of the 18th Annual International Cryptology Conference on Advances in Cryptology*, CRYPTO '98, pages 1–12, London, UK, UK, 1998. Springer-Verlag.

[3]   D. E. R. Denning. *Encryption Algorithms*, chapter 2, pages 59–133. Addison-Wesley Publishing Company, Inc., Reading, Massachusetts, 1982.

[4]   DigiCert. DigiCert statement on trustico certificate revocation. `www.digicert.com/blog/digicert-statement-trustico-certificate-revocation/`, 2 2018.

[5]   F. Fischer, K. Bttinger, H. Xiao, C. Stransky, Y. Acar, M. Backes, and S. Fahl. Stack overflow considered harmful? the impact of copy&paste on android application security. In *IEEE Symposium on Security and Privacy*, pages 121–136. IEEE Computer Society, 2017.

[6]   M. Green. Wonk post: chosen ciphertext security in public-key encryption, 3 2016. `https://blog.cryptographyengineering.com/2016/03/21/attack-of-week-apple-imessage/`.

[7]   M. Green. Wonk post: chosen ciphertext security in public-key encryption, 4 2018. `https://blog.cryptographyengineering.com/2018/04/21/wonk-post-chosen-ciphertext-security-in-public-key-encryption-part-1/`.

© Seth James Nielson, Christopher K. Monson 2019
S. J. Nielson and C. K. Monson, *Practical Cryptography in Python*,
https://doi.org/10.1007/978-1-4842-4900-0

[8]   H. Hoogstraaten. Black tulip report of the investigation into the diginotar certificate authority breach, 08 2012.

[9]   Jacob Hoffman-Andrews. ETS isn't TLS and you shouldn't use it, February 2019.

[10] B. Marr. How much data do we create every day? the mind-blowing stats everyone should read. `www.forbes.com/sites/bernardmarr/2018/05/21/how-much-data-do-we-create-every-day-the-mind-blowing-stats-everyone-should-read`. Accessed 2018-10-06.

[11] A. J. Menezes, S. A. Vanstone, and P. C. V. Oorschot. *Handbook of Applied Cryptography*. CRC Press, Inc., Boca Raton, FL, USA, 1st edition, 1996.

[12] Y. Sasaki and K. Aoki. Finding preimages in full md5 faster than exhaustive search. In A. Joux, editor, *Advances in Cryptology - EUROCRYPT 2009*, pages 134–152, Berlin, Heidelberg, 2009. Springer Berlin Heidelberg.

[13] M. Stevens, E. Bursztein, P. Karpman, A. Albertini, and Y. Markov. The first collision for full sha-1. Cryptology ePrint Archive, Report 2017/190, 2017. `https://eprint.iacr.org/2017/190`.

[14] A. J. H. Vinck. Introduction to public key cryptography. `www.uni-due.de/imperia/md/images/dc/crypto_chapter_5_public_key.pdf`. Accessed 2018-10-08.

[15] D. Waitzman. Standard for the transmission of ip datagrams on avian carriers. RFC 1149, RFC Editor, April 1990.

[16] D. Waitzman. Standard for the transmission of ip datagrams on avian carriers. RFC 7914, RFC Editor, August 2016.

[17] X. Wang and H. Yu. How to break md5 and other hash functions. In *Proceedings of the 24th Annual International Conference on Theory and Applications of Cryptographic Techniques*, EUROCRYPT'05, pages 19–35, Berlin, Heidelberg, 2005. Springer-Verlag.

Index

© Seth James Nielson, Christopher K. Monson 2019
S. J. Nielson and C. K. Monson, *Practical Cryptography in Python*,
https://doi.org/10.1007/978-1-4842-4900-0